Reading Women's Lives

Contributing Editors:
The Faculty of the Department of Women's Studies at The Ohio State University

Compiled by

Dr. Anne Mulvey
47.335 Psychology and Women Readings
Sections 201& 202
University of Massachusetts Lowell

Director of Database Publishing: Michael Payne
Sponsoring Editor: Natalie Danner
Development Editor: Katherine R. Gehan and Mary Kate Aveni
Editorial Assistant: Abbey Briggs
Marketing Coordinator: Kelly Forsberg
Operations Manager: Eric M. Kenney
Production Project Manager: Jennifer M. Berry
Rights Editor: Francesca Marcantonio
Cover Designer: Renée Sartell

Printed in the United States of America.

Please visit our website at *www.pearsoncustom.com.*
Attention bookstores: For permission to return any unsold stock, contact us at *pe-uscustomreturns@pearsoncustom.com.*

ISBN-13: 978-0-536-22809-3 ISBN-10: 0-536-22809-4

PEARSON CUSTOM PUBLISHING
501 Boylston St., Suite 900
Boston, MA 02116

Contents

CHALLENGING FALSE DICHOTOMIES & SOCIAL INEQUALITIES

VI. ENVISIONING & CREATING

THE SELVES & THE COMMUNITIES WE WANT & NEED

Sex in Education: A Fair Chance for the Girls (1873)

Edward Clarke

In this excerpt from Sex in Education; or, A Fair Chance for the Girls, *Dr. Edward H. Clarke, a professor at Harvard College and chair of Harvard Medical School from 1855 to 1872, writes about the harmful effects of education on the sexual development and reproductive capacities of women. This study was published in 1873 and went through seventeen editions over the next thirty years—a time when women were campaigning for suffrage and equal education.*

Spending Her Force in Intellectual Labor

Miss G_____ worked her way through New-England primary, grammar, and high schools to a Western college, which she en-

Excerpts from *Sex in Education; or, A Fair Chance for the Girls*, by Edward H. Clarke, 1873, Arno Press.

tered with credit to herself, and from which she graduated, confessedly its first scholar, leading the male and female youth alike. All that need be told of her career is that she worked as a student, continuously and perseveringly, through the years of her first critical epoch, and for a few years after it, without any sort of regard to the periodical type of her organization. It never appeared that she studied excessively in other respects, or that her system was weakened while in college by fevers or other sickness. Not a great while after graduation, she began to show signs of failure, and some years later died under the writer's care. A post-mortem examination was made, which disclosed no disease in any part of the body, except in the brain, where the microscope revealed commencing degeneration.

This was called an instance of death from over-work. Like the preceding case, it was not so much the result of over-work as of un-physiological work. She was unable to make a good brain, that could stand the wear and tear of life, and a good reproductive system that should serve the race, at the same time that she was continuously spending her force in intellectual labor. Nature asked for a periodical remission, and did not get it. And so Miss G_____ died, not because she had mastered the wasps of Aristophanes and the Mécanique Céleste, not because she had made the acquaintance of Kant and Kölliker, and ventured to explore the anatomy of flowers and the secrets of chemistry, but because, while pursuing these studies, while doing all this work, she steadily ignored her woman's make. Believing that woman can do what man can, for she held that faith, she strove with noble but ignorant bravery to compass man's intellectual attainment in a man's way, and died in the effort. . . .

In our schools it is the ambitious and conscientious girls, those who have in them the stuff of which the noblest women are made, that suffer, not the romping or lazy sort; and thus our modern ways of education provide for the "non-survival of the fittest." A speaker told an audience of women at Wesleyan Hall not long ago, that he once attended the examination of a Western college, where a girl beat the boys in unravelling the intricacies [*sic*] of Juvenal. He did not report the consumption of blood and wear of brain tissue that in her college way of study correlated her Latin, or hint at the possibility of arrested development. Girls of bloodless skins and intellectual faces may be seen any day, by those who desire the spectacle, among the scholars of our high and normal schools,—faces that crown, and skins that cover, curving spines, which should be straight, and neuralgic nerves that should know no pain. Later on, when marriage and maternity overtake these girls, and they "live laborious days" in a sense not intended by Milton's line, they bend and break beneath the labor, like loaded grain before a storm, and bear little fruit again. A training that yields this result is neither fair to the girls nor to the race.

Let us quote the authority of such an acute and sagacious observer as Dr. Maudsley, in support of the physiological and pathological views that have been here presented. Referring to the physiological condition and phenomena of the first critical epoch, he says, "In the great mental revolution caused by the development of the sexual system at puberty, we have the most striking example of the intimate and essential sympathy between the brain, as a mental organ, and other organs of the body. The change of character at this period is not by any means *limited to the appearance of the sexual feelings,* and their sympathetic ideas, but, when traced to its ultimate reach, will be found to extend to the highest feelings of mankind, social, moral, and even religious." He points out the fact that is very easy by improper training and forced work, during this susceptible period, to turn a psychological into a pathological state. "The great mental revolution which occurs at puberty may go beyond its physiological limits in some instances, and become pathological." "The time of this mental revolution is at best a trying period for youth." "The monthly activity of the ovaries, which marks the advent of puberty in women, has a notable effect upon the mind and body; wherefore it may become an important cause of mental and physical derangement." With regard to the physiological effects of arrested development of the reproductive apparatus in women, Dr. Maudsley uses the following plain and empathetic language: "The forms and habits of mutilated men approach those of women; and women, whose ovaries and uterus remain for some cause in a state of complete inaction, approach the forms and habits of men. It is said, too, that, in hermaphrodites, the mental character, like the physical, participates equally in that of both sexes. While woman preserves her sex, she will necessarily be feebler than man, and, having her special bodily and mental characters, will have, to a certain extent, her own sphere of activity; where she has become thoroughly masculine in nature, or hermaphrodite in mind,—when, in fact, she has pretty well divested herself of her sex,—then she may take his ground, and do his work; but she will have lost her feminine attractions, and probably also her chief feminine functions." It has been reserved for our age and country, by its methods of female education, to demonstrate that it is possible in some cases to divest a woman of her chief feminine functions; in others, to produce grave and even fatal disease of the brain and nervous system; in others, to engender torturing derangements and imperfections of the reproductive apparatus that imbitter [*sic*] a lifetime. . . .

The number of these graduates who have been permanently disabled to a greater or less degree, or fatally injured, by these causes, is such as to excite the *gravest alarm,* and to demand the serious attention of the community.

QUESTIONS

1. What is Dr. Clarke's central argument? What evidence does he use to support his claim?
2. Why do you think this study is entitled . . . *A Fair Chance for the Girls*?
3. What are some of the social factors that may have contributed to the popularity of Clarke's findings during this time period?

The Doctors' Stake in Women's Illness (1973)

Barbara Ehrenreich and Deidre English

Social ideology and gender beliefs shape medical practice and treatments in any age; In the 19th century, women's "nervous disorders" and reputation for "frailty" kept doctors supplied with a steady flow of ailing patients and justified women's exclusion from higher education and medical training. This excerpt from Barbara Ehrenreich and Deidre English's books Complaints and Disorders *explores some of these 19th century medical beliefs, providing an opportunity to better understand the subjectivity of a discipline hailed for its objectivity and the costs of such practices to women's development and potential. The essay also stimulates inquiry into 20th century practices for the ideology lurking there.*

The myth of female frailty, and the very real cult of female hypochondria that seemed to support the myth, played directly to the financial interests of the medical profession. In the late nineteenth and early twentieth centuries, the "regular" AMA doctors (members of the American Medical Association—the intellectual ancestors of today's doctors) still had no legal monopoly over medical practice and no legal control over the number of people who called themselves "doctors." Competition from lay healers of both sexes, and from what the AMA saw as an excess of formally trained male physicians, had the doctors running scared. A good part of the competition was female: women lay healers and midwives dominated the urban ghettos and the countryside in many areas; suffragists were beating on the doors of the medical schools.

For the doctors, the myth of female frailty thus served two purposes. It helped them to disqualify women as healers, and, of course, it made women highly qualified as patients.* In 1900 there were 173 doctors (engaged in primary patient care) per 100,000 population, compared to 50 per 100,000 today. So, it was in the interests of doctors to cultivate the illnesses of their patients with frequent home visits and drawn-out "treatments." A few dozen well-heeled lady customers were all that a doctor needed for a successful urban practice. Women—at least, women whose husbands could pay the bills—became a natural "client caste" to the developing medical profession.

In many ways, the upper-middle-class woman was the ideal patient: her illnesses—and her husband's bank account— seemed almost inexhaustible. Furthermore, she was usually submissive and obedient to the "doctor's orders." The famous Philadelphia doctor S. Weir Mitchell expressed his profession's deep appreciation of the female invalid in 1888:

> With all her weakness, her unstable emotionality, her tendency to morally warp when long nervously ill, she is then far easier to deal with, far more amenable to reason, far more sure to be comfortable as a patient, than the man who is relatively in a like position. The reasons for this are too obvious to delay me here, and physicians accustomed to deal with both sexes as sick people will be apt to justify my position.

In Mitchell's mind women were not only easier to relate to, but sickness was the very key to femininity: "The man who does not know sick women does not know women."

"The Doctors' Stake in Women's Illness," and "The Scientific Explanation of Female Frailty," by Barbara Ehrenreich, and Deidre English reprinted from *Complaints and Disorders: The Sexual Politics of Sickness*, The Feminist Press, 1973.

Some women were quick to place at least some of the blame for female invalidism on the doctors' interests. Dr. Elizabeth Garrett Anderson, an American woman doctor, argued that the extent of female invalidism was much exaggerated by male doctors and that women's natural functions were not really all that debilitating. In the working classes, she observed, work went on during menstruation "without intermission, and, as a rule, without ill effects." (Of course, working-class women could not have afforded the costly medical attention required for female invalidism.) Mary Livermore, a women's suffrage worker, spoke against "the monstrous assumption that woman is a natural invalid," and denounced "the unclean army of 'gynecologists' who seem desirous to convince women that they possess but one set of organs—and that these are always diseased." And Dr. Mary Putnam Jacobi put the matter most forcefully when she wrote in 1895, "I think, finally, it is in the increased attention paid to women, and especially in their new function as lucrative patients, scarcely imagined a hundred years ago, that we find explanation for much of the ill-health among women, freshly discovered today. . . .

The "Scientific" Explanation of Female Frailty

As a businessman, the doctor had a direct interest in a social role for women that encouraged them to be sick; as a doctor, he had an obligation to find the causes of female complaints. The result was that, as a "scientist," he ended up proposing medical theories that were actually justifications of women's social role.

This was easy enough to do at the time: no one had a very clear idea of human physiology. American medical education, even at the best schools, put few constraints on the doctors' imaginations, offering only a scant introduction to what was known of physiology and anatomy and no training in rigorous scientific method. So doctors had considerable intellectual license to devise whatever theories seemed socially appropriate.

Generally, they traced female disorders either to women's inherent "defectiveness" or to any sort of activity beyond the mildest "feminine" pursuits—especially sexual, athletic, and mental activity. Thus promiscuity, dancing in hot rooms, and subjection to an overly romantic husband were given as the origins of illness, along with too much reading, too much seriousness or ambition, and worrying.

The underlying medical theory of women's weakness rested on what doctors considered the most basic physiological law: "conservation of energy." According to the first postulate of this theory, each human body contained a set quantity of energy that was directed variously from one organ or function to another. This meant that you could develop one organ or ability only at the expense of others, drawing energy away from the parts not being developed. In particular, the sexual organs competed with the other organs for the body's fixed supply of vital energy. The second postulate of this theory—that reproductivity was central to a woman's biological life—made this competition highly unequal, with the reproductive organs in almost total command of the whole woman.

The implications of the "conservation of energy" theory for male and female roles are important. Let's consider them.

Curiously, from a scientific perspective, *men* didn't jeopardize their reproductivity by engaging in intellectual pursuits. On the contrary, since the mission of upper- and upper- middle-class men was to be doers, not breeders, they had to be careful not to let sex drain energy away from their "higher functions." Doctors warned men not to "spend their seed" (i.e., the essence of their energy) recklessly, but to conserve themselves for the "civilizing endeavors" they were embarked upon. College youths were jealously segregated from women—except on rare sexual sprees in town—and virginity was often prized in men as well as women. Debilitated sperm would result from too much "indulgence," and this in turn could produce "runts," feeble infants, and girls.

On the other hand, because reproduction was woman's grand purpose in life, doctors agreed that women ought to concentrate their physical energy internally, toward the womb. All other activity should be slowed down or stopped during the peak periods of sexual energy use. At the onset of menstruation, women were told to take a great deal of bed rest in order to help focus their strength on regulating their periods—though this might take years. The more time a pregnant woman spent lying down quietly, the better. At menopause, women were often put to bed again.

Doctors and educators were quick to draw the obvious conclusion that, for women, higher education could be physically dangerous. Too much development of the brain, they counseled, would atrophy the uterus. Reproductive development was totally antagonistic to mental development. In a work entitled *Concerning the Physiological and Intellectual Weakness of Women*, the German scientist P. Moebius wrote:

> If we wish woman to fulfill the task of motherhood fully she cannot possess a masculine brain. If the feminine abilities were developed to the same degree as those of the male, her material organs would suffer and we should have before us a repulsive and useless hybrid.

In the United States this thesis was set forth most cogently by Dr. Edward Clarke of Harvard College. He warned, in his influential book *Sex in Education* (1873), that higher education was *already* destroying the reproductive abilities of American women.

Even if a woman should choose to devote herself to intellectual or other "unwomanly" pursuits, she could hardly hope to escape the domination of her uterus and ovaries. In *The Diseases of Women* (1849), Dr. F. Hollick wrote: "The Uterus, it must be remembered, is the *controlling* organ in the female body, being the most excitable of all, and so intimately connected, by the ramifications of its numerous nerves, with every other part." To other medical theorists, it was the ovaries that occupied center stage. This passage, written in 1870 by Dr. W. W. Bliss, is, if somewhat overwrought, nonetheless typical:

> Accepting, then, these views of the gigantic power and influence of the ovaries over the whole animal economy of woman,—that they are the most powerful agents in all the commotions of her system; that on them rest her intellectual standing in society, her physical perfection, and all that lends beauty to those fine and delicate contours which are constant objects of admiration, all that is great, noble and beautiful, all that is voluptuous, tender, and endearing: that her fidelity, her devotedness, her perpetual vigilance, forecast, and all those qualities of mind and disposition which inspire respect and love and fit her as the safest counselor and friend of man, spring from the ovaries,—*what must be their influence and power over the great vocation of woman and the august purposes of her existence when these organs have become compromised through disease!* Can the record of woman's mission on earth be otherwise than filled with tales of sorrow, sufferings, and manifold infirmities, all through the influence of these important organs?

This was not mere textbook rhetoric. In their actual medical practices, doctors found uterine and ovarian "disorders" behind almost every female complaint, from headaches to sore throats and indigestion. Curvature of the spine, bad posture, or pains anywhere in the lower half of the body could be the result of "displacement" of the womb, and one doctor ingeniously explained how constipation results from the pressure of the uterus on the rectum.

Notes

*See *Witches, Midwives and Nurses* by Barbara Ehrenreich and Deirdre English. Glass Mountain Pamphlets, no. 1 (Old Westbury. N.Y.: The Feminist Press, 1973).

QUESTIONS

1. What was "Doctors' Stake in Women's Illness" in the 19th century? What advantages would a reputation for "frailty" and "illness" offer women?
2. According to 19th century doctors, what was the source of women's disorders? What different implications did the Conservation of Energy Theory have for men and women? How did these differing implications serve social norms?
3. Why might a 19th century woman buy into this ideology so easily? Can you identify comparable ideology today? What stake might modern doctors have in illness, whether male or female? How do we separate legitimate differences in illness and disease from differences that serve social norms? Can individuals serve social norms unconsciously?

THE YELLOW WALLPAPER (1892)

Charlotte Perkins Gilman

Charlotte Perkins Gilman (1869-1935) was a prolific 19th century writer, economist and women's rights advocate. Although born a member of the well-known New England Beecher family, Gilman grew up near-destitute after her father abandoned the family. Gilman suffered from intense clinical depression during her adult years and the common medical treatment prescribed for women's psychological afflictions at this time—avoiding physical and intellectual activity—only served to intensify Gilman's malaise. Gilman published a number of acclaimed works, including an investigation into women's status at the turn of the century entitled Women and Economics *(1898), an entertaining feminist utopian novel entitled* Herland *(1915), and over 200 short stories. After her second husband's death and her diagnosis with breast cancer, Gilman committed suicide in 1935. "The Yellow Wallpaper," Gilman's most well-known work, was published in 1892. It explores a fictional female character's experience with nervous depression and its treatment, often called the "rest cure," in the 19th century.*

It is very seldom that mere ordinary people like John and myself secure ancestral halls for the summer.

A colonial mansion, a hereditary estate, I would say a haunted house, and reach the height of romantic felicity—but that would be asking too much of fate!

Still I will proudly declare that there is something queer about it.

Else, why should it be let so cheaply? And why have stood so long untenanted?

John laughs at me, of course, but one expects that in marriage.

John is practical in the extreme. He has no patience with faith, an intense horror of superstition, and he scoffs openly at any talk of things not to be felt and seen and put down in figures.

John is a physician, and *perhaps*—(I would not say it to a living soul, of course, but this is dead paper and a great relief to my mind)—*perhaps* that is one reason I do not get well faster.

You see, he does not believe I am sick! And what can one do?

If a physician of high standing, and one's own husband, assures friends and relatives that there is really nothing the matter with one but temporary nervous depression—a slight hysterical tendency—what is one to do?

My brother is also a physician, and also of high standing, and he says the same thing.

So I take phosphates or phosphites—whichever it is, and tonics, and journeys, and air, and exercise, and am absolutely forbidden to "work" until I am well again.

Personally, I disagree with their ideas.

Personally, I believe that congenial work, with excitement and change, would do me good.

But what is one to do?

I did write for a while in spite of them; but it *does* exhaust me a good deal—having to be so sly about it, or else meet with heavy opposition.

I sometimes fancy that in my condition if I had less opposition and more society and stimulus—but John says the very worst thing I can do is to think about my condition, and I confess it always makes me feel bad.

So I will let it alone and talk about the house.

The most beautiful place! It is quite alone, standing well back from the road, quite three miles from the village. It makes me think of English places that you read about, for there are hedges and walls and gates that lock, and lots of separate little houses for the gardeners and people.

There is a *delicious* garden! I never saw such a garden—large and shady, full of box-bordered paths, and lined with long grape-covered arbors with seats under them.

There were greenhouses, too, but they are all broken now.

There was some legal trouble, I believe, something about the heirs and co-heirs; anyhow, the place has been empty for years.

That spoils my ghostliness, I am afraid, but I don't care—there is something strange about the house—I can feel it.

I even said so to John one moonlight evening, but he said what I felt was a *draught*, and shut the window.

I get unreasonably angry with John sometimes. I'm sure I never used to be so sensitive. I think it is due to this nervous condition.

But John says if I feel so I shall neglect proper self-control; so I take pains to control myself—before him, at least, and that makes me very tired.

I don't like our room a bit. I wanted one downstairs that opened onto the piazza and had roses all over the window, and such pretty old-fashioned chintz hangings! but John would not hear of it.

He said there was only one window and not room for two beds, and no near room for him if he took another.

He is very careful and loving, and hardly lets me stir without special direction.

I have a schedule prescription for each hour in the day; he takes all care from me, and so I feel basely ungrateful not to value it more.

He said we came here solely on my account, that I was to have perfect rest and all the air I could get. "Your exercise depends on your strength, my dear," said he, "and your food somewhat on your appetite; but air you can absorb all the time." So we took the nursery at the top of the house.

It is a big, airy room, the whole floor nearly, with windows that look all ways, and air and sunshine galore. It was nursery first, and then playroom and gymnasium, I should judge, for the windows are barred for little children, and there are rings and things in the walls.

The paint and paper look as if a boys' school had used it. It is stripped off—the paper—in great patches all around the head of my bed, about as far as I can reach, and in a great place on the other side of the room low down. I never saw a worse paper in my life.

One of those sprawling, flamboyant patterns committing every artistic sin.

It is dull enough to confuse the eye in following, pronounced enough constantly to irritate and provoke study, and when you follow the lame uncertain curves for a little distance they suddenly commit suicide—plunge off at outrageous angles, destroy themselves in unheard-of contradictions.

The color is repellent, almost revolting; a smouldering unclean yellow, strangely faded by the slow-turning sunlight.

It is a dull yet lurid orange in some places, a sickly sulphur tint in others.

No wonder the children hated it! I should hate it myself if I had to live in this room long.

There comes John, and I must put this away—he hates to have me write a word.

We have been here two weeks, and I haven't felt like writing before, since that first day.

I am sitting by the window now, up in this atrocious nursery, and there is nothing to hinder my writing as much as I please, save lack of strength.

John is away all day, and even some nights when his cases are serious.

I am glad my case is not serious!

But these nervous troubles are dreadfully depressing.

John does not know how much I really suffer. He knows there is no *reason* to suffer, and that satisfies him.

Of course it is only nervousness. It does weigh on me so not to do my duty in any way!

I meant to be such a help to John, such a real rest and comfort, and here I am a comparative burden already!

Nobody would believe what an effort it is to do what little I am able—to dress and entertain, and order things.

It is fortunate Mary is so good with the baby. Such a dear baby!

And yet I *cannot* be with him, it makes me so nervous.

I suppose John never was nervous in his life. He laughs at me so about this wallpaper!

At first he meant to repaper the room, but afterward he said that I was letting it get the better of me, and that nothing was worse for a nervous patient than to give way to such fancies.

He said that after the wallpaper was changed it would be the heavy bedstead, and then the barred windows, and then that gate at the head of the stairs, and so on.

"You know the place is doing you good," he said, "and really, dear, I don't care to renovate the house just for a three months' rental."

"Then do let us go downstairs," I said. "There are such pretty rooms there."

Then he took me in his arms and called me a blessed little goose, and said he would go down cellar, if I wished, and have it whitewashed into the bargain.

But he is right enough about the beds and windows and things.

It is as airy and comfortable a room as anyone need wish, and, of course, I would not be so silly as to make him uncomfortable just for a whim.

I'm really getting quite fond of the big room, all but that horrid paper.

Out of one window I can see the garden—those mysterious deep-shaded arbors, the riotous old-fashioned flowers, and bushes and gnarly trees.

Out of another I get a lovely view of the bay and a little private wharf belonging to the estate. There is a beautiful shaded lane that runs down there from the house. I always fancy I see people walking in these numerous paths and arbors, but John has cautioned me not to give way to fancy in the least. He says that with my imaginative power and habit of story-making, a nervous weakness like mine is sure to lead to all manner of excited fancies, and that I ought to use my will and good sense to check the tendency. So I try.

I think sometimes that if I were only well enough to write a little it would relieve the press of ideas and rest me.

But I find I get pretty tired when I try.

It is so discouraging not to have any advice and companionship about my work. When I get really well, John says we will ask Cousin Henry and Julia down for a long visit; but he says he would as soon put fireworks in my pillow-case as to let me have those stimulating people about now.

I wish I could get well faster.

But I must not think about that. This paper looks to me as if it *knew* what a vicious influence it had!

There is a recurrent spot where the pattern lolls like a broken neck and two bulbous eyes stare at you upside down.

I get positively angry with the impertinence of it and the everlastingness. Up and down and sideways they crawl, and those absurd unblinking eyes are everywhere. There is one place where two breadths didn't match, and the eyes go all up and down the line, one a little higher than the other.

I never saw so much expression in an inanimate thing before, and we all know how much expression they have! I used to lie awake as a child and get more entertainment and terror out of blank walls and plain furniture than most children could find in a toy-store.

I remember what a kindly wink the knobs of our big old bureau used to have, and there was one chair that always seemed like a strong friend.

I used to feel that if any of the other things looked too fierce I could always hop into that chair and be safe.

The furniture in this room is no worse than inharmonious, however, for we had to bring it all from downstairs. I suppose when this was used as a playroom they had to take the nursery things out, and no wonder! I never saw such ravages as the children have made here.

The wallpaper, as I said before, is torn off in spots, and it sticketh closer than a brother—they must have had perseverance as well as hatred.

Then the floor is scratched and gouged and splintered, the plaster itself is dug out here and there, and this great heavy bed, which is all we found in the room, looks as if it had been through the wars.

But I don't mind it a bit—only the paper.

There comes John's sister. Such a dear girl as she is, and so careful of me! I must not let her find me writing.

She is a perfect and enthusiasitic housekeeper, and hopes for no better profession. I verily believe she thinks it is the writing which made me sick!

But I can write when she is out, and see her a long way off from these windows.

There is one that commands the road, a lovely shaded winding road, and one that just looks off over the country. A lovely country, too, full of great elms and velvet meadows.

This wallpaper has a kind of subpattern in a different shade, a particularly irritating one, for you can only see it in certain lights, and not clearly then.

But in the places where it isn't faded and where the sun is just so—I can see a strange, provoking, formless sort of figure that seems to skulk about behind that silly and conspicuous front design.

There's sister on the stairs!

Well, the Fourth of July is over! The people are all gone, and I am tired out. John thought it might do me good to see a little company, so we just had Mother and Nellie and the children down for a week.

Of course I didn't do a thing. Jennie sees to everything now.

But it tired me all the same.

John says if I don't pick up faster he shall send me to Weir Mitchell in the fall.

But I don't want to go there at all. I had a friend who was in his hands once, and she says he is just like John and my brother, only more so!

Besides, it is such an undertaking to go so far.

I don't feel as if it was worthwhile to turn my hand over for anything, and I'm getting dreadfully fretful and querulous.

I cry at nothing, and cry most of the time.

Of course I don't when John is here, or anybody else, but when I am alone.

And I am alone a good deal just now. John is kept in town very often by serious cases, and Jennie is good and lets me alone when I want her to.

So I walk a little in the garden or down that lovely lane, sit on the porch under the roses, and lie down up here a good deal.

I'm getting really fond of the room in spite of the wallpaper. Perhaps *because* of the wallpaper.

It dwells in my mind so!

I lie here on this great immovable bed—it is nailed down, I believe—and follow that pattern about by the hour. It is as good as gymnastics, I assure you. I start, we'll say, at the bottom, down in the corner over there where it has not been touched, and I determine for the thousandth time that I *will* follow that pointless pattern to some sort of a conclusion.

I know a little of the principle of design, and I know this thing was not arranged on any laws of radiation, or alternation, or repetition, or symmetry, or anything else that I ever heard of.

It is repeated, of course, by the breadths, but not otherwise.

Looked at in one way, each breadth stands alone; the bloated curves and flourishes—a kind of "debased Romanesque" with *delirium tremens*—go waddling up and down in isolated columns of fatuity.

But, on the other hand, they connect diagonally, and the sprawling outlines run off in great slanting waves of optic horror, like a lot of wallowing sea-weeds in full chase.

The whole thing goes horizontally, too, at least it seems so, and I exhaust myself trying to distinguish the order of its going in that direction.

They have used a horizontal breadth for a frieze, and that adds wonderfully to the confusion.

There is one end of the room where it is almost intact, and there, when the crosslights fade and the low sun shines directly upon it, I can almost fancy radiation after all—the interminable grotesque seem to form around a common center and rush off in headlong plunges of equal distraction.

It makes me tired to follow it. I will take a nap, I guess.

I don't know why I should write this.

I don't want to.

I don't feel able.

And I know John would think it absurd. But I *must* say what I feel and think in some way—it is such a relief!

But the effort is getting to be greater than the relief.

Half the time now I am awfully lazy, and lie down ever so much.

John says I mustn't lose my strength, and has me take cod liver oil and lots of tonics and things, to say nothing of ale and wines and rare meat.

Dear John! He loves me very dearly, and hates to have me sick. I tried to have a real earnest reasonable talk with him the other day, and tell him how I wish he would let me go and make a visit to Cousin Henry and Julia.

But he said I wasn't able to go, not able to stand it after I got there; and I did not make out a very good case for myself, for I was crying before I had finished.

It is getting to be a great effort for me to think straight. Just this nervous weakness, I suppose.

And dear John gathered me up in his arms, and just carried me upstairs and laid me on the bed, and sat by me and read to me till it tired my head.

He said I was his darling and his comfort and all he had, and that I must take care of myself for his sake, and keep well.

He says no one but myself can help me out of it, that I must use my will and self-control and not let any silly fancies run away with me.

There's one comfort—the baby is well and happy, and does not have to occupy this nursery with the horrid wallpaper.

If we had not used it, that blessed child would have! What a fortunate escape! Why, I wouldn't have a child of mine, an impressionable little thing, live in such a room for worlds.

I never thought of it before, but it is lucky that John kept me here after all; I can stand it so much easier than a baby, you see.

Of course I never mention it to them anymore—I am too wise—but I keep watch of it all the same.

There are things in the wallpaper that nobody knows but me, or ever will.

Behind that outside pattern the dim shapes get clearer every day.

It is always the same shape, only very numerous.

And it is like a woman stooping down and creeping about behind that pattern. I don't like it a bit. I wonder—I begin to think—I wish John would take me away from here!

It is so hard to talk with John about my case, because he is so wise, and because he loves me so.

But I tried it last night.

It was moonlight. The moon shines in all around just as the sun does.

I hate to see it sometimes, it creeps so slowly, and always comes in by one window or another.

John was asleep and I hated to waken him, so I kept still and watched the moonlight on that undulating wallpaper till I felt creepy.

The faint figure behind seemed to shake the pattern, just as if she wanted to get out.

I got up softly and went to feel and see if the paper *did* move, and when I came back John was awake.

"What is it, little girl?" he said. "Don't go walking about like that—you'll get cold."

I thought it was a good time to talk, so I told him that I really was not gaining here, and that I wished he would take me away.

"Why, darling!" said he. "Our lease will be up in three weeks, and I can't see how to leave before."

"The repairs are not done at home, and I cannot possibly leave town just now. Of course, if you were in any danger, I could and would, but you really are better, dear, whether you can see it or not. I am a doctor, dear, and I know. You are gaining flesh and color, your appetite is better, I feel really much easier about you."

"I don't weigh a bit more," said I, "nor as much; and my appetite may be better in the evening when you are here but it is worse in the morning when you are away!"

"Bless her little heart!" said he with a big hug. "She shall be as sick as she pleases! But now let's improve the shining hours by going to sleep and talk about it in the morning!"

"And you won't go away?" I asked gloomily.

"Why, how can I, dear? It is only three weeks more and then we will take a nice little trip for a few days while Jennie is getting the house ready. Really, dear, you are better!"

"Better in body perhaps—" I began, and stopped short, for he sat up straight and looked at me with such a stern, reproachful look that I could not say another word.

"My darling," said he, "I beg you, for my sake and for our child's sake, as well as for your own, that you will never for one instant let that idea enter your mind! There is nothing so dangerous, so fascinating, to a temperament like yours. It is a false and foolish fancy. Can you not trust me as a physician when I tell you so?" So of course I said no more on that score, and we went to sleep before long. He thought I was asleep first, but I wasn't, and lay there for hours trying to decide whether that front pattern and the back pattern really did move together or separately.

On a pattern like this, by daylight, there is a lack of sequence, a defiance of law, that is a constant irritant to a normal mind.

The color is hideous enough, and unreliable enough, and infuriating enough, but the pattern is torturing.

You think you have mastered it, but just as you get well under way in following, it turns a back-somersault and there you are. It slaps you in the face, knocks you down, and tramples upon you. It is like a bad dream.

The outside pattern is a florid arabesque, reminding one of a fungus. If you can imagine a toadstool in joints, an interminable string of toadstools, budding and sprouting in endless convolutions—why, that is something like it.

That is, sometimes!

There is one marked peculiarity about this paper, a thing nobody seems to notice but myself, and that is that it changes as the light changes.

When the sun shoots in through the east window—I always watch for that first long, straight ray—it changes so quickly that I never can quite believe it.

That is why I watch it always.

By moonlight—the moon shines in all night when there is a moon—I wouldn't know it was the same paper.

At night in any kind of light, in twilight, candlelight, lamplight, and worst of all by moonlight, it becomes bars! The outside pattern, I mean, and the woman behind it is as plain as can be.

I didn't realize for a long time what the thing was that showed behind, that dim subpattern, but now I am quite sure it is a woman.

By daylight she is subdued, quiet. I fancy it is the pattern that keeps her so still. It is so puzzling. It keeps me quiet by the hour.

I lie down ever so much now. John says it is good for me, and to sleep all I can.

Indeed he started the habit by making me lie down for an hour after each meal.

It is a very bad habit, I am convinced, for you see, I don't sleep.

And that cultivates deceit, for I don't tell them I'm awake—Oh, no!

The fact is I am getting a little afraid of John.

He seems very queer sometimes, and even Jennie has an inexplicable look.

It strikes me occasionally, just as a scientific hypothesis, that perhaps it is the paper!

I have watched John when he did not know I was looking, and come into the room suddenly on the most innocent excuses, and I've caught him several times *looking at the paper*! And Jennie too. I caught Jennie with her hand on it once.

She didn't know I was in the room, and when I asked her in a quiet, a very quiet voice, with the most restrained manner possible, what she was doing with the paper, she turned around as if she had been caught stealing, and looked quite angry—asked me why I should frighten her so!

Then she said that the paper stained everything it touched, that she had found yellow smooches on all my clothes and John's and she wished we would be more careful!

Did not that sound innocent? But I know she was studying that pattern, and I am determined that nobody shall find it out but myself!

Life is very much more exciting now than it used to be. You see, I have something more to expect, to look forward to, to watch. I really do eat better, and am more quiet than I was.

John is so pleased to see me improve! He laughed a little the other day, and said I seemed to be flourishing in spite of my wallpaper.

I turned it off with a laugh. I had no intention of telling him it was *because* of the wallpaper—he would make fun of me. He might even want to take me away.

I don't want to leave now until I have found it out. There is a week more, and I think that will be enough.

I'm feeling ever so much better!

I don't sleep much at night, for it is so interesting to watch developments; but I sleep a good deal in the daytime.

In the daytime it is tiresome and perplexing.

There are always new shoots on the fungus, and new shades of yellow all over it. I cannot keep count of them, though I have tried conscientiously.

It is the strangest yellow, that wallpaper! It makes me think of all the yellow things I ever saw—not beautiful ones like buttercups, but old, foul, bad yellow things.

But there is something else about that paper—the smell! I noticed it the moment we came into the room, but with so much air and sun it was not bad. Now we have had a week of fog and rain, and whether the windows are open or not, the smell is here.

It creeps all over the house.

I find it hovering in the dining-room, skulking in the parlor, hiding in the hall, lying in wait for me on the stairs.

It gets into my hair.

Even when I go to ride, if I turn my head suddenly and surprise it—there is that smell!

Such a peculiar odor, too! I have spent hours in trying to analyze it to find what it smelled like.

It is not bad—at first—and very gentle, but quite the subtlest, most enduring odor I ever met.

In this damp weather it is awful. I wake up in the night and find it hanging over me.

It used to disturb me at first. I thought seriously of burning the house—to reach the smell.

But now I am used to it. The only thing I can think of that it is like is the *color* of the paper! A yellow smell.

There a very funny mark on this wall, low down, near the mopboard. A streak that runs round the room. It goes behind every piece of furniture, except the bed, a long, straight, even *smooch*, as if it had been rubbed over and over.

I wonder how it was done and who did it, and what they did it for. Round and round and round—round and round and round—it makes me dizzy!

I really have discovered something at last.

Through watching so much at night, when it changes so, I have finally found out.

The front pattern *does* move—and no wonder! The woman behind shakes it!

Sometimes I think there are a great many women behind, and sometimes only one, and she crawls around fast, and her crawling shakes it all over.

Then in the very bright spots she keeps still, and in the very shady spots she just takes hold of the bars and shakes them hard.

And she is all the time trying to climb through. But nobody could climb through that pattern—it strangles so; I think that is why it has so many heads.

They get through and then the pattern strangles them off and turns them upside down, and makes their eyes white!

If those heads were covered or taken off it would not be half so bad.

I think that woman gets out in the daytime!

And I'll tell you why—privately—I've seen her!

I can see her out of every one of my windows!

It is the same woman, I know, for she is always creeping and most women do not creep by daylight.

I see her in that long shaded lane, creeping up and down. I see her in those dark grape arbors, creeping all round the garden.

I see her on that long road under the trees, creeping along, and when a carriage comes she hides under the blackberry vines.

I don't blame her a bit. It must be very humiliating to be caught creeping by daylight!

I always lock the door when I creep by daylight. I can't do it at night, for I know John would suspect something at once.

And John is so queer now that I don't want to irritate him. I wish he would take another room! Besides, I don't want anybody to get that woman out at night but myself.

I often wonder if I could see her out of all the windows at once.

But, turn as fast as I can, I can only see out of one at one time.

And though I always see her, she *may* be able to creep faster than I can turn!

I have watched her sometimes away off in the open country, creeping as fast as a cloud shadow in a high wind.

If only that top pattern could be gotten off from the under one! I mean to try it, little by little.

I have found out another funny thing, but I shan't tell it this time! It does not do to trust people too much.

There are only two more days to get this paper off, and I believe John is beginning to notice. I don't like the look in his eyes.

And I heard him ask Jennie a lot of professional questions about me. She had a very good report to give.

She said I slept a good deal in the daytime.

John knows I don't sleep very well at night, for all I'm so quiet!

He asked me all sorts of questions too, and pretended to be very loving and kind.

As if I couldn't see through him!

Still, I don't wonder he acts so, sleeping under this paper for three months.

It only interests me, but I feel sure John and Jennie are affected by it.

Hurrah! This is the last day, but it is enough. John is to stay in town over night, and won't be out until this evening.

Jennie wanted to sleep with me—the sly thing! but I told her I should undoubtedly rest better for a night all alone.

That was clever, for really I wasn't alone a bit! As soon as it was moonlight and that poor thing began to crawl and shake the pattern, I got up and ran to help her.

I pulled and she shook. I shook and she pulled, and before morning we had peeled off yards of that paper.

A strip about as high as my head and half around the room.

And then when the sun came and that awful pattern began to laugh at me, I declared I would finish it today!

We go away tomorrow, and they are moving all my furniture down again to leave things as they were before.

Jennie looked at the wall in amazement, but I told her merrily that I did it out of pure spite at the vicious thing.

She laughed and said she wouldn't mind doing it herself, but I must not get tired.

How she betrayed herself that time!

But I am here, and no person touches this paper but me—not *alive*!

She tried to get me out of the room—it was too patent! But I said it was so quiet and empty and clean now that I believed I would lie down again and sleep all I could, and not to wake me even for dinner—I would call when I woke.

So now she is gone, and the servants are gone, and the things are gone, and there is nothing left but that great bedstead nailed down, with the canvas mattress we found on it.

We shall sleep downstairs tonight, and take the boat home tomorrow.

I quite enjoy the room, now it is bare again.

How those children did tear about here!

This bedstead is fairly gnawed!

But I must get to work.

I have locked the door and thrown the key down into the front path.

I don't want to go out, and I don't want to have anybody come in, till John comes.

I want to astonish him.

I've got a rope up here that even Jennie did not find. If that woman does get out, and tries to get away, I can tie her!

But I forgot I could not reach far without anything to stand on!

This bed will *not* move!

I tried to lift and push it until I was lame, and then I got so angry I bit off a little piece at one corner—but it hurt my teeth.

Then I peeled off all the paper I could reach standing on the floor. It sticks horribly and the pattern just enjoys it! All those strangled heads and bulbous eyes and waddling fungus growths just shriek with derision!

I am getting angry enough to do something desperate. To jump out of the window would be admirable exercise, but the bars are too strong even to try.

Besides I wouldn't do it. Of course not. I know well enough that a step like that is improper and might be misconstrued.

I don't like to *look* out of the windows even—there are so many of those creeping women, and they creep so fast.

I wonder if they all come out of that wallpaper as I did?

But I am securely fastened now by my well-hidden rope—you don't get *me* out in the road there!

I suppose I shall have to get back behind the pattern when it comes night, and that is hard!

It is so pleasant to be out in this great room and creep around as I please!

I don't want to go outside. I won't, even if Jennie asks me to.

For outside you have to creep on the ground, and everything is green instead of yellow.

But here I can creep smoothly on the floor, and my shoulder just fits in that long smooch around the wall, so I cannot lose my way.

Why, there's John at the door!

It is no use, young man, you can't open it!

How he does call and pound!

Now he's crying to Jennie for an axe.

It would be a shame to break down that beautiful door!

"John, dear!" said I in the gentlest voice. "the key is down by the front steps, under a plantain leaf!"

That silenced him for a few moments.

Then he said—very quietly indeed, "Open the door, my darling!"

"I can't," said I. "The key is down by the front door under a plantain leaf!"

And then I said it again, several times, very gently and slowly, and said it so often that he had to go and see, and he got it of course, and came in. He stopped short by the door.

"What is the matter?" he cried. "For God's sake, what are you doing!"

I kept on creeping just the same, but I looked at him over my shoulder.

"I've got out at last," said I, "in spite of you and Jane? And I've pulled off most of the paper, so you can't put me back!"

Now why should that man have fainted? But he did, and right across my path by the wall, so that I had to creep over him every time!

QUESTIONS

1. What does the narrator in the tale seem to suffer from? What are her symptoms? How do they change as the story progresses? What words would you use to describe the narrator's personality?
2. What medical treatment is administered to the narrator? How does she feel about it? What activities does she think will aid her recovery?
3. Why does the narrator hate the wallpaper so much? What is the role of the wallpaper in this story? Who is the woman in the paper? How does the narrator's response to the wallpaper change over time?
4. What does the narrator mean when she says, "John is a physician and perhaps that is one reason I do not get well faster"? Isn't it the job of a physician to heal? Does John love his wife? How do you know? How does he treat her?
5. Is the narrator of the story sane or insane? Why do you take that position? What evidence do you have? What is the narrator's fate?

ON VOLUNTARY MOTHERHOOD (1855)

Sarah Grimké

Grimké (1792–1873) was an abolitionist and women's rights activist, who pioneered in the development of feminist theory in the U.S. Denied a college education because of her sex, she studied the condition and status of women throughout history and wrote a number of essays justifying women's demands for equality and autonomy. In her essay, "Marriage," she argued that women's oppression in marriage resulted from their economic dependence and their inability to control pregnancies. Grimké's demand for women's control of their own bodies, for their right to say no to their husbands' sexual desires, was radical in its day. In an era when contraception was unreliable and abortion dangerous, she advocated that women control reproduction by sexual abstinence. Sarah Grimké, who never married, lived with her sister Angelina Grimké Weld and her husband and helped care for their three children.

"On Voluntary Motherhood," by Sarah Grimké, reprinted from *Marriage, Weld Grimké Papers*, 1855. The William L. Clements Library, University of Michigan

An eminent physician of Boston once remarked that if in the economy of nature, the sexes alternated in giving birth to children no family would ever have more than three, the husband bearing one & the wife two. But the *right* to decide this matter has been almost wholly denied to woman. How often is she forced into an untimely motherhood which compels her to wean her babe, thus depriving it of that nutriment provided by nature as the most bland & fitting, during the period of dentition. Thousands of deaths from this cause, in infancy, are attributed by superstition & ignorance to the dispensations of Divine Providence. How many thousand, too, of miscarriages are forced upon woman by the fact that man lives down that law of his being which would protect her from such terrible consequences just as animal instinct protects the female among brutes. To save woman from legalized licentiousness is then one of the reasons why we plead for *equality of rights*.

No one can fail to see that this condition of things results from several causes:

1. Ignorance of those physical laws which every man & woman *ought* to know before marriage, the knowledge of which has been withheld from the young, under a false & fatal idea of delicacy. Many a man ruins his own health & that of his wife & his children too, thro' ignorance. A diffusion of knowledge respecting these laws would greatly defuse existing evils.

2. A false conception in man & woman of *his* nature & necessities. The great truth that the most concentrated fluid of the body has an office to perform in the product of *great tho'ts & original ideas*, as well as in the reproduction of the species is known to few & too little appreciated by all. The prodigal waste of this by legalized licentiousness has dwarfed the intellect of man. . . .

3. The fact that many legal marriages are not love marriages. In a pure, true relation between the sexes, no difficulties can ever arise, but a willing recognition of each other's right & mutual wants, naturally & spontaneously resulting in voluntary motherhood, a joyful appreciation of the blessedness of parentage, the birth of healthy, comely children & a beautiful home.

But it may be asked, what is to be done in cases of uncongenial marriages. Are not such men & women to follow their attractions outside of the legal relation. I unhesitatingly answer No! Where two persons have established a false marriage relation, *they are bound to abide by the consequences* of the mistake they have made.

Perhaps they did love each other, but a nearer intimacy has frozen this love or changed it into disgust. Or, theirs may have been a marriage of *convenience*, or one for the sake of obtaining a house, a fortune, a position in life: or it may have been a mere act of obedience to parents, or of gratitude, or a means of canceling a monied obligation. Multiform are the *unworthy* motives which seduce men & women into this sacred relation. In all these cases, let them abide the consequences of their own perversion of marriage, in exchanging personal chastity for the pride of life, vanity in dress, position or a house to live in, without that *love* which alone can make that house a *home*.

In some cases, it may be duty for the parties to separate, but let both keep themselves pure, so long as both are living. Let them accept the discipline thus afforded, & spiritual strength & growth will be their reward.

The Doctrine that human beings are to follow their attractions, which lies at the base of that miscalled "free love" system, is fraught with infinite danger. We are too low down to listen for one moment to its syren voice. . . .

Let me then exculpate "the woman's rights movement," from the charge of "tending directly and rapidly to the Free Love system, & nullifying the very idea of Marriage as anything more than a partnership at will." On the contrary our great desire is to purify & exalt the marriage relation & destroy *all* licentiousness. . . .

. . . Man seems to feel that Marriage gives him the control of Woman's person just as the Law gives him the control of her property. Thus are her most sacred rights destroyed by that very act, which, under the laws of Nature should enlarge, establish & protect them. In marriage is the origin of Life—in it woman finds herself endowed with a creative energy she never possessed before. In it new aspirations take possession of her, an indescribable longing after motherhood as the felt climax of her being. She joyfully gives herself away, that she may receive the germ of a new being, & true to nature, would fain retire within herself & absorb & expend all her energies in the development of this precious germ. But alas! How few are permitted, unmolested to pursue that end, which for the time being, has become the great object of life. How often is she compelled by various considerations to yield to the *unnatural* embraces of her husband, & thus to endanger the very existence of her embryo babe. How often is it sacrificed to the ungoverned passion of its own father, & the health of the mother seriously impaired. Every unnatural process is deleterious, hence abortions are destructive to the constitution & many women are broken down in the prime of life by them alone, & their haggard countenances too plainly reveal their secret sorrows. A lady once said to me I have but one child, but I have had 12 miscarriages—another had 4 children & 15 abortions. And why I would ask this untimely casting of her fruit? Do the beasts of the field miscarry? Why not? *They* are governed by instinct. Are the *brutes* safe during the period of gestation whilst *Woman* is not! . . .

. . . Again—look at the burdens imposed upon her by the care of many children following in quick succession. How can any mother do her duty to her family, if in 8 years she have 6 children. Look at the unnatural tug upon her constitution, her night watches, her sore vexations & trials & causes nameless & numberless, that wear away her life. If men had to alternate with their wives, the duties of the nursery, fewer & further between would be its inmates.

QUESTIONS

1. What are the arguments that Grimké makes for voluntary motherhood, or women's right to control pregnancy? What does she cite as consequences resulting from women's inability to control her body?
2. What assumptions does Grimké make about male sexuality and female sexuality?
3. How does Grimké respond to the charge that feminists advocate "free love?"
4. Why do you think Grimké advocates that voluntary motherhood be practiced through sexual abstinence? How does that position separate her from most contemporary feminists?

THE MYTH OF THE VAGINAL ORGASM (1968)

Anne Koedt

Anne Koedt's classic essay, published at the start of the 1970s women's movement, makes an essential connection between women's sexuality and women's liberation. Koedt challenges the long-held myth that "real" women experience sexual pleasure primarily through heterosexual intercourse—through vaginal, rather than clitoral, orgasms. This misconception viewed women's sexual lives in terms of a male-centered model of sex, and had serious consequences for women, including scientific and popular blaming of couples' sexual problems on women's supposed "frigidity," reducing female sexual pleasure and preventing the examinations of women's own varied erotic feelings. Koedt reviews the factors that have sustained this "myth"—a myth that persists today—and calls for a re-definition of sexuality that emphasized mutual enjoyment between partners.

"The Myth of the Vaginal Orgasm," by Anne Koedt, reprinted from the *First National Women's Liberation Confrence*, 1968, New England Free Press.

Whenever female orgasm and frigidity is discussed, a false distinction is made between the vaginal and the clitoral orgasm. Frigidity has generally been defined by men as the failure of women to have vaginal orgasms. Actually the vagina is not a highly sensitive area and is not constructed to achieve orgasm. It is the clitoris which is the center of sexual sensitivity and which is the female equivalent of the penis.

I think this explains a great many things: First of all, the fact that the so-called frigidity rate among women is phenomenally high. Rather than tracing female frigidity to the false assumptions about female anatomy, our "experts" have declared frigidity a psychological problem of women. Those women who complained about it were recommended psychiatrists, so that they might discover their "problem"–diagnosed generally as a failure to adjust to their role as women.

The facts of female anatomy and sexual response tell a different story. There is only one area for sexual climax, although there are many areas for sexual arousal; that area is the clitoris. All orgasms are extensions of sensation from this area. Since the clitoris is not necessarily stimulated sufficiently in the conventional sexual positions, we are left "frigid".

Aside from physical stimulation, which is the common cause of orgasm for most people, there is also stimulation through primarily mental processes. Some women, for example, may achieve orgasm through sexual fantasies or through fetishes. However, while the stimulation may be psychological, the orgasm manifests itself physically. Thus, while the cause is psychological, the *effect* is still physical, and the orgasm necessarily takes place in the sexual organ equipped for sexual climax–the clitoris. The orgasm experience may also differ in degree of intensity–some more localized, and some more diffuse and sensitive. But they are all clitoral orgasms.

All this leads to some interesting questions about conventional sex and our role in it. Men have orgasms essentially by friction with the vagina, not the clitoral area, which is external and not able to cause friction the way penetration does. Women have thus been defined sexually in terms of what pleases men; our own biology has not been properly analyzed. Instead, we are fed the myth of the liberated woman and her vaginal orgasm–an orgasm which in fact does not exist.

What we must do is redefine our sexuality. We must discard our "formal" concepts of sex and create new guidelines which take into account mutual sexual enjoyment. While the idea of mutual enjoyment is liberally applauded in marriage manuals, it is not followed to its logical conclusion. We must begin to demand that if certain sexual positions now defined as "standard" are not mutually conducive to orgasm, they no longer be defined as standard. New techniques must be used or devised or transform this particular aspect of our current sexual exploitation.

FREUD—A FATHER OF THE VAGINAL ORGASM

Freud contended that the clitoral orgasm was adolescent, and that upon puberty, when women began having intercourse with men, women should transfer the center of orgasm to the vagina. The vagina, it was assumed, was able to produce a parallel, but more mature, orgasm than the clitoris. Much work was done to elaborate on this theory, but little was done to challenge the basic assumptions.

To fully appreciate this incredible invention, perhaps Freud's general attitude about women should first be recalled. Mary Ellman in *Thinking About Women,* summed it up this way:

> Everything in Freud's patronizing and fearful attitude toward women follows from their lack of a penis, but it is only in his essay *The Psychology of Women* that Freud makes explicit . . . the deprecations of women which are implicit in his work. He then prescribes for them the abandonment of the life of the mind, which will interfere with their sexual function. When the psychoanalyzed patient is male, the analyst sets himself the task of developing the man's capacities; but with women patients, the job is to resign them to the limits of their sexuality. As Mr. Rieff puts it: For Freud, "Analysis cannot encourage in women new energies for success and achievement, but only teach them the lesson of rational resignation."

It was Freud's feelings about women's secondary and inferior relationship to men that formed that basis for his theories on female sexuality.

Once having laid down the law about the nature of our sexuality, Freud not so strangely discovered a tremendous problem of frigidity in women. His recommended cure for a woman who was frigid was psychiatric care. She was suffering from failure to mentally adjust to her "natural" role as a woman. Frank S. Caprio, contemporary follower of these ideas, states:

> . . . whenever a woman is incapable of achieving an orgasm via coitus, provided her husband is an adequate partner, and prefers clitoral stimulation to any other form of sexual activity, she can be regarded as suffering from frigidity and requires psychiatric assistance. (*The Sexually Adequate Female,* p. 64)

The explanation given was that women were envious of men– "renunciation of womanhood". Thus it was diagnosed as an anti-male phenomenon.

It is important to emphasize that Freud did not base his theory upon a study of woman's anatomy, but rather upon his assumptions of woman as an inferior appendage to man, and her consequent social and psychological role. In their attempts to deal with the ensuing problem of mass frigidity, Freudians created elaborate mental gymnastics. Marie Bonaparte, in *Female Sexuality,* goes so far as to suggest surgery to help women back on their rightful path. Having discovered a strange connection between the non-frigid woman and the location of the clitoris near the vagina,

> it then occurred to me that where, in certain women, this gap was excessive, and clitoral fixation obdurate, a clitoral-vaginal reconciliation might be effected by surgical means, which would then benefit the normal erotic function. Professor Halban, of Vienna, as much a biologist as surgeon, became interested in the problem and worked out a simple operative technique. In this, the suspensory ligament of the clitoris was severed and the clitoris secured to the underlying structures, thus fixing it in a lower position, with eventual reduction of the labia minora (p. 148)

But the severest damage was not in the area of surgery, where Freudians ran around absurdly trying to change female anatomy to fit their basic assumptions. The worst damage was done to the mental health of women, who either suffered silently with self-blame, or flocked to the psychiatrists looking desperately for the hidden and terrible repression that kept from them their vaginal destiny.

LACK OF EVIDENCE?

One may perhaps at first claim that these are unknown and unexplored areas, but upon closer examination this is certainly not true today, nor was it true even in the past. For example, men have known that women suffered from frigidity often during intercourse. So the problem was there. Also, there is much specific evidence. Men knew that the clitoris was and is the essential organ for masturbation, whether in children or adult women. So obviously women made it clear where *they* thought their sexuality was located. Men also seem suspiciously aware of the clitoral powers during "foreplay", when they want to arouse women and produce the necessary lubrication for penetration. Foreplay is a concept created for male purposes, but works to the disadvantage of many women, since as soon as the woman is aroused the man changes to vaginal stimulation, leaving her both aroused and unsatisfied.

It has also been known that women need no anesthesia inside the vagina during surgery, thus pointing to the fact that the vagina is in fact not a highly sensitive area.

Today, with extensive knowledge of anatomy, with Kinsey, and Masters and Johnson, to mention just a few sources, there is no ignorance on the subject. There are, however, social reasons why this knowledge has not been popularized. We are living in a male society which has not sought change in women's role.

ANATOMICAL EVIDENCE

Rather than starting with what women *ought* to feel, it would seem logical to start out with the anatomical facts regarding the clitoris and vagina.

The Clitoris–is a small equivalent of the penis, except for the fact that the urethra does not go through it as in the man's penis. Its erection is similar to the male erection, and the head of the clitoris has the same type of structure and function as the head of the penis. G. Lombard Kelley, in *Sexual Feelings in Married Men and Women,* says:

> The head of the clitoris is also composed of erectile tissue, and it possesses a very sensitive epithelium or surface covering, supplied with special nerve endings called genital corpuscles, which are peculiarly adapted for sensory stimulation that under proper mental conditions terminates in the sexual orgasm. No other part of the female generative tract has such corpuscles. (Pocketbooks; p. 35)

The clitoris has no other function than that of sexual pleasure.

The Vagina–Its functions are related to the reproductive function. Principally, 1) menstruation, 2) receive penis, 3) hold semen, and 4) birth passage. The interior of the vagina, which according to the defenders of the vaginally caused orgasm is the center and product of the orgasm, is:

> like nearly all other internal body structures, poorly supplied with end organs of touch. The internal entodermal origin of the lining of the vagina makes it similar in this respect to the rectum and other parts of the digestive tract. (Kinsey, *Sexual Behavior in the Human Female*, p. 580)

The degree of insensitivity inside the vagina is so high that "Among the women who were tested in our gynecological sample, less than 14% were at all conscious that they had been touched." (Kinsey, p. 580)

Even the importance of the vagina as an *erotic* center (as opposed to an orgasmic center) has been found to be minor.

Other areas–Labia minora and the vestibule of the vagina. These two sensitive areas may trigger off a clitoral orgasm. Because they can be effectively stimulated during "normal" coitus, though infrequent, this kind of stimulation is incorrectly thought to be vaginal orgasm. However, it is important to distinguish between areas which can stimulate the clitoris, incapable of producing the orgasm themselves, and the clitoris:

> Regardless of what means of excitation is used to bring the individual to the state of sexual climax, the sensation is perceived by the genital corpuscles and is localized where they are situated: in the head of the clitoris or penis. (Kelly, p. 49)

Psychologically Stimulated Organsm–Aside from the above mentioned direct and indirect stimulations of the clitoris, there is a third way an orgasm may be triggered. This is through mental (cortical) stimulation, where the imagination stimulates the brain, which in turn stimulates the genital corpuscles of the glans to set off an orgasm.

WOMEN WHO SAY THEY HAVE VAGINAL ORGASMS

Confusion–Because of the lack of knowledge of their own anatomy, some women accept the idea that an orgasm felt during "normal" intercourse was vaginally caused. This confusion is caused by a combination of two factors. One, failing to locate the center of the orgasm, and two, by a desire to fit her experience to the male-defined idea of sexual normalcy. Considering that women know little about their anatomy, it is easy to be confused.

Deception–The vast majority of women who pretend vaginal orgasm to their men are faking it to, as Ti-Grace Atkinson says "get the job". In a new best-selling Danish book, *I Accuse* (my own translation), Mette Ejlersen specifically deals with this common problem, which she calls the "sex comedy". This comedy has many causes. First of all, the man brings a great deal of pressure to bear on the woman, because he considers his ability as a lover at stake. So as not to offend his ego, the woman will comply with the prescribed role and go through simulated ecstasy. In some of the other Danish women mentioned, women who were left frigid were turned off to sex, and pretended vaginal orgasm to hurry up the sex act. Others admitted that they had faked vaginal orgasm to catch a man. In one case, the woman pretended vaginal orgasm to get him to leave his first wife, who admitted being vaginally frigid. Later she was forced to continue the deception, since obviously she couldn't tell him to stimulate her clitorally.

Many more women were simply afraid to establish their right to equal enjoyment, seeing the sexual act as being primarily for the man's benefit, and any pleasure that the woman got as an added extra.

Other women, with just enough ego to reject the man's idea that they needed psychiatric care, refused to admit their frigidity. They wouldn't accept self-blame, but they didn't know how to solve the problem, not knowing the physiological facts about themselves. So they were left in a peculiar limbo.

Again, perhaps one of the most infuriating and damaging results of this whole charade has been that women who were perfectly healthy sexually were taught that they were not. So in addition to being sexually deprived, these women were told to blame themselves when they deserved no blame. Looking for a cure to a problem that has none can lead a woman on an endless path of self-hatred and insecurity. For she is told by her analyst that not even in her one role allowed in a male society–the role of a woman– is she successful. She is put on the defensive, with phony data as evidence that she better try to be even more feminine, think more feminine, and reject her envy of men. That is, shuffle even harder, baby.

WHY MEN MAINTAIN THE MYTH

1. *Sexual Penetration is Preferred*–The best stimulant for the penis is the woman's vagina. It supplies the necessary friction and lubrication. From a strictly technical point of view this position offers the best physical conditions, even though the man may try other positions for variation.
2. *The Invisible Woman*–One of the elements of male chauvinism is the refusal or inability to see women as total, separate human beings. Rather, men have chosen to define women only in terms of how they benefited men's lives. Sexually, a woman was not seen as an individual wanting to share equally in the sexual act, any more than she was seen as a person with independent desires when she did anything else in society. Thus, it was easy to make up what was convenient about women; for on top of that, society has been a function of male interests, and women were not organized to form even a vocal opposition to the male experts.
3. *The Penis as Epitome of Masculinity*–Men define their lives greatly in terms of masculinity. It is a *universal,* as opposed to racial, ego boosting, which is localized by the geography of racial mixtures.

The essence of male chauvinism is not the practical, economic services women supply. It is the psychological superiority. This kind of negative definition of self, rather than positive definition based upon one's own achievements and development, has of course chained the victim and the oppressor both. But by far the most brutalized of the two is the victim.

An analogy is racism, where the white racist compensates his feelings of unworthiness by creating an image of the black man (it is primarily a male power structure, the white man can socially enforce this mythical division. To the extent that men try to rationalize and justify male superiority through physical differentiation, masculinity may be symbolized by being the *most* muscular, the most hairy, the deepest voice, and the biggest penis. Women, on the other hand, are approved of (i.e., called feminine) if they are weak, petite, shave their legs, have high soft voices, and no penis.

Since the clitoris is almost identical to the penis, one finds a great deal of evidence of men in various societies trying to either ignore the clitoris and emphasize the vagina (as did Freud), or, as in some places in the Mideast, actually performing clitoridectomy. Freud saw this ancient and still practiced custom as a way of further "feminizing" the female by removing this cardinal vestige of her masculinity. It should be noted also that a big clitoris is considered ugly and masculine. Some cultures engage in the practice of pouring a chemical on the clitoris to make it shrivel up to proper size.

It seems clear to me that men in fact fear the clitoris as a threat to their masculinity.

4. *Sexually Expendable Male*–Men fear that they will become sexually expendable if the clitoris is substituted for the vagina as the center of pleasure for women. Actually this has a great deal of validity if one considers *only* the anatomy. The position of the penis inside the vagina, while perfect for reproduction, does not necessarily stimulate an orgasm in women because the clitoris is locally externally and higher up. Women must rely upon indirect stimulation in the "normal" position.

Lesbian sexuality could make an excellent case, based upon anatomical data, for the extinction of the male organ. Albert Ellis says something to the effect that a man without a penis can make a woman an excellent lover.

Considering that the vagina is very desirable from a man's point of view, purely on physical grounds, one begins to see the dilemma for men. And it forces us as well to discard many "physical" arguments explaining why women select men at the exclusion of women as sexual partners.

5. *Control of Women*–One reason given to explain the Mideastern practice of clitoridectomy is that it will keep the women from straying. By removing the sexual organ capable of orgasm, it must be assumed that her sexual drive will diminish. Considering how men look upon their women as property, particularly in very backward nations, we should begin to consider a great deal more why it is not in the men's interest to have women totally free sexually. The double standard, as practiced for example in Latin America, is set up to keep the woman as total property of the husband, while he is free to have affairs as he wishes.

6. *Lesbianism and Bisexuality*–Aside from the strictly anatomical reasons why women might equally seek other women as lovers, there is a fear on men's part that women will seek the company of other women on a full, human basis. The establishment of clitoral orgasm as fact would threaten the heterosexual *institution*. For it would indicate that sexual pleasure was obtainable from either men *or* women, thus making heterosexuality not an absolute, but an option. It would thus open up the whole question of *human* sexual relationships beyond the confines of the present male-female role system.

Questions

1. What is the "myth of the vaginal orgasm"? From what source does it originate? What anatomical evidence does Koedt offer to challenge this myth?
2. What forces have sustained this myth? How has it been damaging to women? What evidence can you point to in popular culture that demonstrate the persistence of this myth even today?
3. What cultural assumptions make women's sexuality and pleasure a difficult topic to discuss? How is sexual anatomy and equal sexual satisfaction tied to personhood?
4. Why is sexuality a key element to women's oppression and therefore "liberation," according to Koedt?

Ain't I a Woman? (1851)

Sojourner Truth

This eloquent 1851 address was given by Sojourner Truth at a women's convention in Akron, Ohio, and recorded by Frances Gage almost ten years later. Born into slavery around 1795, Truth spent years traveling and speaking on behalf of abolitionism and women's rights after she gained her freedom in 1827. Truth's extemporaneous speech responds to women's rights opponents of the Akron convention, and also reveals the inadequacy of the nineteenth century ideals like the "Cult of True Womanhood" to account for all women's experiences.

Well, children, where there is so much racket there must be something out of kilter. I think that 'twixt the negroes of the South and the women of the North, all talking about rights, the white men will be in a fix pretty soon. But what's all this here talking about?

That man over there says that women need to be helped into carriages, and lifted over ditches, and to have the best place everywhere. Nobody ever helps me into carriages, or over mud-

"Ain't I a Woman?" by Sojourner Truth. Reprinted from *Feminism: The Essential Historical Writings,* Miriam Schneir, Editor.

puddles, or gives me any best place! An ain't I a woman? Look at me! Look at my arm! I have ploughed and planted, and gathered into barns, and no man could head me! And ain't I a woman? I could work as much and eat as much as a man—when I could get it— and bear the lash as well! And ain't I a woman? I have borne thirteen children, and seen them most all sold off to slavery, and when I cried out with my mother's grief, none but Jesus heard me! And ain't I a woman?

Then they talk about this thing in the head; what's this they call it? [Intellect, someone whispers.] That's it, honey. What's that got to do with women's rights or negro's rights? If my cup won't hold but a pint, and yours holds a quart, wouldn't you be mean not to let me have my little half-measure full?

Then that little man in black there, he says women can't have as much rights as men, 'cause Christ wasn't a woman! Where did your Christ come from? Where did your Christ come from? From God and a woman! Man had nothing to do with Him.

If the first woman God ever made was strong enough to turn the world upside down all alone, these women together ought to be able to turn it back, and get it right side up again! And now they is asking to do it, the men better let them.

Obliged to you for hearing me, and now old Sojourner ain't got nothing more to say.

Questions

1. What is Truth trying to accomplish in this speech? What is her speaking style? What arguments does she use to combat women's rights opponents? What sources does she draw from to make her points?

2. What might have been the audience reaction to Truth's speech? How would the speech have helped women's rights activists? How might it have hindered them?

3. How does Truth's speech contradict the "Cult of True Womanhood" as a feminine ideal? What issues does she introduce about race and class?

4. How does this address fit into the nineteenth century women's movement? Why does it remain a touchstone for twentieth century feminists?

Morality on a New Scale (1982)

Judith Kegan Gardiner

This brief article describes the work of Harvard Professor and Psychologist Carol Gilligan who has contributed over 20 years of research on adolescence and women's moral development to the field of Psychology. In the 1980s Gilligan questioned why women were often judged to be "less developed" or "inferior" to men on scales of moral development and discovered that the majority of studies on moral development had been done on men and their results generalized to women. Gilligan's own research, published in her well known text In a Different Voice *(1979), found that women were not less moral than men but made their moral decisions differently than men. Although her research overemphasized gender at the expense of other types of differences among women, it changed the face of Psychology 15 years ago and has been essential to rethinking how gender shapes cognitive development. Gilligan's most recent book is* Between Voice and Silence: Women and Girls, Race and Relationship *(1995).*

"Morality on a New Scale," by Judith Kegan Gardiner. Reprinted from *In These Times*, October 20–26, 1982.

Many Victorians believed that women were angelic beings, morally superior to men although incapable of dealing with worldly affairs. Then along came Freud who insisted that women were ethically deficient and unable to make abstract moral judgments. Jean Piaget, Erik Erikson and Lawrence Kohlberg followed, devising models of human development in which women appear deviant or morally stunted.

Now, Harvard psychologist Carol Gilligan challenges all these views. With her study of "women's voices" as expressed in literature and personal interviews, she says there is a different model for moral development that is complementary to the "male" model. This model appeals to responsibilities rather than to rights. It fears isolation rather than aggression. Its emphasis is to care for others before oneself.

Gilligan developed her views under the tutelage of, and in partial opposition to, Kohlberg. His scale for determining moral development starts with egocentric individual needs and climbs past strict adherence to social conventions on the way to the moral pinnacle of the individual conscience judging on the basis of abstract principles. Gilligan noticed that women in Kohlberg's studies stayed on the "conventional" middle rungs of the moral scale much more often than men. She surmised that the rating system was geared to men and that it failed to understand women's approaches to moral questions.

Kohlberg tests children by posing a hypothetical problem: should poor Heinz steal the drug needed to save his dying wife if the druggist won't sell it for a price he can afford? Boys rate high when they answer "yes": the right to life is greater than the right to property. Girls rate low when they refuse to judge in this matter. Instead, many of them want Heinz to talk over the situation with the druggist until the two work out a mutually-satisfactory arrangement. Gilligan suggests that men and women might see moral dilemmas differently and construct different kinds of solutions. Often the men see competing principles and set them up in a hierarchy of values. Many women add details to make the situation concrete. Then they empathize with all its participants and seek to respond in such a way that all are cared for, none are left out, and the consequences don't harm anyone.

Based on interview data, Gilligan builds a scale of moral development more applicable to women than Kohberg's. The lowest rung emphasizes personal survival. At the next stage, survival needs are seen as selfish, so individuals turn to an opposite ideal of selflessness in the service of others. This ideal is rarely attainable. It is closely associated with the anxieties and ambivalences of traditional female roles, and its impossibility generates guilt. The highest stage of moral development on Gilligan's scale integrates the demand for personal integrity with the need to care for others. It includes the self in the group that must not be harmed and recognizes the interdependence of the self and others. Gilligan calls this "the ethic of care." At its broadest, it condemns all forms of exploitation. "The moral imperative that emerges repeatedly in interviews with women," Gilligan writes, "is an injunction to care, a responsibility to discern and alleviate the 'real and recognizable trouble' of this world."

Gilligan argues that men and women achieve a similar maturity, but that they come to it from different directions. Male identity is based on the ideals of individuality and autonomy. Female identity is based on immersion in personal relationships. Often men must learn tolerance and generosity in midlife if they are to avoid despair. However, their adolescence and early manhood trains them to value success over intimacy. On the other hand, many women at midlife have been deeply embedded in the intimate generosity of family relationships. They are taught to subordinate their own achievements to the care of others. Their midlife crisis is likely to be one of separation, not one of attachment. That contemporary women feel peculiarly adrift at this stage in their lives, Gilligan thinks, is "more a commentary on the society than a problem in women's development."

Gilligan shows that both popular psychology and academic theory about the life cycle must be changed to include women equally with men. She implies that the female moral voice gives invaluable lessons to both sexes. For example, she reviews studies of children's games: girls change the rules to preserve their relationships, whereas boys abide by the rules, but think of relationships as easily replaced. Gilligan criticizes those who conclude that girls should be taught to play like boys. They assume "the male model is the better one since it fits the requirements for modern corporate success. In contrast, the sensitivity and care for the feelings of others that girls develop through their play have little market value." As adolescents and adults, men often associate power with aggression, while women see nurturing as powerful. It is not clear from this analysis whether the male model is the invariable product of social power or if it is a special development of capitalism today.

Gilligan makes her thesis with a clear and careful style. She avoids rash generalizations and polarizations, and admits that the small size of her interview samples means additional studies are necessary to confirm her results. She did not analyze her data for class, race or other cultural variables, and this seems an important area for further research. The repeated notion in her study that aggression represents a failure of communication, for example, may reflect the popular humanistic psychology of the '70s as much as it manifests a constant of female psychology.

But this study still has important and immediate political implications. Gilligan shows, for instance, that women respond to the moral crisis of abortion in their own lives with decisions based on an ethic of responsibility. However, as she observed in a recent panel discussion, the public discourse about abortion is posed entirely in "male" terms of abstract rights—"the right to life" versus "the right to choose." The public men speak a different language than the private women. The male legislators misunderstand and therefore devalue the moral standards underlying the decisions of the pro-choice women.

Gilligan demonstrates that developmental psychology based exclusively on a male model is inadequate. She shows how apparently abstract notions of virtue and justice can be culturally biased. Perhaps more importantly, she builds a moral megaphone that enables us to hear women's voices with all their complexity and integrity.

QUESTIONS

1. How does Gilligan alter her moral development scale to more accurately fit the lives of women? How do women make moral decisions differently than men?
2. What social circumstances might contribute to women's different ways of making moral decisions? Why does Gilligan believe it is important to include women's perspective in our thinking about the life cycle?

3. How does the language of the abortion debate fit a male perspective on rights? How might women think about abortion differently than just these terms?

Who Is Female? Science Can't Say (1992)

Gina Kolata

Dividing gender into two distinct categories is problematic when even scientists admit they aren't sure how to be certain if an individual is either male or female. As described in the following New York Times *article, this very dilemma was confronted by researchers involved with testing athletes for competitions like the Olympic games.*

For decades, rumors have persisted that some of the best female athletes have in fact been men. As a result women have been subjected to tests, requiring certificates of femininity before they can compete in national or international events. But the very idea of certifying femaleness raises a thorny question: Who is a man and who is a woman?

For all its dazzling discoveries about the genes that guide a human embryo along its path to maleness or femaleness, science, it appears, cannot provide a simple answer.

Scientists say that dozens of birth defects can blur gender and impossibly complicate the search for a simple genetic test to certify someone as female. A person can be born with "male" sex chromosomes, but because of a mutation in a gene on another chromosome be unable to respond to those hormones. She will look like a woman and see herself as one. Other women will have normal female sex chromosomes, but due to defects in hormone production, have a man's muscles and masculinized genitals, usually an enlarged clitoris. Still others will have the two X chromosomes that most women have, but also a Y chromosome, like most men.

Recognizing the problem, a medical committee of the International Athletic Federation recommended that sports directors abandon their increasingly complex genetic tests. Instead, the committee said in a published statement, doctors should simply look at an athlete's genitals. Their advice runs counter to that of the International Olympic Committee, which recently adopted a technologically sophisticated test that searches for a "male" gene in cells.

The committee's recommendation touches on the essence of human identity, asserting that gender is more a matter of external appearance than of genes and chromosomes.

Dr. Maria New, head of the pediatrics department at New York Hospital-Cornell Medical Center, applauded the recommendation. It is unfair to single out X and Y chromosomes as sole determinants of gender and who has a genetic advantage in sports, she said.

Dr. New said her patients include hundreds of little girls with normal sex chromosomes who have male-muscle patterns and masculinized genitals. This defect occurs in 1 in 13,000 births in the general population, she said, adding that a number of women who won Olympic gold medals have the disorder. She said a milder form occurs in 1 in 30 Ashkenazi Jews. Dr. New also said she often sees boys and men who, despite stereotypically male chromosomes, are, unexpectedly, found to have a uterus.

A Subtle Message

The idea of certifying female athletes as females originated more than 25 years ago. Athletic directors said they were trying to guard against male imposters, but a more subtle message was also being sent, said Alison Carlson, a member of the athletic federation's committee and a tennis coach. A successful female athlete "challenges society's notion of femininity," Ms. Carlson said, so both the athletic directors and the women themselves felt it important to prove they were real women.

In 1965, female athletes had to parade nude in front of doctors. Later that decade, sports discovered science. The athletic federations, including the International Olympic Committee, began testing for the female XX chromosomes, using cells taken from the athlete's mouth.

Despite rumors of men masquerading as women in sports events, only one man has as yet admitted to the ruse. In 1957 Herman Artjen of Bremen, Germany, said the Nazis forced him to enter the Olympic high jump in 1936. He placed fourth.

Since 1968, when the XX chromosome test was instituted by the Olympics, two or three women have failed the test at virtually every Olympic competition and been disqualified for life, Ms. Carlson said. And that, she added, "is just the tip of the iceberg—this trickles down to national, regional and local competitions." The women, almost always too humiliated to fight the tests publicly, take the advice of their coaches and quietly withdraw from competition, Ms. Carlson said.

Other athletes were nearly undone by laboratory errors, she said. Kristen Wengler, a swimmer, took her first gender test in 1985, before an international competition. After the test, the swimmers lined up for their femininity cards, and every woman except Ms. Wengler was handed one. Ms. Wengler was told, in front of the group, that she needed to return to the lab. The results of a second test, showing pieces of a Y chromosome on her X chromosome, were wrong, but Ms. Wengler only discovered this after undergoing more detailed tests at her own expense and waiting four months for the results.

But the real question, scientists said, is: Do chromosome tests of gender address the right issue? And the answer, they said, is no.

If there is any justification at all for testing athletes, it is to bar those with male-muscle mass, said Dr. David C. Page of the Whitehead Institute at the Massachusetts Institute of Technology. But, he said, there are many steps along the way from a Y chromosome to male muscles, the bulky build that results primarily from testosterone.

Dr. Page said, "The connection between the presence or absence of a Y chromosome and muscle mass is very indirect and requires a number of intervening steps."

For that reason, he said, "to focus on one of the first features in sexual differentiation—the presence or absence of a Y chromosome—when what you actually care about is hormonal differences that underlie muscle mass really misses the mark."

QUESTIONS

1. What are some of the ways in which the medical profession determines the sex of an individual?
2. What are some of the implications for masculine and feminine gender roles when the boundaries between male and female become blurred?
3. Should this kind of testing be done for athletes? What kinds of issues does it raise? What implications does it have for the individuals involved?

"Night to His Day": The Social Construction of Gender (1994)

Judith Lorber

In this essay from Paradoxes of Gender, *sociologist Judith Lorber presents us with a new way to think about something we all take for granted—gender. She argues that gender is a paradox: something that is culturally assigned to us at birth and at the same time something we actively create throughout our lives. Gender organizes our social relations and our basic institutions, like religion, education, work and the state. We understand the cultural significance of gender only when our expectations about gender are disrupted in some way.*

Talking about gender for most people is the equivalent of fish talking about water. Gender is so much the routine ground of everyday activities that questioning its taken-for-granted assumptions and presuppositions is like thinking about whether the sun will come up.[1] Gender is so pervasive that in our society we assume it is bred into our genes. Most people find it hard to believe that gender is constantly created and re-created out of human interaction, out of social life, and is the texture and order of that social life. Yet gender, like culture, is a human production that depends on everyone constantly "doing gender" (West and Zimmerman 1987).

And everyone "does gender" without thinking about it. Today, on the subway, I saw a well-dressed man with a year-old child in a stroller. Yesterday, on a bus, I saw a man with a tiny baby in a carrier on his chest. Seeing men taking care of small children in public is increasingly common—at least in New York City. But both men were quite obviously stared at—and smiled at, approvingly. Everyone was doing gender—the men who were changing the role of fathers and the other passengers, who were applauding them silently. But there was more gendering going on that probably fewer people noticed. The baby was wearing a white crocheted cap and white clothes. You couldn't tell if it was a boy or a girl. The child in the stroller was wearing a dark blue T-shirt and dark print pants. As they started to leave the train, the father put a Yankee baseball cap on the child's head. Ah, a boy, I thought. Then I noticed the gleam of tiny earrings in the child's ears, and as they got off, I saw the little flowered sneakers and lace-trimmed socks. Not a boy after all. Gender done.

Gender is such a familiar part of daily life that it usually takes a deliberate disruption of our expectations of how women and men are supposed to act to pay attention to how it is produced. Gender signs and signals are so ubiquitous that we usually fail to note them—unless they are missing or ambiguous. Then we are uncomfortable until we have successfully placed the other person in a gender status; otherwise, we feel socially dislocated. In our society, in addition to man and woman, the status can be *transvestite* (a person who dresses in opposite gender clothes) and *transsexual* (a person who has had sex-change surgery). Transvestites and transsexuals carefully construct their gender status by dressing, speaking, walking, gesturing in the ways prescribed for women or men—whichever they want to be taken for—and so does any "normal" person.

For the individual, gentler construction starts with assignment to a sex category on the basis of what the genitalia look like at birth.[2] Then babies are dressed or adorned in a way that displays the category because parents don't want to be constantly asked whether their baby is a girl or a boy. A sex category becomes a gentler status through naming, dress, and the use of other gender markers. Once a child's gender is evident, others treat those in one gender differently from those in the other, and the children respond to the different treatment by feeling different and behaving differently. As soon as they can talk, they start to refer to themselves as members of their gender. Sex doesn't come into play again until puberty, but by that time, sexual feelings and desires and practices have been shaped by gendered norms and expectations. Adolescent boys and girls approach and avoid each other in an elaborately scripted and gendered mating dance. Parenting is gendered, with different expectations for mothers and for fathers, and people of different genders work at different kinds of jobs. The work adults do as mothers and fathers and as low-level workers and high-level bosses, shapes women's and men's life experiences, and these experiences produce different feelings, consciousness, relationships, skills—ways of being that we call feminine or masculine.[3] All of these processes constitute the social construction of gender.

Gendered roles change—today fathers are taking care of little children, girls and boys are wearing unisex clothing and getting the same education, women and men are working at the same jobs. Although many traditional social groups are quite strict about maintaining gender differences, in other social groups they seem to be blurring. Then why the one-year-old's earrings? Why is it still so important to mark a child as a girl or a boy, to make sure she is not taken for a boy or he for a girl? What would happen if they were? They would, quite literally, have changed places in their social world.

To explain why gendering is done from birth, constantly and by everyone, we have to look not only at the way individuals experience gender but at gender as a social institution. As a social institution, gender is one of the major ways that human beings organize their lives. Human society depends on a predictable division of labor, a designated allocation of scarce goods, assigned responsibility for children and others who cannot care for themselves, common values and their systematic transmission to new members, legitimate leadership, music, art, stories, games, and other symbolic productions. One way of choosing people for the different tasks of society is on the basis of their talents, motivations, and competence—their demonstrated achievements. The other way is on the basis of gender, race, ethnicity—ascribed membership in a category of people. Although societies vary in the extent to which they use one or the other of these ways of allocating people to work and to carry out other responsibilities, every society uses gender and age grades. Every society classifies people as "girl and boy children," "girls and boys ready to be married," and "fully adult women and men," constructs similarities among them and differences between them, and assigns them to different roles and responsibilities. Personality characteristics, feelings, motivations, and ambitions flow from these different life experiences so that the members of these different groups become different kinds of people. The process of gendering and its outcome are legitimated by religion, law, science, and the society's entire set of values. . . .

Western society's values legitimate gendering by claiming that it all comes from physiology—female and male procreative differences. But gender and sex are not equivalent, and gender as a social construction does not flow automatically from genitalia and reproductive organs, the main physiological differences of females and males. In the construction of ascribed social statuses, physiological differences such as sex, stage of development, color of skin, and size are crude markers. They are not the source of the social statuses of gender, age, grade, and race. Social statuses are carefully constructed through prescribed processes of teaching, learning, emulation, and enforcement. Whatever genes, hormones, and biological evolution contribute to human social institutions is materially as well as qualitatively transformed by social practices. Every social institution has a material base, but culture and social practices transform that base into something with qualitatively different patterns and constraints. The economy is much more than producing food and goods and distributing them to eaters and users; family and kinship are not the equivalent of having sex and procreating; morals and religions cannot be equated with the fears and ecstasies of the brain; language goes far beyond the sounds produced by tongue and larynx. No one eats "money" or "credit"; the concepts of "god" and "angels" are the subjects of theological disquisitions; not only words but objects, such as their flag, "speak" to the citizens of a country.

Similarly, gender cannot be equated with biological and physiological differences between human females and males. The building blocks of gender are *socially constructed statuses.* Western societies have only two genders, "man" and "woman." Some societies have three genders—men, women, and *berdaches* or *hijras* or *xaniths.* Berdaches, hijras, and xaniths are biological males who behave, dress, work, and are treated in most respects as social women; they are therefore not men, nor are they female women; they are, in our language, "male women."[4] There are African and American Indian societies that have a gender status called *manly hearted women*—biological females who work, marry, and parent as men; their social status is "female men" (Amadiume 1987; Blackwood 1984). They do not have to behave or dress as men to have the social responsibilities and prerogatives of husbands and fathers; what makes them men is enough wealth to buy a wife.

Modern Western societies' *transsexuals* and *transvestites* are the nearest equivalent of these crossover genders, but they are not institutionalized as third genders (Bolin 1987). Transsexuals are biological males and females who have sex-change operations to alter their genitalia. They do so in order to bring their physical anatomy in congruence with the way they want to live and with their own sense of gender identity. They do not become a third gender; they change genders. Transvestites are males who live as women and females who live as men but do not intend to have sex-change surgery. Their dress, appearance, and mannerisms fall within the range of what is expected from members of the opposite gender, so that they "pass." They also change genders, sometimes temporarily, some for most of their lives. Transvestite women have fought in wars as men soldiers as recently as the nineteenth century; some married women, and others went back to being women and married men once the war was over.[5] Some were discovered when their wounds were treated; others not until they died. In order to work as a jazz musician, a man's occupation, Billy Tipton, a woman, lived most of her life as a man. She died recently at seventy-four, leaving a wife and three adopted sons for whom she was husband and father, and musicians with whom she had played and traveled, for whom she was "one of the boys" (*New York Times* 1989).[6] There have been many other such occurrences of women passing as men to do more prestigious or lucrative men's work (Matthaei 1982, 192–93).[7]

Genders, therefore, are not attached to a biological substratum. Gender boundaries are breachable, and individual and socially organized shifts from one gender to another call attention to "cultural, social, or aesthetic dissonances" (Garber 1992, 16). These odd or deviant or third genders show us what we ordinarily take for granted—that people have to learn to be women and men. Men who cross-dress for performances or for pleasure often learn from women's magazines how to "do femininity" convincingly (Garber 1992, 41–51). Because transvestism is direct evidence of how gender is constructed, Marjorie Garber claims it has "extraordinary power . . . to disrupt, expose, and challenge, putting in question the very notion of the 'original' and of stable identity" (1992, 16).

GENDER BENDING

It is difficult to see how gender is constructed because we take it for granted that it's all biology, or hormones, or human nature. The differences between women and men seem to be self-evident, and we think they would occur no matter what society did. But in actuality, human females and males are physiologically more similar in appearance than are the two sexes of many species of animals and are more alike than different in traits and behavior (C. F. Epstein 1988). Without the deliberate use of gendered clothing, hairstyles, jewelry, and cosmetics, women and men would look far more alike.[8] Even societies that do not cover women's breasts have gender-identifying clothing, scarification, jewelry, and hairstyles.

The ease with which many transvestite women pass as men and transvestite men as women is corroborated by the common gender misidentification in Westernized societies of people in jeans, T-shirts, and sneakers. Men with long hair may be addressed as "miss," and women with short hair are often taken for men unless they offset the potential ambiguity with deliberate gender markers (Devor 1987, 1989). Jan Morris, in *Conundrum,* an autobiographical account of events just before and just after a sex-change operation, described how easy it was to shift back and forth from being a man to being a woman when testing how it would feel to change gender status. During this time, Morris still had a penis and wore more or less unisex clothing; the context alone made the man and the woman:

> Sometimes the arena of my ambivalence was uncomfortably small. At the Travellers' Club, for example, I was obviously known as a man of sorts—women were only allowed on the

> premises at all during a few hours of the day, and even then were hidden away as far as possible in lesser rooms or alcoves. But I had another club, only a few hundred yards away, where I was known only as a woman, and often I went directly from one to the other, imperceptibly changing roles on the way—"Cheerio, sir," the porter would say at one club, and "Hello, madam," the porter would greet me at the other. (1975, 132)

Gentler shifts are actually a common phenomenon in public roles as well. Queen Elizabeth II of England bore children, but when she went to Saudi Arabia on a state visit, she was considered an honorary man so that she could confer and dine with the men who were heads of a state that forbids unrelated men and women to have face-to-unveiled-face contact. In contemporary Egypt, lower-class women who run restaurants or shops dress in men's clothing and engage in unfeminine aggressive behavior, and middle-class educated women of professional or managerial status can take positions of authority (Rugh 1986, 131). In these situations, there is an important status change: These women are treated by the others in the situation as if they are men. From their own point of view, they are still women. From the social perspective, however, they are men.[9]

In many cultures, gender bending is prevalent in theater or dance—the Japanese kabuki are men actors who play both women and men; in Shakespeare's theater company, there were no actresses. Juliet and Lady Macbeth were played by boys. Shakespeare's comedies are full of witty comments on gender shifts. Women characters frequently masquerade as young men, and other women characters fall in love with them; the boys playing these masquerading women, meanwhile, are acting out pining for the love of men characters.[10] . . .

But despite the ease with which gender boundaries can be traversed in work, in social relationship, and in cultural productions, gender statuses remain. Transvestites and transsexuals do not challenge the social construction of gender. Their goal is to be feminine women and masculine men. (Kando 1973). Those who do not want to change their anatomy but do want to change their gender behavior fare less well in establishing their social identity.

Paradoxically, then, bending gender rules and passing between genders does not erode but rather preserves gender boundaries. In societies with only two genders, the gender dichotomy is not disturbed by transvestites, because others feel that a transvestite is only transitorily ambiguous—is "really a man or woman underneath." After sex change surgery, transsexuals end up in a conventional gender status—a "man" or a "woman" with the appropriate genitals (Eichler 1989). When women dress as men for business reasons, they are indicating that in that situation, they want to be treated the way men are treated; when they dress as women, they want to be treated as women:

> By their male dress, female entrepreneurs signal their desire to suspend the expectations of accepted feminine conduct without losing respect and reputation. By wearing what is "unattractive" they signify that they are not intending to display their physical charms while engaging in public activity. Their loud, aggressive banter contrasts with the modest demeanor that attracts men. . . . Overt signalling of a suspension of the rules preserves normal conduct from eroding expectations. (Rugh 1986, 131)

FOR INDIVIDUALS, GENDER MEANS SAMENESS

Although the possible combinations of genitalia, body shapes, clothing, mannerisms, sexuality, and roles could produce infinite varieties in human beings, the social institution of gender depends on the production and maintenance of a limited number of gender statuses and of making the members of these statuses similar to each other. Individuals are born sexed but not gendered, and they have to be taught to be masculine or feminine.[11] As Simone de Beauvoir said: "One is not born, but rather becomes, a woman . . . ; it is civilization as a whole that produces this creature . . . which is described as feminine." (1952, 267).

Children learn to walk, talk, and gesture the way their social group says girls and boys should. Ray Birdwhistell, in his analysis of body motion as human communication, calls these learned gender displays *tertiary* sex characteristics and argues that they are needed to distinguish genders because humans are a weakly dimorphic species—their only sex markers are genitalia (1970, 39–46). Clothing, paradoxically, often hides the sex but displays the gender.

In early childhood, humans develop gendered personality structures and sexual orientations through their interactions with parents of the same and opposite gender. As adolescents, they conduct their sexual behavior according to gendered scripts. Schools, parents, peers, and the mass media guide young people into gendered work and family roles. As adults, they take on a gendered social status in their society's stratification system. Gender is thus both ascribed and achieved (West and Zimmerman 1987).

The achievement of gender was most dramatically revealed in a case of an accidental transsexual—a baby boy whose penis was destroyed in the course of a botched circumcision when he was seven months old (Money and Ehrhardt 1972, 118–23). The child's sex category was changed to "female," and a vagina was surgically constructed when the child was seventeen months old. The parents were advised that they could successfully raise the child, one of identical twins, as a girl. Physicians assured them that the child was too young to have formed a gender identity. Children's sense of which gender they belong to usually develops around the age of three, at the time that they start to group objects and recognize that the people around them also fit into categories big, little; pink-skinned, brown-skinned; boys, girls. Three has also been the age when children's appearance is ritually gendered, usually by cutting a boy's hair or dressing him in distinctively masculine clothing. In Victorian times, English boys wore dresses up to the age of three, when they were put into short pants (Garber 1992, 1–2).

The parents of the accidental transsexual bent over backward to feminize the child—and succeeded. Frilly dresses, hair ribbons, and jewelry created a pride in looks, neatness, and "daintiness." More significant, the child's dominance was also feminized:

> The girl had many tomboyish traits, such as abundant physical energy, a high level of activity, stubbornness, and being often the dominant one in a girls' group. Her mother tried to modify her tomboyishness: " . . . I teach her to be more polite and quiet. I always wanted those virtues. I never did manage, but I'm going to try to manage them—to my daughter—to be more quiet and ladylike." From the beginning the girl had been the dominant twin. By the age of three, her dominance over her brother was, as her mother described it, that of a mother hen. The boy in turn took up for his sister, if anyone threatened her. (Money and Ehrhardt 1972, 122).

This child was not a tomboy because of male genes or hormones; according to her mother, she herself had also been a tomboy. What the mother had learned poorly while growing up as a "natural" female she insisted that her physically reconstructed son-daughter learn well. For both mother and child, the social construction of gender overrode any possibly inborn traits.

People go along with the imposition of gender norms because the weight of morality as well as immediate social pressure enforces them. Consider how many instructions for properly gendered behavior are packed into this mother's admonition to her daughter: "This is how to hem a dress when you see the hem coming down and so to prevent yourself from looking like the slut I know you are so bent on becoming" (Kincaid 1978).

Gender norms are inscribed in the way people move, gesture, and even eat. In one African society, men were supposed to eat with their "whole mouth, wholeheartedly, and not, like women, just with the lips, that is halfheartedly, with reservation and restraint" (Bourdieu [1980], 1990, 70). Men and women in this society learned to walk in ways that proclaimed their different positions in the society:

> The manly man . . . stands up straight into the face of the person he approaches, or wishes to welcome. Ever on the alert, because ever threatened, he misses nothing of what happens around him. . . . Conversely, a well brought-up woman . . . is expected to walk with a slight stoop, avoiding every misplaced movement of her body, her head or her arms, looking down, keeping her eyes on the spot where she will next put her foot, especially if she happens to have to walk past the men's assembly. (70)

Many cultures go beyond clothing, gestures, and demeanor in gendering children. They inscribe gender directly into bodies. In traditional Chinese society, mothers bound their daughters' feet into three-inch stumps to enhance their sexual attractiveness. Jewish fathers circumcise their infant sons to show their covenant with God. Women in African societies remove the clitoris of prepubescent girls, scrape their labia, and make the lips grow together to preserve their chastity and ensure their marriageability. In Western societies, women augment their breast size with silicone and reconstruct their faces with cosmetic surgery to conform to cultural ideals of feminine beauty. . . .

Most parents create a gendered world for their newborn by naming, birth announcements, and dress. Children's relationships with same-gendered and different-gendered caretakers structure their self-identifications and personalities. Through cognitive development, children extract and apply to their own actions the appropriate behavior for those who belong in their own gender, as well as race, religion, ethnic group, and social class, rejecting what is not appropriate. If their social categories are highly valued, they value themselves highly; if their social categories are low status, they lose self-esteem (Chodorow 1974). Many feminist parents who want to raise androgynous children soon lose their children to the pull of gendered norms (T. Gordon 1990, 87–90). My son attended a carefully nonsexist elementary school, which didn't even have girls' and boys' bathrooms. When he was seven or eight years old, I attended a class play about "squares" and "circles" and their need for each other and noticed that all the girl squares and circles wore makeup, but none of the boy squares and circles did. I asked the teacher about it after the play, and she said, "Bobby said he was not going to wear makeup, and he is a powerful child, so none of the boys would either." In a long discussion about conformity, my son confronted me with the question of who the conformists were, the boys who followed their leader or the girls who listened to the woman teacher. In actuality, they both were, because they both followed same-gender leaders and acted in gender-appropriate ways. (Actors may wear makeup, but real boys don't.)

For human beings there is no essential femaleness or maleness, femininity or masculinity, womanhood or manhood, but once gender is ascribed, the social order constructs and holds individuals to strongly gendered norms and expectations. Individuals may vary on many of the components of gender and may shift genders temporarily or permanently, but they must fit into the limited number of gender statuses their society recognizes. In the process, they re-create their society's version of women and men: "If we do gender appropriately, we simultaneously sustain, reproduce, and render legitimate the institutional arrangements. . . . If we fail to do gender appropriately, we as individuals—not the institutional arrangements—may be called to account (for our character, motives, and predispositions)" (West and Zimmerman 1987, 146).

The gendered practices of everyday life reproduce a society's view of how women and men should act (Bourdieu [1980] 1990). Gendered social arrangements are justified by religion and cultural productions and backed by law, but the most powerful means of sustaining the moral hegemony of the dominant gender ideology is that the process is made invisible; any possible alternatives are virtually unthinkable (Foucault 1972; Gramsci 1971).[12]

For Society, Gender Means Difference

The pervasiveness of gender as a way of structuring social life demands that gender statuses be clearly differentiated. Varied talents, sexual preferences, identities, personalities, interests, and ways of interacting fragment the individual's bodily and social experiences. Nonetheless, these are organized in Western cultures into two and only two socially and legally recognized gender statuses, "man" and "woman."[13] In the social construction of gender, it does not matter what men and women actually do; it does not even matter if they do exactly the same thing. The social institution of gender insists only that what they do is *perceived* as different.

If men and women are doing the same tasks, they are usually spatially segregated to maintain gender separation, and often the tasks are given different job titles as well, such as executive secretary and administrative assistant (Reskin 1988). If the differences between women and men begin to blur, society's "sameness taboo" goes into action (G. Rubin 1975, 178). At a rock and roll dance at West Point in 1976, the year women were admitted to the prestigious military academy for the first time, the school's administrators "were reportedly perturbed by the sight of mirror-image couples dancing in short hair and dress gray trousers," and a rule was established that women cadets could dance at these events only if they wore skirts (Barkalow and Raab 1990, 53).[14] Women recruits in the U.S. Marine Corps are required to wear makeup—at a minimum, lipstick and eye shadow—and they have to take classes in makeup, hair care, poise, and etiquette. This feminization is part of a deliberate policy of making them clearly distinguishable from men Marines. Christine Williams quotes a twenty-five-year-old woman drill instructor as saying: "A lot of the recruits who come here don't wear makeup; they're tomboyish or athletic. A lot of them have the preconceived idea that going into the military means they can still be a tomboy. They don't realize that you are a *Woman* Marine" (1989, 76–77).[15]

If gender differences were genetic, physiological, or hormonal, gender bending and gender ambiguity would occur only in hermaphrodites, who are born with chromosomes and genitalia that are not clearly female or male. Since gender differences are socially constructed, all men and all women can enact the behavior of the other, because they know the other's social script: "'Man' and 'woman' are at once empty and overflowing categories. Empty because they have no ultimate, transcendental meaning. Overflowing because even when they appear to be fixed, they still contain within them alternative, denied, or suppressed definitions." (J. W. Scott 1988a, 49). Nonetheless, though individuals may be able to shift gender statuses, the gender boundaries have to hold, or the whole gendered social order will come crashing down.

Pardoxically, it is the social importance of gender statuses and their external markers—clothing, mannerisms, and spatial segregation—that makes gender bending or gender crossing possible—or even necessary. The social viability of differentiated gender statuses produces the need or desire to shift statuses. Without gender differentiation, transvestism and transsexuality would be meaningless. You couldn't dress in the opposite gender's clothing if all clothing were unisex. There would be no need to reconstruct genitalia to match identity if interests and life-styles were not gendered. There would be no need for women to pass as men to do certain kinds of work if jobs were not typed as "women's work" and "men's work." Women would not have to dress as men in public life in order to give orders or aggressively bargain with customers.

Gender boundaries are preserved when transsexuals create congruous autobiographies of always having felt like what they are now. The transvestite's story also "recuperates social and sexual norms" (Garber 1992, 69). In the transvestite's normalized narrative, he or she "is 'compelled' by social and economic forces to disguise himself or herself in order to get a job, escape repression, or gain artistic or political 'freedom'" (Garber 1992, 70). The "true identity" when revealed, causes amazement over how easily and successfully the person passed as a member of the opposite gender, not a suspicion that gender itself is something of a put on. . . .

NOTES

1. Gender is, in Erving Goffman's words, an aspect of *Felicity's Condition:* "any arrangement which leads us to judge an individual's . . . acts not to be a manifestation of strangeness. Behind *Felicity's Condition* is our sense of what it is to be sane" (1983, 27). Also see Bem 1993; Frye 1983, 17–40; Goffman 1977.

2. In cases of ambiguity in countries with modern medicine, surgery is usually performed to make the genitalia more clearly male or female.

3. See J. Butler 1990 for an analysis of how doing gender *is* gender identity.

4. On the hijras of India, see Nanda 1990; on the xaniths of Oman, Wikan 1982, 168–86; on the American Indian berdaches, W. L. Williams 1986. Other societies that have similar institutionalized third-gender men are the Koniag of Alaska, the Tanala of Madagascar, the Mesakin of Nuba, and the Chukchee of Siberia (Wikan 1982, 170).

5. Durova 1989; Freeman and Bond 1992; Wheelwright 1989.

6. Gender segregation of work in popular music still has not changed very much, according to Groce and Cooper 1989, despite considerable androgyny in some very popular figures. See Garber 1992 on the androgyny. She discusses Tipton on pp. 67–70.

7. In the nineteenth century, not only did these women get men's wages, but they also "had male privileges and could do all manner of things other women could not: open a bank account, write checks, own property, go anywhere unaccompanied, vote in elections" (Faderman 1991, 44).

8. When unisex clothing and men wearing long hair came into vogue in the United States in the mid-1960s, beards and mustaches for men also came into style again as gender identifications.

9. For other accounts of women being treated as men in Islamic countries, as well as accounts of women and men cross-dressing in these countries, see Garber 1992, 304–52.
10. Dollimore 1986; Garber 1992, 32–40; Greenblatt 1987, 66–93; Howard 1988. For Renaissance accounts of sexual relations with women and men of ambiguous sex, see Laqueur 1990a, 134–39. For modern accounts of women passing as men that other women find sexually attractive, see Devor 1989, 136–37; Wheelwright 1989, 53–59.
11. For an account of how a potential man-to-woman transsexual learned to be feminine, see Garfinkel 1967, 116–85, 285–88. For a gloss on this account that points out how, throughout his encounters with Agnes, Garfinkel failed to see how he himself was constructing his own masculinity, see Rogers 1992.
12. The concepts of moral hegemony, the effects of everyday activities (praxis) on thought and personality, and the necessity of consciousness of these processes before political change can occur are all based on Marx's analysis of class relations.
13. Other societies recognize more than two categories, but usually no more than three or four (Jacobs and Roberts 1989).
14. Carol Barkalow's book has a photograph of eleven first-year West Pointers in a math class, who are dressed in regulation pants, shirts, and sweaters, with short haircuts. The caption challenges the reader to locate the only woman in the room.
15. The taboo on males and females looking alike reflects the U.S. military's homophobia (Bérubé 1989). If you can't tell those with a penis from those with a vagina, how are you going to determine whether their sexual interest is heterosexual or homosexual unless you watch them having sexual relations?

QUESTIONS

1. What is the first question we ask about the newborn? Why is this important knowledge? What is the relationship between sex and gender? Between biology and culture?
2. What does it mean to say gender is socially constructed? How do individuals "do" gender? Is it possible to change the way you do gender? What are the consequences? How does gender get inscribed on the body?
3. What does gender bending or gender crossing teach us about gender categories and boundaries? What makes gender shifts possible? Have you ever been in a circumstance where you have violated the taken-for-granted norms about your gender? Describe what happened.
4. How does the author interpret the words of Simone de Beauvoir, "One is not born, but rather becomes, a woman"?
5. According to Lorber, "man" and "woman" are at once "empty and overflowing" categories. Discuss what you think she means? Why does she put quotation marks around the words man and woman? Why are they often defined as opposites?

Age, Race, Class, and Sex: Women Redefining Difference (1984)

Audre Lorde

An African-American feminist poet, theorist, and activist, Audre Lorde is the author of 12 collections of poetry and 6 works of prose, including Coal, Sister Outsider, Cables to Rage, Use of the Erotic: The Erotic as Power, *and a memoir about her battle with breast cancer entitled* The Cancer Journals. *She is also credited with co-founding Kitchen Table: Women of Color Press with Barbara Smith. In this 1984 essay, Lorde conveys the difficulties of African American women active in a movement dominated by white women, and a civil rights movement dominated by African American men. Urging the acknowledgment of differences both within and across categories of age, race, class and sex, Lorde emphasizes human diversity as a force to seize and utilize, rather than as an obstacle to unity.*

Much of Western European history conditions us to see human differences in simplistic opposition to each other: dominant/subordinate, good/bad, up/down, superior/inferior.[1,2] In a society where the good is defined in terms of profit rather than in terms of human need, there must always be some group of people who, through systematized oppression, can be made to feel surplus, to occupy the place of the dehumanized inferior. Within this society, that group is made up of Black and Third World people, working-class people, older people and women.

As a 49-year-old Black lesbian feminist socialist mother of two, including one boy, and a member of an interracial couple, I usually find myself a part of some group defined as other, deviant, inferior or just plain wrong. Traditionally, in American society, it is the members of oppressed, objectified groups who are expected to stretch out and bridge the gap between the actualities of our lives and the consciousness of our oppressor. For in order to survive, those of us for whom oppression is as American as apple pie have always had to be watchers, to become familiar with the language and manners of the oppressor, even sometimes adopting them for some illusion of protection. Whenever the need for some pretense of communication arises, those who profit from our oppression call upon us to share our knowledge with them. In other words, it is the responsibility of the oppressed to teach the oppressors their mistakes. I am responsible for educating teachers who dismiss my children's culture in school. Black and Third World people are expected to educate white people as to our humanity. Women are expected to educate men. Lesbians and gay men are expected to educate the heterosexual world. The oppressors maintain their position and evade responsibility for their own actions. There is a constant drain of energy which might be better used in redefining ourselves and devising realistic scenarios for altering the present and constructing the future.

Institutionalized rejection of difference is an absolute necessity in a profit economy which needs outsiders as surplus people. As members of such an economy, we have *all* been programmed to respond to the human differences between us with fear and loathing and to handle that difference in one of three ways: ignore it, and if that is not possible, copy it if we think it is dominant, or destroy it if we think it is subordinate. But we have no patterns for relating across our human differences as equals. As a result, those differences have been misnamed and misused in the service of separation and confusion.

Certainly there are very real differences between us of race, age, and sex. But it is not those differences between us that are separating us. It is rather our refusal to recognize those differences, and to examine the distortions which result from our misnaming them and their effects upon human behavior and expectation.

Racism, the belief in the inherent superiority of one race over all others and thereby the right to dominance. Sexism, the belief in the inherent superiority of one sex over the other and thereby the right to dominance. Ageism. Heterosexism. Elitism. Classism.

It is a lifetime pursuit for each one of us to extract these distortions from our living at the same time as we recognize, reclaim and define those differences upon which they are imposed. For we have all been raised in a society where those distortions were endemic within our living. Too often, we pour the energy needed for recognizing and exploring difference into pretending those differences are insurmountable barriers, or that they do not exist at all. This results in a voluntary isolation, or false and treacherous connections. Either way, we do not develop tools for using human difference as a springboard for creative change within our lives. We speak not of human difference, but of human deviance.

Somewhere, on the edge of consciousness, there is what I call a *mythical norm*, which each one of us within our hearts knows "that is not me." In America, this norm is usually defined as white, thin, male, young, heterosexual, christian and financially secure. It is with this mythical norm that the trappings of power reside within this society. Those of us who stand outside that power often identify one way in which we are different, and we assume that to be the primary cause of all oppression, forgetting other distortions around difference, some of which we ourselves may be practicing. By and large within the woman's movement today, white women focus upon their oppression as women and ignore differences of race, sexual preference, class and age. There is a pretense to a homogeneity of experience covered by the word *sisterhood* that does not in fact exist.

Unacknowledged class differences rob women of each other's energy and creative insight. Recently a women's magazine collective made the decision for one issue to print only prose, saying poetry was a less "rigorous" or "serious" art form. Yet even the form our creativity takes is often a class issue. Of all the art forms, poetry is the most economical. It is the one which is the most secret, which requires the least physical labor, the least material, and the one which can be done between shifts, in the hospital pantry, on the subway, and on scraps of surplus paper. Over the last few years, writing a novel on tight finances, I came to appreciate the enormous differences in the material demands between poetry and prose. As we reclaim our literature, poetry has been the major voice of poor, working-class and Colored women. A room of one's own may be a necessity for writing prose, but so are reams of paper, a typewriter and plenty of time. The actual requirements to produce the visual arts also help determine, along class lines, whose art is whose. In this day of inflated prices for material, who are our sculptors, our painters, our photographers? When we speak of a broadly based women's culture, we need to be aware of the effect of class and economic differences on the supplies available for producing art.

As we move toward creating a society within which we can each flourish, ageism is another distortion of relationship which interferes without vision. By ignoring the past, we are encouraged to repeat its mistakes. The "generation gap" is an important social tool for any repressive society. If the younger members of a community view the older members as contemptible or suspect or excess, they will never be able to join hands and examine the living memories of the community, nor ask the all important question, "Why?" This gives rise to a historical amnesia that keeps us working to invent the wheel every time we have to go to the store for bread.

We find ourselves having to repeat and relearn the same old lessons over and over that our mothers did because we do not pass on what we have learned, or because we are unable to listen. For instance, how many times has this all been said before? For another, who would have believed that once again our daughters are allowing their bodies to be hampered and purgatoried by girdles and high heels and hobble skirts?

Ignoring the differences of race between women and the implications of those differences presents the most serious threat to the mobilization of women's joint power.

As white women ignore their built-in privilege of whiteness and define *woman* in terms of their own experience alone, then women of Color become "other," the outsider whose experience and tradition is too "alien" to comprehend. An example of this is the signal absence of the experience of women of Color as a resource for women's studies courses. The literature of women of Color is seldom included in women's literature courses and almost never in other literature courses, nor in women's studies as a whole. All too often, the excuse given is that the literatures of women of Color can only be taught by Colored women, or that they are too difficult to understand, or that classes cannot "get into" them because they come out of experiences that are "too different." I have heard this argument presented by white women of otherwise quite clear intelligence, women who seem to have no trouble at all teaching and reviewing work that comes out of the vastly different experiences of Shakespeare, Molière, Dostoyevsky and Aristophanes. Surely there must be some other explanation.

This is a very complex question, but I believe one of the reasons white women have such difficulty reading Black women's work is because of their reluctance to see Black women as women and different from themselves. To examine Black women's literature effectively requires that we be seen as whole people in our actual complexities—as individuals, as women, as human—rather than as one of those problematic but familiar stereotypes provided in this society in place of genuine images of Black women. And I believe this holds true for the literatures of other women of Color who are not Black.

The literatures of all women of Color recreate the textures of our lives, and many white women are heavily invested in ignoring the real differences. For as long as any difference between us means one of us must be inferior, then the recognition of any difference must be fraught with guilt. To allow women of Color to step out of stereotypes is too guilt provoking, for it threatens the complacency of those women who view oppression only in terms of sex.

Refusing to recognize difference makes it impossible to see the different problems and pitfalls facing us as women.

Thus, in a patriarchal power system where white skin privilege is a major prop, the entrapments used to neutralize Black women and white women are not the same. For example, it is easy for Black women to be used by the power structure against Black men, not because they are men, but because they are Black. Therefore, for Black women, it is necessary at all times to separate the needs of the oppressor from our own legitimate conflicts within our communities. This same problem does not exist for white women. Black women and men have shared racist oppression and still share it, although in different ways. Out of that shared oppression we have developed joint defenses and joint vulnerabilities to each other that are not duplicated in the white community, with the exception of the relationship between Jewish women and Jewish men.

On the other hand, white women face the pitfall of being seduced into joining the oppressor under the pretense of sharing power. This possibility does not exist in the same way for women of Color. The tokenism that is sometimes extended to us is not an invitation to join power; our racial "otherness" is a visible reality that makes that quite clear. For white women there is a wider range of pretended choices and rewards for identifying with patriarchal power and its tools.

Today, with the defeat of ERA, the tightening economy and increased conservatism, it is easier once again for white women to believe the dangerous fantasy that if you are good enough, pretty enough, sweet enough, quiet enough, teach the children to behave, hate the right people, and marry the right men, then you will be allowed to co-exist with patriarchy in relative peace, at least until a man needs your job or the neighborhood rapist happens along. And true, unless one lives and loves in the trenches it is difficult to remember that the war against dehumanization is ceaseless.

But Black women and our children know the fabric of our lives is stitched with violence and with hatred, that there is no rest. We do not deal with it only on the picket lines, or in the dark midnight alleys, or in the places where we dare to verbalize our resistance. For us, increasingly, violence weaves through the daily tissues of our living—in the supermarket, in the classroom, in the elevator, in the clinic and the schoolyard, from the plumber, the baker, the sales woman, the bus driver, the bank teller, the waitress who does not serve us.

Some problems we share as women, some we do not. You fear your children will grow up to join the patriarchy and testify against you, we fear our children will be dragged from a car and shot down in the street, and you will turn your backs upon the reasons they are dying.

The threat of difference has been no less blinding to people of Color. Those of us who are Black must see that the reality of our lives and our struggle does not make us immune to the errors of ignoring and misnaming difference. Within Black communities where racism is a living reality; differences among us often seem dangerous and suspect. The need for unity is often misnamed as a need for homogeneity, and a Black feminist vision mistaken for betrayal of our common interests as a people. Because of the continuous battle against racial erasure that Black women and Black men share, some Black women still refuse to recognize that we are also oppressed as women, and that sexual hostility against Black women is practiced not only by the white racist society, but implemented within our Black communities as well. It is a disease striking the heart of Black nationhood, and silence will not make it disappear. Exacerbated by racism and the pressures of powerlessness, violence against Black women and children often becomes a standard within our communities, one by which manliness can be measured. But these women-hating acts are rarely discussed as crimes against Black women.

As a group, women of Color are the lowest-paid wage earners in America. We are the primary targets of abortion and sterilization abuse, here and abroad. In certain parts of Africa, small girls are still being sewed shut between their legs to keep them docile and for men's pleasure. This is known as female circumcision, and it is not a cultural affair as the late Jomo Kenyatta insisted, it is a crime against Black women.

Black women's literature is full of the pain of frequent assault, not only by racist patriarchy, but also by Black men. Yet the necessity for and history of shared battle have made us, Black women, particularly vulnerable to the false accusation that anti-sexist is anti-Black. Meanwhile, womanhating as a recourse of the powerless is sapping strength from Black communities, and our very lives. Rape is on the increase, reported and unreported, and rape is not aggressive sexuality, it is sexualized aggression. As Kalamu ya Salaam, a Black male writer, points out, "As long as male domination exists, rape will exist. Only women revolting and men made conscious of their responsibility to fight sexism can collectively stop rape."[3]

Differences between ourselves as Black women are also being misnamed and used to separate us from one another. As a Black lesbian feminist comfortable with the many different ingredients of my identity, and a woman committed to racial and sexual freedom from oppression, I find I am constantly being encouraged to pluck out some one aspect of myself and present this as the meaningful whole, eclipsing or denying the other parts of self. But this is a destructive and fragmenting way to live. My fullest concentration of energy is available to me only when I integrate all the parts of who I am, openly, allowing power from particular sources of my living to flow back and forth freely through all my different selves, without the restrictions of externally imposed definition. Only then can I bring myself and my energies as a whole to the service of those struggles which I embrace as part of my living.

A fear of lesbians, or of being accused of being a lesbian, has led many Black women into testifying against themselves. It has led some of us into destructive alliances, and others into despair and isolation. In the white women's communities, heterosexism is sometimes a result of identifying with the white patriarchy, a rejection of that interdependence between women-identified women which allows the self to be, rather than to be used in the service of men. Sometimes it reflects a die-hard belief in the protective coloration of heterosexual relationships, sometimes a self-hate which all women have to fight against, taught us from birth.

Although elements of these attitudes exist for all women, there are particular resonances of heterosexism and homophobia among Black women. Despite the fact that woman-bonding has a long and honorable history in the African and African-American communities, and despite the knowledge and accomplishments of many strong and creative women-identified Black women in the political, social and cultural fields, heterosexual Black women often tend to ignore or discount the existence and work of Black lesbians. Part of this attitude has come from an understandable terror of Black male attack within the close confines of Black society, where the punishment for any female self-assertion is still to be accused of being a lesbian and therefore unworthy of the attention or support of the scarce Black male. But part of this need to misname and ignore Black lesbians comes from a very real fear that openly women-identified Black women who are no longer dependent upon men for their self-definition may well reorder our whole concept of social relationships.

Black women who once insisted that lesbianism was a white woman's problem now insist that Black lesbians are a threat to Black nationhood, are consorting with the enemy, are basically un-Black. These accusations, coming from the very women to whom we look for deep and real understanding, have served to keep many Black lesbians in hiding, caught between the racism of white women and the homophobia of their sisters. Often, their work has been ignored, trivialized or misnamed, as with the work of Angelina Grimké, Alice Dunbar-Nelson, Lorraine Hansberry. Yet women-bonded women have always been some part of the power of Black communities, from our unmarried aunts to the amazons of Dahomey.

And it is certainly not Black lesbians who are assaulting women and raping children and grandmothers on the streets of our communities.

Across this country, as in Boston during the spring of 1979 following the unsolved murders of 12 Black women, Black lesbians are spearheading movements against violence against Black women.

What are the particular details within each of our lives that can be scrutinized and altered to help bring about change? How do we redefine difference for all women? It is not our differences which separate women, but our reluctance to recognize those differences and to deal effectively with the distortions which have resulted from the ignoring and misnaming of those differences.

As a tool of social control, women have been encouraged to recognize only one area of human difference as legitimate, those differences which exist between women and men. And we have learned to deal across those differences with the urgency of all oppressed subordinates. All of us have had to learn to live or work or co-exist with men, from our fathers on. We have recognized and negotiated these differences, even when this recognition only continued the old dominant/subordinate mode of human relationship, where the oppressed must recognize the masters' difference in order to survive.

But our future survival is predicated upon our ability to relate within equality. As women, we must root out internalized patterns of oppression within ourselves if we are to move beyond the most superficial aspects of social change. Now we must recognize differences among women who are our equals, neither inferior nor superior, and devise ways to use each other's difference to enrich our visions and our joint struggles.

The future of our earth may depend upon the ability of all women to identify and develop new definitions of power and new patterns of relating across difference. The old definitions have not served us, nor the earth that supports us. The old patterns, no matter how cleverly rearranged to imitate progress, still condemn us to cosmetically altered repetitions of the same old exchanges, the same old guilt, hatred, recrimination, lamentation and suspicion.

For we have, built into all of us, old blueprints of expectation and response, old structures of oppression, and these must be altered at the same time as we alter the living conditions which are a result of those structures. For the master's tools will never dismantle the master's house.

As Paulo Freire shows so well in *The Pedagogy of the Oppressed*,[4] the true focus of revolutionary change is never merely the oppressive situations which we seek to escape, but that piece of the oppressor which is planted deep within each of us, and which knows only the oppressors' tactics, the oppressors' relationships.

Change means growth, and growth can be painful. But we sharpen self-definition by exposing the self in work and struggle together with those whom we define as different from ourselves, although sharing the same goals. For Black and white, old and young, lesbian and heterosexual women alike, this can mean new paths to our survival.

> *We have chosen each other*
> *and the edge of each others battles*
> *the war is the same*
> *if we lose*
> *someday women's blood will congeal*
> *upon a dead planet*
> *if we win*
> *there is no telling*
> *we seek beyond history*
> *for a new and more possible meeting.*[5]

NOTES

1. The editors and publishers gratefully acknowledge permission of Crossing Press © 1984 and Audre Lorde to reproduce "Age, Race, Class, and Sex: Women Redefining Difference" from *Sister Outsider*.
2. This paper was delivered at the Copeland Colloquium, Amherst College, April 1980.
3. From "Rape: A Radical Analysis, An African-American Perspective" by Kalamu ya Salaam in *Black Books Bulletin*, Vol. 6, no. 4 (1980).

4. Seabury Press: New York, 1970.
5. From "Outlines," unpublished poem.

QUESTIONS

1. What is the tone of Lorde's writing in this essay? How does she feel about her argument? What textual evidence can you offer for your assessment?
2. What does Lorde mean by a mythical norm? How does this norm work in our society? What are the three most common ways to deal with difference, according to Lorde? Why are these problematic?
3. Why does Lorde focus so much on "difference" in this piece? Why does she urge us to acknowledge differences among people? What are the consequences for African American women if differences get obscured, or if a "homogeneity of experience" among women is assumed?
4. What concrete differences does Lorde pinpoint between women of color and white women's experiences?

WHITE PRIVILEGE: UNPACKING THE INVISIBLE KNAPSACK (1989)

Peggy McIntosh

This well-known consciousness-raising essay, written in 1988, examines the advantages that can come from being white in U.S. society. Although often unrecognized or unacknowledged, these advantages have a direct relationship to the disadvantages and oppression people of color face. McIntosh pinpoints concrete examples from her own experience that illustrate how even daily activities of white people reflect invisible privileges upon which other racial groups cannot depend. Peggy McIntosh, an educator and activist, is the Associate Director of the Center for Research on Women at Wellesley College.

Through work to bring materials from women's studies into the rest of the curriculum, I have often noticed men's unwillingness to grant that they are overprivileged, even though they may grant that women are disadvantaged. They may say they will work to improve women's status, in the society, the university, or the

"White Privilege: Unpacking the Invisible Knapsack," by Peggy McIntosh, reprinted from *Independent School*, Winter, 1990.

curriculum, but they can't or won't support the idea of lessening men's. Denials that amount to taboos surround the subject of advantages that men gain from women's disadvantages. These denials protect male privilege from being fully acknowledged, lessened, or ended.

Thinking through unacknowledged male privilege as a phenomenon, I realized that, since hierarchies in our society are interlocking, there was most likely a phenomenon of white privilege that was similarly denied and protected. As a white person, I realized I had been taught about racism as something that puts others at a disadvantage, but had been taught not to see one of its corollary aspects, white privilege, which puts me at an advantage.

I think whites are carefully taught not to recognize white privilege, as males are taught not to recognize male privilege. So I have begun in an untutored way to ask what it is like to have white privilege. I have come to see white privilege as an invisible package of unearned assets that I can count on cashing in each day, but about which I was "meant" to remain oblivious. White privilege is like an invisible weightless knapsack of special provisions, maps, passports, codebooks, visas, clothes, tools, and blank checks.

Describing white privilege makes one newly accountable. As we in women's studies work to reveal male privilege and ask men to give up some of their power, so one who writes about having white privilege must ask. "Having described it, what will I do to lessen or end it?"

After I realized the extent to which men work from a base of unacknowledged privilege, I understood that much of their oppressiveness was unconscious. Then I remembered the frequent charges from women of color that white women whom they encounter are oppressive. I began to understand why we are justly seen as oppressive, even when we don't see ourselves that way. I began to count the ways in which I enjoy unearned skin privilege and have been conditioned into oblivion about its existence.

My schooling gave me no training in seeing myself as an oppressor, as an unfairly advantaged person, or as a participant in a damaged culture. I was taught to see myself as an individual whose moral state depended on her individual moral will. My schooling followed the pattern my colleague Elizabeth Minnich has pointed out: whites are taught to think of their lives as morally neutral, normative, and average, and also ideal, so that when we work to benefit others, this is seen as work that will allow "them" to be more like "us."

DAILY EFFECTS OF WHITE PRIVILEGE

I decided to try to work on myself at least by identifying some of the daily effects of white privilege in my life. I have chosen those conditions that I think in my case *attach somewhat more to skin-color privilege* than to class, religion, ethnic status, or geographic location, though of course all these other factors are intricately intertwined. As far as I can tell, my African American coworkers, friends, and acquaintances with whom I come into daily or frequent contact in this particular time, place, and line of work cannot count on most of these conditions.

1. I can, if I wish, arrange to be in the company of people of my race most of the time.
2. If I should need to move, I can be pretty sure of renting or purchasing housing in an area that I can afford and in which I would want to live.
3. I can be pretty sure that my neighbors in such a location will be neutral or pleasant to me.
4. I can go shopping alone most of the time, pretty well assured that I will not be followed or harassed.
5. I can turn on the television or open to the front page of the paper and see people of my race widely represented.
6. When I am told about our national heritage or about "civilization," I am shown that people of my color made it what it is.
7. I can be sure that my children will be given curricular materials that testify to the existence of their race.
8. If I want to, I can be pretty sure of finding a publisher for this piece on white privilege.

9. I can go into a music shop and count on finding the music of my race represented, into a supermarket and find the staple foods that fit with my cultural traditions, into a hairdresser's shop and find someone who can deal with my hair.

10. Whether I use checks, credit cards, or cash, I can count on my skin color not to work against the appearance of financial reliability.

11. I can arrange to protect my children most of the time from people who might not like them.

12. I can swear, or dress in second-hand clothes, or not answer letters without having people attribute these choices to the bad morals, the poverty, or the illiteracy of my race.

13. I can speak in public to a powerful male group without putting my race on trial.

14. I can do well in a challenging situation without being called a credit to my race.

15. I am never asked to speak for all the people of my racial group.

16. I can remain oblivious of the language and customs of persons of color, who constitute the world's majority, without feeling in my culture any penalty for such oblivion.

17. I can criticize our government and talk about how much I fear its policies and behavior without being seen as a cultural outsider.

18. I can be pretty sure that if I ask to talk to "the person in charge" I will be facing a person of my race.

19. If a traffic cop pulls me over, or if the IRS audits my tax return, I can be sure I haven't been singled out because of my race.

20. I can easily buy posters, postcards, picture books, greeting cards, dolls, toys, and children's magazines featuring people of my race.

21. I can go home from most meetings of organizations I belong to feeling somewhat tied in rather than isolated, out

of place, outnumbered, unheard, held at a distance, or feared.

22. I can take a job with an affirmative action employer without having coworkers on the job suspect that I got it because of race.
23. I can choose public accommodation without fearing that people of my race cannot get in or will be mistreated in the places I have chosen.
24. I can be sure that if I need legal or medical help my race will not work against me.
25. If my day, week, or year is going badly, I need not ask of each negative episode or situation whether it has racial overtones.
26. I can choose blemish cover or bandages in "flesh" color that more or less match my skin.

Elusive and fugitive

I repeatedly forgot each of the realizations on this list until I wrote it down. For me white privilege has turned out to be an elusive and fugitive subject. The pressure to avoid it is great, for in facing it I must give up the myth of meritocracy. If these things are true, this is not such a free country; one's life is not what one makes it; many doors open for certain people through no virtues of their own.

In unpacking this invisible knapsack of white privilege, I have listed conditions of daily experience that I once took for granted. Nor did I think of any of these perquisites as bad for the holder. I now think that we need a more finely differentiated taxonomy of privilege, for some of these varieties are only what one would want for everyone in a just society, and others give license to be ignorant, oblivious, arrogant, and destructive.

I see a pattern running through the matrix of white privilege, a pattern of assumptions that were passed on to me as a white person. There was one main piece of cultural turf; it was my own turf, and I was among those who could control the turf. *My skin color was an asset for any move I was educated to want to make.* I could think of myself as belonging in major ways and of making social systems work for me. I could freely disparage, fear, neglect, or be oblivious to anything outside of the dominant cultural forms. Being of the main culture, I could also criticize it fairly freely.

In proportion as my racial group was being made confident, comfortable, and oblivious, other groups were likely being made unconfident, uncomfortable, and alienated. Whiteness protected me from many kinds of hostility, distress, and violence, which I was being subtly trained to visit, in turn, upon people of color.

For this reason, the word "privilege" now seems to me misleading. We usually think of privilege as being a favored state, whether earned or conferred by birth or luck. Yet some of the conditions I have described here work systematically to overempower certain groups. Such privilege simply *confers dominance* because of one's race or sex.

Earned strength, unearned power

I want, then, to distinguish between earned strength and unearned power conferred systemically. Power from unearned privilege can look like strength when it is in fact permission to escape or to dominate. But not all of the privileges on my list are inevitably damaging. Some, like the expectation that neighbors will be decent to you, or that your race will not count against you in court, should be the norm in a just society. Others, like the privilege to ignore less powerful people, distort the humanity of the holders as well as the ignored groups.

We might at least start by distinguishing between positive advantages, which we can work to spread, and negative types of advantage, which unless rejected will always reinforce our present hierarchies. For example, the feeling that one belongs within the human circle, as Native Americans say, should not be seen as privilege for a few. Ideally it is an *unearned entitlement*. At present, since only a few have it, it is an *unearned advantage* for them. This paper results from a process of coming to see that some of the power that I originally saw as attendant on being a human being in the United States consisted in *unearned advantage* and *conferred dominance*.

I have met very few men who are truly distressed about systemic, unearned male advantage and conferred dominance. And so one question for me and others like me is whether we will be like them, or whether we will get truly distressed, even outraged, about unearned race advantage and conferred dominance, and, if so, what we will do to lessen them. In any case, we need to do more work in identifying how they actually affect our daily lives. Many, perhaps most, of our white students in the United States think that racism doesn't affect them because they are not people of color; they do not see "whiteness" as a racial identity. In addition, since race and sex are not the only advantaging systems at work, we need similarly to examine the daily experience of having age advantage, or ethnic advantage, or physical ability, or advantage related to nationality, religion, or sexual orientation.

Difficulties and dangers surrounding the task of finding parallels are many. Since racism, sexism, and heterosexism are not the same, the advantages associated with them should not be seen as the same. In addition, it is hard to disentangle aspects of unearned advantage that rest more on social class, economic class, race, religion, sex, and ethnic identity than on other factors. Still, all of the oppressions are interlocking, as the members of the Combahee River collective pointed out in their "Black Feminist Statement" of 1977.

One factor seems clear about all of the interlocking oppressions. They take both active forms, which we can see, and embedded forms, which as a member of the dominant group one is taught not to see. In my class and place, I did not see myself as a racist because I was taught to recognize racism only in individual acts of meanness by members of my group, never in invisible systems conferring unsought racial dominance on my group from birth.

Disapproving of the systems won't be enough to change them. I was taught to think that racism could end if white individuals changed their attitudes. But a "white" skin in the United States opens many doors for whites whether or not we approve of the way dominance has been conferred on us. Individual acts can palliate, but cannot end, these problems.

To redesign social systems we need first to acknowledge their colossal unseen dimensions. The silences and denials surrounding privilege are the key political tool here. They keep the thinking about equality or equity incomplete, protecting unearned advantage and conferred dominance by making these subjects taboo. Most talk by whites about equal opportunity seems to me now to be about equal opportunity to try to get into a position of dominance while denying that *systems* of dominance exist.

It seems to me that obliviousness about white advantage, like obliviousness about male advantage, is kept strongly inculturated in the United States so as to maintain the myth of meritocracy, the myth that democratic choice is equally available to all. Keeping most people unaware that freedom of confident action is there for just a small number of people props up those in power and serves to keep power in the hands of the same groups that have most of it already.

Although systemic change takes many decades, there are pressing questions for me and, I imagine, for some others like me if we raise our daily consciousness on the perquisites of being light-skinned. What will we do with such knowledge? As we know from watching men, it is an open question whether we will choose to use unearned advantage to weaken hidden systems of advantage, and whether we will use any of our arbitrarily awarded power to try to reconstruct power systems on a broader base.

QUESTIONS

1. What is "white privilege"? How is white privilege connected to the disadvantages and oppression people of color face? What distinction does McIntosh make between "positive" and "negative" advantages?

2. How do racism and white privilege differ? How do individual and institutional racism differ?

3. Why is whiteness, and the advantages that come from being white, so often unrecognized? What examples does McIntosh offer that resonate with your experience?

Why Boys Don't Play With Dolls (1995)

Katha Pollitt

The power of gender socialization is examined by Katha Pollitt in the following essay. She comments on the viability of various theories that attempt to explain why boys and girls seem so dissimilar. In considering the role adults play in reinforcing the gendered behavior of children, Pollitt wonders whether or not change is possible.

It's 28 years since the founding of NOW, and boys still like trucks and girls still like dolls. Increasingly, we are told that the source of these robust preferences must lie outside society—in prenatal hormonal influences, brain chemistry, genes—and that feminism has reached its natural limits. What else could possibly explain the love of preschool girls for party dresses or the desire of toddler boys to own more guns than Mark from Michigan.

True, recent studies claim to show small cognitive differences between the sexes: he gets around by orienting himself in space, she does it by remembering landmarks. Time will tell if any

---

deserve the hoopla with which each is invariably greeted, over the protests of the researchers themselves. But even if the results hold up (and the history of such research is not encouraging), we don't need studies of sex-differentiated brain activity in reading, say, to understand why boys and girls still seem so unalike.

The feminist movement has done much for some women, and something for every woman, but it has hardly turned America into a playground free of sex roles. It hasn't even got women to stop dieting or men to stop interrupting them.

Instead of looking at kids to "prove" that differences in behavior by sex are innate, we can look at the ways we raise kids as an index to how unfinished the feminist revolution really is, and how tentatively it is embraced even by adults who fully expect their daughters to enter previously dominated professions and their sons to change diapers.

I'm at a children's birthday party. "I'm sorry," one mom silently mouths to the mother of the birthday girl, who has just torn open her present—Tropical Splash Barbie. Now, you can love Barbie or you can hate Barbie, and there are feminists in both camps. But *apologize* for Barbie? Inflict Barbie, against your own convictions, on the child of a friend you know will be none too pleased?

Every mother in that room had spent years becoming a person who had to be taken seriously, not least by herself. Even the most attractive, I'm willing to bet, had suffered over her body's failure to fit the impossible American ideal. Given all that, it seems crazy to transmit Barbie to the next generation. Yet to reject her is to say that what Barbie represents—being sexy, thin, stylish—is unimportant, which is obviously not true, and children know it's not true.

Women's looks matter terribly in their society, and so Barbie, however ambivalently, must be passed along. After all, there are worse toys. The Cut and Style Barbie styling head, for example, a grotesque object intended to encourage "hair play." The grown-ups who give that probably apologize, too.

How happy would most parents be to have a child who flouted sex conventions? I know a lot of women, feminists, who complain in a comical, eyeball-rolling way about their sons' passion for sports: the ruined weekends, obnoxious coaches, macho values. But they would not think of discouraging their sons from participating in this activity they find so foolish. Or do they? Their husbands are sports fans, too, and they like their husbands a lot.

Could it be that even sports-resistant moms see athletics as part of manliness? That if their sons wanted to spend the weekend writing up their diaries, or reading, or baking, they'd find it disturbing? Too antisocial? Too lonely? Too gay?

Theories of innate differences in behavior are appealing. They let parents off the hook—no small recommendation in a culture that holds moms, and sometimes even dads, responsible for their children's every misstep on the road to bliss and success.

They allow grown-ups to take the path of least resistance to the dominant culture, which always requires less psychic effort, even if it means more actual work: just ask the working mother who comes home exhausted and nonetheless finds it easier to pick up her son's socks than make him do it himself. They let families buy for their children, without *too* much guilt, the unbelievably sexist junk that the kids, who have been watching commercials since birth, understandably crave.

But the thing the theories do most of all is tell adults that the *adult* world—in which moms and dads still play by many of the old rules even as they question and fidget and chafe against them—is the way it's supposed to be. A girl with a doll and a boy with a truck "explain" why men are from Mars and women are from Venus, why wives do housework and husbands just don't understand.

The paradox is that the world of rigid and hierarchical sex roles evoked by determinist theories is already passing away. Three-year-olds may indeed insist that doctors are male and nurses are female, even if their own mother is a physician. Six-year-olds know better. These days, something like half of all medical students are female, and male applications to nursing school are inching upward. When tomorrow's 3-year-olds play doctor who's to say how they'll assign the roles?

With sex roles, as in every area of life, people aspire to what is possible, and conform to what is necessary. But these are not fixed, especially today. Biological determinism may reassure some adults about their present, but it is feminism, the ideology of flexible and converging sex roles, that fits our children's future. And the kids, somehow, know this.

That's why, if you look carefully, you'll find that for every kid who fits a stereotype, there's another who's breaking one down. Sometimes it's the same kid—the boy who skateboards *and* takes cooking in his after-school program; the girl who collects stuffed animals *and* A-pluses in science.

Feminists are often accused of imposing their "agenda" on children. Isn't that what adults always do, consciously and unconsciously? Kids aren't born religious, or polite, or kind, or able to remember where they put their sneakers. Inculcating these behaviors and the values behind them is a tremendous amount of work, involving many adults. We don't have a choice, really, about *whether* we should give our children messages about what it means to be male and female—they're bombarded with them from morning till night.

The question, as always, is what do we want those messages to be?

QUESTIONS

1. What are some of the agents of socialization described in this essay?
2. How does Pollitt connect feminism to her thoughts about gender socialization?
3. What reasoning does Pollitt use to explain why biological essentialism is, for many, an appealing approach to explaining gender differences?
4. What is Pollitt's conclusion about "why boys don't play with dolls"? Do you agree or disagree with her viewpoint? Why?

MEASURING UP: WHY WOMEN ARE NOT INFERIOR TO MEN (1992)

Carol Tavris

In this chapter from her popular book The Mismeasure of Woman, *Social Psychologist Carol Tavris investigates androcentrism in research on women's bodies, brains and psychology. The tendency to view men as the "norm," and women as "deviations" from that male norm is a widespread, often unconscious assumption underlying research studies that at first glance appear unbiased and noteworthy. That these studies based on a male standard receive mass media attention only propels the assumption that women, biologically and psychologically, do not "measure up" to men.*

Do you sometimes feel inadequate and worthless? Do you dislike your body? Are you nagged by the fear that you don't really deserve to be happy and successful? Do you frequently compare yourself to others and come up short? When things go wrong, do you automatically blame yourself? . . . If you can answer yes to one or several of these questions, you're probably suffering from low self-esteem, a problem that plagues large numbers of women.[1]

"Measuring Up," by Carol Tavris, reprinted from *The Mismeasure of Woman*, 1992, Simon & Schuster.

If you were to flip through a random selection of research articles, magazines, and popular books about differences between the sexes, you would encounter many problems that apparently plague large numbers of women. For instance:

- Women have lower self-esteem than men do.
- Women do not value their efforts as much as men do, even when they are doing the same work.
- Women are less self-confident than men; when asked to predict how they will do in the future, they are less optimistic than men about their abilities.
- Women are more likely than men to repress their anger and to say they are "hurt" than to admit they are angry.
- Women have more difficulty than men in developing a separate identity, a sense of self.

Well, these are all things to worry about, aren't they? Surely it is desirable for women to have high self-esteem, value their work, be self-confident, express anger clearly, and develop autonomy. Surely it is important to explore the problem of why women are so insecure and what can be done about it.[2]

To find the premises underlying these well-meaning efforts to understand women's problems, let's dissect a very good recent study. The researcher asked some young women and men to take tests of creativity, such as inventing uses for ordinary objects. She was not actually interested in whether men or women are more creative (in this case, they did not differ), but in the reasons they give for their success or failure on the tests during a mock job interview afterward.

The investigator reported that women are less self-confident than men: The women attributed their successes less often to their own abilities than to luck, and they reported less overall confidence in their present and future performance. Why, she asked, do women make "less self-serving" explanations than men do? "The feminine social goal of appearing modest," she concluded, "inhibits women in making self-promoting attributions in an achievement situation which involves face-to-face interaction."[3]

Now, ignore the lumpy language of research psychology and notice that the goal of this study was to explain why the women didn't behave like the men. To see this more clearly, simply rephrase the question and its answer. The investigator might have said: "Why do men make *more self-serving* explanations than women do? The masculine social goal of appearing self-confident inhibits them from making modest explanations of their abilities or acknowledging the help of others and the role of chance."

Of course, the habit of seeing women's behavior as something to be explained in relation to the male norm makes sense in a world that takes the male norm for granted. In this case, the researcher showed that the female habit of modesty actually does women a disservice in job interviews, because they appear to be unconcerned with achievement and unwilling to promote themselves. This bit of information would be useful to women *and* men from England, Japan, and other cultures that value modesty, if they want to do business in America.

Nevertheless, in this study, as in many others, the men's responses are used to define the norm, framing the very questions and solutions that investigators explore. But suppose for a moment that we lived in a world where psychologists used women as the basis of comparison. We might then be reading articles and books that analyze the following problems that plague men:

- Men are more conceited than women.
- Men overvalue the work they do.
- Men are not as realistic and modest as women in assessing their abilities.
- Men are more likely than women to accuse and attack others when they are unhappy, instead of stating that they feel hurt and inviting sympathy.
- Men have more difficulty than women in forming and maintaining attachments.

Now the same "problems" have to do with male overconfidence, unrealistic self-assessment, aggression, and isolation, not with women's inadequacies. But you won't find many popular books trying to help men like George Steinbrenner or Donald Trump, who, as far as I'm concerned, suffer from excessive self-esteem.

In recent years, women have been uncovering many of the implicit biases that resulted from using men as the human standard. But the universal man is deeply embedded in our lives and habits of thought, and women who deviate from his ways are still regarded as, well, deviant. To illustrate the persistence of the normal man and the difficulty he poses for women who hope to measure up, I offer three stories of how he affects the evaluation of women's bodies, psychology, and brains.

BODY: BEAUTY AND THE BUST

The cartoonist Nicole Hollander once described what she thought the world would be like without men. "There would be no crime." she said, "and lots of happy, fat women."

Its a wonderful line, funny because it strikes at the heart of the guilty secret (or outright worry) of most women: the endless obsession with weight and body shape. Every woman I know has a "weight problem." My thin friends worry about gaining weight, my plumper friends struggle to lose it. My friends are governed by diets: they are either on one, about to start one, delighted at having finished one, or miserable that they can't stick with one. I sympathize with them; I'm that way too. This obsession, which is so damaging to women's self-concept, happiness, and self-esteem, perfectly highlights the dilemma for women of being like men or different from them, and the origins of that dilemma in the larger social picture.

Over the years, the ideal figure for a woman has changed, from eras that accentuate the differences from the male body to those that minimize them. In this century alone we have seen rapid shifts from the Lillian Russell/Marilyn Monroe standard, which was voluptuous and curvaceous, to the 1920s Flapper/1960s Twiggy standard, which was unisex slim, to today's odd hybrid: full-breasted but harrow-hipped. Psychologist Brett Silverstein and his associates have cleverly documented this changing female ideal by calculating "bust-to-waist" and "waist-to-hip" ratios of the measurements of women in popular women's magazines.[4] You get larger ratios in eras that celebrate the big-breasted figure, and a smaller ratio in eras that endorse the boyish shape.

In the 1950s, for instance, *Playboy* centerfolds, beauty contest winners, and fashion models weighed much more and were several inches more ample in bust and hips than they were in the

1970s and 1980s. The 1951 Miss Sweden was 5′7″ tall and weighed 151 pounds; the 1983 Miss Sweden was 5′9″ tall and weighed 109 pounds.[5] The phrase "pleasantly plump," which was still a compliment in the 1950s, became an oxymoron in the 1960s Actress Valerie Harper, who truly was pleasantly plump, was not happy with her body until she became alarmingly gaunt.

Why do these ideals change? Curvy, full-breasted women are in fashion during pro-maternal eras, in which motherhood and domesticity are considered women's most important roles: this was the case in the early 1900s, the 1950s, and, increasingly, today. In contrast, thin, muscular boyish bodies are in fashion whenever women have entered the work force, specifically the traditionally male occupations: this was the case in the 1920s and again in the late 1960s and 1970s. In the 1920s, women used to bind their breasts with tape so their breasts would not be prominent in the dress styles of the day. The 1970s "working girl" that Mary Tyler Moore played for seven years on television didn't have to do this; she was as thin as a reed. Jane Fonda transformed her voluptuous Barbarella shape into an aerobically toned muscular one.

Why should the kind of work that people do affect ideal body image? Men and women, Silverstein discovered, associate the round, big-breasted body with femininity. And they associate femininity with nurturance, dependence, passivity, domesticity—and, unhappily, incompetence. The normal male body, in contrast, conveys intelligence, strength, and ability. Therefore, women who want to be thought intelligent, professional, and competent—i.e., "masculine"—must look more male-ish. (Men, too, have fallen prey to this equation. Fat, once a sign of a man's wealth and success in the early decades of this century, now signifies womanly softness and lack of masculinity.)

Indeed, in every era when educational and occupational opportunities for women have increased, the ideal body for women became thin, athletic, small-busted, and narrow-hipped. A 1935 *Fortune* article described the professional, "intelligently dressed woman," contrasting her with the "blond stenographer with the slick sleazy stockings and the redundant breasts." Redundant breasts? The idea returned in the careerist 1970s and 1980s. A 1984 career guide for women advised its readers: "The sex goddess look is at odds with a professional business look. If you have a large bust don't accentuate it."

In such egalitarian times, the number of articles and books on dieting increases astronomically, and eating disorders and "fat panic" among women and girls became epidemic. Most white teenage girls no longer regard normal and necessary adolescent weight gain as normal signs of maturation, but as signs of (unpleasant) fatness. A representative survey of more than 2,000 girls in Michigan, ages eleven to eighteen, found that nearly 40 percent considered themselves overweight; dieting and dissatisfaction with body image were the typical responses to the onset of puberty.[6] Many other studies of nationally representative samples find that dieting, unrealistic body image, and dissatisfaction with weight are chronic stressors for women.[7]

Women who value achievement, higher education, and professional careers are especially likely to be obsessed with thinness and to suffer from various eating disorders, such as anorexia and bulimia. "Eating disorders and the obsession with weight control," says Silverstein, "are an ironic price of 'women's liberation.' They occur when the level of discrimination against women decreases enough to let women into higher education and professions—but not enough to break the association between femininity and incompetence."[8]

This link seems to be particularly troubling for women who are insecure about their competence and who feel that their fathers did not think they were intelligent and did not support their ambitions. To resolve this dilemma, they try literally to measure up: to become as thin as a man, since they can't actually become one. According to O. Wayne Wooley and Susan Wooley, who direct a research program and eating-disorders clinic at the University of Cincinnati's College of Medicine, many bulimic young women are seeking their fathers' recognition of their competence, which they don't get because they are female. "To become like their fathers, our patients feel compelled to be thin," they observe, "—not just to minimize their womanliness, but also because thinness, in this culture, is a sign of achievement and mastery."[9]

All women remain affected to some degree by the portrayals of the ideal woman in the media, and those portrayals, in spite of the popularity of Roseanne Barr, are getting worse. "Women receive more messages to be slim and stay in shape than do men," says Silverstein, who analyzed popular television characters and articles and ads in magazines. On television in the late 1980s, 69 percent of the female characters were very thin, compared to only

17.5 percent of the male characters. Only five percent of the female characters were heavy, compared to 25.5 percent of the males. In 48 issues of popular women's magazines that Silverstein surveyed, the total number of ads for diet foods was 63; the comparable number in popular men's magazines was 1. As for articles dealing with body shape or size, the score was women's magazines 96, men's 8.

With the dawn of the 1990s, media images of women began to celebrate a hybrid form that is all but impossible for most women: big-breasted but narrow-hipped. (Accordingly, Jane Fonda got breast implants.) This hybrid reflects the ambivalence in American society toward women's roles and the expectation that women must be both professionally competent *and* maternal. The majority of women, including mothers of young children, work outside the home, yet we are also in an era of strong pro-maternal sentiment.

As one sign of the times, those "redundant breasts" are back in vogue: After a decade of the popularity of breast-reduction surgeries, breast-enlargement procedures are on the increase. "Be Your Best," blares an ad for the "Breast Enhancement Medical Center" in Los Angeles. These three words are placed across the model's breasts, as if to convey the real message, "Be Your Bust." The message is catching on. More than 70,000 women in the United States had breast augmentation surgery in 1988 alone, and that number jumped to 150,000 in 1990. Eighty percent are for cosmetic purposes; indeed, breast implants have become the most popular form of cosmetic surgery for women in the nation. They are more popular than liposuction, nose jobs, or face lifts, in spite of the considerable expense and a significant degree of risk of ruptured implants, repeat surgery for complications, infections, allergic reactions, tumors, and disruption of the autoimmune system.[10]

The fashion industry, both haute couture and ready-to-wear, now features the breast, offering swimwear with padded bust lines and underwire bras, dresses with plunging necklines, padded corsets, and bustiers, and fabrics that cling to the bosom to emphasize its curves. "Curves are natural to a woman's form," explained a designer for Van Buren, whose dresses nevertheless now include built-in push-up bras for women who need help being natural. "We're definitely moving in the direction of a softer, more feminine curvaceousness," said a representative of

Lancôme cosmetics in New York. "It's much sexier to have some flesh to hold on to," said Gale Hayman, who is president of her own cosmetics company. As if to prove her point, for their respective roles in *Green Card* and *Alice,* Andie MacDowell and Mia Farrow gained ten pounds.[11]

So the cycle is making another turn. A reporter writing on this trend explained, "after years of stick-thin cover girls, their fuller figures [of bigger-breasted models] provided a refreshing, ultra-feminine look."[12] Today the big-breasted "refreshing and ultra-feminine" look competes with "a professional business look." But if breasts are ultrafeminine and also redundant, what's a woman to do?

If she accepts nature's body—the one with breasts, fat deposits, and curves—and throws away the diet books, she risks being regarded as incompetent and best suited for motherhood. If she wishes to enter the business and political world, she struggles to have a man's body, one without those nurturing, feminine breasts. It is no wonder that contemporary dress styles dramatically reflect this ambivalence: many business outfits consist of a "male" tailored jacket and a "feminine" miniskirt. It's an effort to be businesslike and sexy.

Many women justify their efforts to be thin on medical grounds, but even here many of the warnings about the dangers of fat have been based on studies of men. Women are biologically programmed to store fat reserves in the thighs, buttocks, and hips, and fat in these areas is not generally a health risk. On the contrary, this reserve of fat is necessary for menstruation, childbearing, nursing, and after menopause, for production and storage of estrogen. This is one reason that moderate weight gain after menopause is not as risky to women's health as excess weight can be for men; indeed, excessive thinness increases the risk of osteoporosis.[13]

Joel Gurin, co-author with physician William Bennett of *The Dieter's Dilemma,* believes that much of the research on health and weight has been heavily biased by reliance on a male norm. "The risks of dieting have been underestimated," he maintains, "and the risks of fatness have been overestimated." Of course, obesity does increase the risk of diabetes and high blood pressure, and a diet rich in fats has been implicated in numerous diseases (such as breast cancer). But being very thin is also unhealthy: The risks to longevity show up in the extremes of fat and thin. Moreover, the location of fat is more important than the number of pounds: abdominal fat is implicated in a greater risk of diabetes in women and of heart disease in men.[14] "The irony," says Silverstein, "is that it is men who are at greater risk from obesity, but it is women who diet."

And diets themselves carry physical and psychological risks. Up-and-down dieting changes the body's metabolism, making it easier to gain weight and harder to lose it, and possibly also increasing the chances of becoming hypertensive. When rats are put on a regimen of yo-yo dieting, their blood pressures rise significantly and dangerously after the third "crash diet." The link between hypertension and being overweight that doctors warn about may be the result of the person's having been on several crash diets, not a result of the weight per se.[15] Dieting is also psychologically debilitating. "Food fantasies, obsession with talking about food, depression and irritability, and bingeing when the diet is broken are not signs of failed willpower," says Gurin. "They are signs of hunger." Women who are chronically dieting are in a constant state of stress, which affects their emotional and physical health.[16]

O. Wayne Wooley considers women's obsession with dieting and excess weight to be largely a political matter, not a medical one. "It is political," he argues, "because it keeps women attending to their looks instead of the circumstances of their lives, it pits woman against woman, it destroys physical fitness and energy. And, saddest of all, it represents a rejection of the female body"[17]—the real female body, that is; the one with those "redundant" breasts. The same may be said of efforts to change an equally real female body—the one with small breasts. It is small consolidation to be able to throw away the diet books and gain a few pounds if the trade-off is being thought mindless and incompetent.

Nicole Hollander's joke—that in a world without men, women would be fat and happy—reminds us exactly why it is that women subject their bodies to surgery, dieting, and deprivation, and how women might feel about their normal bodies if the world were designed and run by women. As it is, women keep trying to look the right way, but the ideal they aspire to is not based on the normal varieties of the female body. The fact that the large majority of women who have breast implants for cosmetic reasons are in their thirties and forties, and married, reveals a more likely motive than vanity. A news reporter interviewed one woman, age forty-four, who "recently went form 'barely a 32-A' to a 34-C. Before her surgery, she said, her father used to say he 'couldn't tell the difference between the front or the back' when he looked at her. Her husband often joined in the jokes."[18]

Many women today feel superior to Victorian women, who wore excruciating corsets to force their bodies into exaggerated hourglass shapes. (In a woman-centered world, the demise of the corset and the girdle would rank right up there with the electric razor as a major contribution to human welfare.) But modern women who are forcing their bodies into exaggeratedly slim shapes, or, increasingly, into exaggeratedly voluptuous shapes, are no less subject to social pressures and the standards of fashion. These alternating standards, which reflect the perception that the woman's body is never right as it is and always needs to be fixed, will continue as long as women model themselves after the impossible male norm: to be opposite from the male body, or to be like the male body, but never satisfied with the woman's body they have.

PSYCHE: THE PROBLEM OF WOMEN

> It all goes back, of course, to Adam and Eve—a story which shows, among other things, that if you make a woman out of a man, you are bound to get into trouble. In the life cycle, as in the Garden of Eden, the woman has been the deviant.[19]
>
> Carol Gilligan, *In a Different Voice*

Women not only fail to measure up to having the right body; they also fail to measure up to having the right life. I remember how annoyed I felt, as a college student, when I first read Erik Erikson's theory of the "Eight Stages of Man." Every few years throughout their lives, Erikson said, people have a psychological crisis to resolve and overcome. Children, for example, must resolve the crisis of "competence" versus "inferiority." Teenagers must resolve the famous identity crisis of adolescence, or they will wallow around in "role diffusion" and aimlessness. Once you have your identity, you must learn to share it; if you don't master your "intimacy" crisis, you become lonely and isolated. Middle-aged adults face the problems of "stagnation" versus "generativity," and, in old age, "ego integrity" versus "despair."

It turned out, of course, that Erikson meant the ages of "man" literally, but none of us knew that then. The fact that female readers were grumbling that their stages didn't seem to fit the pattern was just further evidence of how peculiar and irritating women were. Erikson's theory was assumed to be a brilliant expansion of Freud's stage theory, which stopped at puberty. If women didn't fit, it was their own fault.

It was worrying. I wasn't having any of my crises in the right order. My sense of competence was plummeting, a result of being a lowly student, and I was supposed to have resolved *that* one at around age seven. My identity was shaky, although I was no longer a teenager, and I hadn't married when I was supposed to, which was putting my intimacy and generativity crises on hold.

Uncertain about my career prospects and having missed the college-age marriage boat, I applied to graduate school. Many graduate schools were reluctant to accept women in the late 1960s, and the reason, they said, was that women were so unpredictable, idiosyncratic, and unreliable—so, in a word, unmasculine. Women were forever dropping out to support their husbands, or have children, or take jobs that allowed them to eat. I remember how relieved I felt to read the research of the time, which provided reassuring evidence to administrators that yes, women would finish their training if you gave them the chance, and yes, they would eventually do as well as men.

In those days, theorists writing on adult development assumed that adults were male. Healthy "adults" follow a single line from childhood to old age, a steady path of school, career, marriage, advancement, a child or two, retirement, and wisdom–in that order. Everyone was supposed to grow "up," not sideways, down, or, God forbid, in circles. In the 1970s and 1980s, popular stage theories offered road maps that plotted a way through the thicket of adult adventures. Psychiatrist George Vaillant wrote *Adaptation to Life,* based on a longitudinal study of privileged Harvard (male) students, and concluded that men go through orderly stages even if the circumstances of their lives differ. Psychiatrist Daniel Levinson and his associates followed with *Seasons of a Man's Life,* which argued that the phases of (a man's) life unfold in a natural sequence, like the four seasons of the year. This book had nothing to say about women's seasons, possibly because women were continuing to irritate academics by doing things unseasonably.

Moreover, almost everyone assumed that healthy adult development meant progress toward autonomy, independence, and separation. It was bad and unhealthy to remain too attached to your parents. Indeed, to many psychologists, the continuing attachment that many women have with their families is a sign of immaturity and their "weak sense of self." Proponents of the "turmoil theory" of adolescent development explained that teenagers must go through a few years of ranting, railing, disobedience, and craziness or they wouldn't become calm, sane, mature adults—the kind who had separated from their parents.

But once a critical mass of women entered psychology, they began asking different questions. Why, they wondered, is it so desirable for an academic career to be uninterrupted by experience, family life, and outside work? So what if women's life paths were less linear than men's? Wasn't this way of structuring one's life as logical as, and more humanly beneficial than, the straight-up-the-ladder model? Shouldn't administrators be worrying about the deficient education of male students, so woefully unweathered by real life? And why, as psychologist Carol Gilligan argued to great acclaim, do we focus so much on the importance of separation from parents, instead of on the continuing affectionate bond that is the norm almost everywhere in the world, the bond that females promote?[20]

These questions and the new research they generated, have transformed our understanding of human development. We now know that women and men do not resolve crises of competence, identity, nurturance, stagnation, autonomy, and connection once and for all; these issues bubble up throughout life. There is no right time or only time to go to school, change careers, have a baby, retire, or marry. The continuing connection between parent and child throughout life is healthy, a sign of strength rather than immaturity.

Even turmoil theories of adolescence are on the way out. Large-scale studies of normal adolescent males and females show that turmoil is only one way, and not the most common way at that, for getting through the teenage years. Most teenagers of both sexes remain close to and admiring of their parents, and experience a minimum of conflict and rebellion.[21] (This doesn't mean they aren't driving their parents crazy, and vice versa; just that these conflicts are ultimately trivial, to both sides, in the larger scheme of things.)

"We need a new model of adolescent development, one which makes sense of the continued love between child and parent," argues psychologist Terri Apter.[22] Apter, who began her research with mothers and daughters on the (male) assumption that the task of adolescence is to separate from the parent, expected that daughters would talk frequently of their needs for separation, to be their "own person," to have more freedom. Instead, the daughters talked much more about their connection to their mothers: Their conversations were dotted with "her view is," "she thinks I'm," "the way she sees things." Mid-adolescence is generally thought to be the time of greatest conflict between parent and child, Apter found, yet most of the teenaged girls she interviewed said "the person they felt closest to, the person they felt most loved by, the person who offered them the greatest support, was their mother."[23]

All of these challenges to traditional theories proved to be good news for men and women, but particularly for the women who for so long had compared themselves to the male life pattern and come away feeling guilty for not matching it. "What's the right way to do it?" women often ask the "experts." "When should I have a baby—before, after, or during a career?" Or "When should I go to school—before, after, or during the baby?" The questioners assume that there is a right answer, and a right answer in turn assumes a single linear standard that will fit everybody—or rather, every man. But, as psychologists Grace Baruch and Rosalind Barnett have found, "there is no one lifeprint that ensures all women a perpetual sense of well-being—nor one that guarantees misery, for that matter. Adult American women today are finding satisfying lives in any number of different role patterns. Most involve tradeoffs at different points in the life cycle."[24] The fact that it is women who tend to be making the tradeoffs and not men is another matter.

In the last decade, new interpretations of many other old theories in psychology have flourished like mushrooms after rainfall. No area of investigation has been immune from scrutiny for male bias. For example, the left side of the list below represents the traditional way of looking at sex differences; the list on the right, another way of interpreting the same findings:

Most people will see at once that the negative terms in the righthand column are biased and derogatory, but that is the point.

What's wrong with women	*What's wrong with men*
Low self-esteem	Inflated self-esteem
Undervalues her work	Overvalues his work
Gullible	Rigid
Too modest	Too overconfident
No sense of humor	Offensive sense of humor
Selflessness	Selfishness
Works too hard	Doesn't work hard enough
Career line irregular	Career path too narrow
Adult development too erratic	Adult development too conformist
Dependent	Aloof
Too connected, fused with others; weak ego boundary	Too autonomous, isolated, narcissistic
Penis envy	Penis insecurity
Suggestible	Inflexible
Conformist	Unyielding
Too emotional	Too remote, unfeeling
Weak leadership style	Authoritarian leadership style
Unwilling to dominate	Unwilling to negotiate
Stunted moral reasoning	Narrow moral reasoning
Not competitive enough	Not cooperative enough

Why has it been so difficult to notice the same degree of bias and denigration in the lefthand list? The answer is that we are used to seeing women as the problem, to thinking of women as being different *from men,* and to regarding women's differences from men as deficiencies and weaknesses.

So it is understandable that many women have responded to the transformation of the list on the left into the list on the right with considerable mirth and relief. It was enormously liberating to believe that women weren't the problem; men were. By smoking the universal male out of his lair, we saw in daylight that he and his ways were not the center of all things. Most women have greeted each attempt to reevaluate him—finding after finding, popular book after popular book—with "At last! That's us!"

My personal favorite is the reanalysis of the perennial male lament, "Why can't women take a joke?" Studies have consistently shown that men and women don't differ in their capacity for humor, but they disagree about what's funny. In general, what's funny has to do with the target of the joke. On the average, men think it is funnier when a male disparages someone else than when he disparages himself, but women generally prefer self-deprecating humor. One psychologist asked men and women to think of funny endings to stories that involved themselves or others. Most of the men took longer to think of endings to jokes in which the humor was directed at themselves than when it was directed at someone else, while for women the opposite was true.[25] Studies like these transform the problem from "Why can't women take a joke?" into "Why don't men know what's funny?"

As a woman, I like to play the reversal game too. But replacing the "woman as problem" bias with a "woman as solution" bias doesn't take us very far in solving the problem of the universal male. For one thing, it tends to confuse differences in what women and men do in their lives with differences in their basic psychological capacities. It is a small jump from saying "Women's lives are less linear than men's, and that is fine" to saying "Women think in a less linear way than men do, and that is fine too." As soon as we are in the realm of psychological qualities rather than in the activities of life, replacing "woman as problem" with "man as problem" obscures the reality of their human similarities. When the public hears news that men and women differ psychologically in some way, they immediately imagine two nonoverlapping groups that look like this:

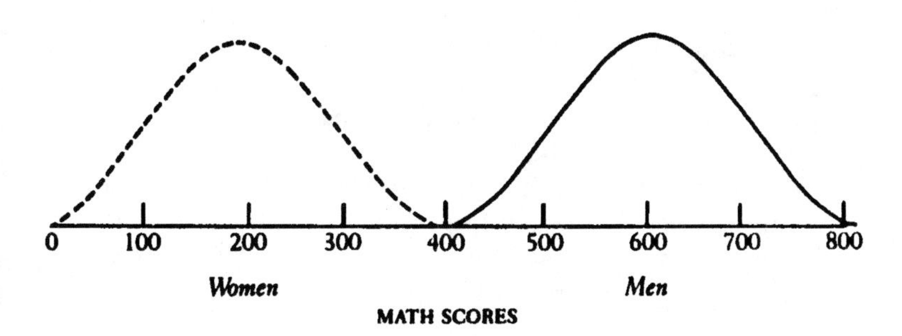

Sometimes two such nonoverlapping groups occur. As scientist Robert M. Sapolsky has observed, if you take two groups of anthrax victims, only one group of which has been treated with antibiotics, there will be no overlap in survival rates at all: The untreated victims will die within forty-eight hours. Period. This is an example of what Sapolsky calls a "powerful fact": By knowing which group an anthrax victim is in—treated or untreated—you will be able to predict with absolute certainty whether he or she will die of the disease.[26]

But when we get into the realm of abilities and qualities—such as doing well in math, the likelihood of roaring at the children, having a sense of humor, needing friends and family, being able to love, or being able to pack a suitcase—the overlap between men and women is always far greater than the difference, if any. Sapolsky plotted the actual results of a famous study that claimed to find clear evidence of a male superiority in math among junior high school students, and the result looked like this:

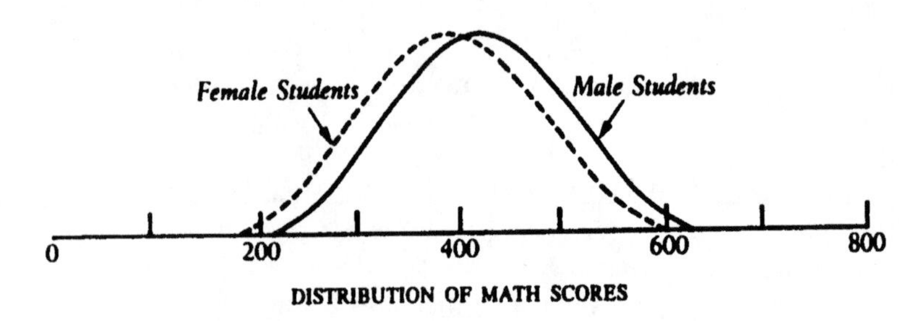

DISTRIBUTION OF MATH SCORES

"Anyone who can look at the graph," Sapolsky says, "and claim that it provides any predictiveness about how an *individual* boy or girl will do in math either has an ideological axe to grind or his own ability to reason mathematically is severely impaired." Moreover, if the small percentage of males who are math prodigies is removed from this sample, the distribution of scores for males and females is identical.

Thus, male "superiority" in math is an example of a "fact" that is not powerful at all, because it does not help us predict how an *individual* boy or girl, man or woman, will do. "Yet how many people ever see the data this way?" Sapolsky asks. "In most branches of science, reporting a difference with this little predictiveness would get you laughed out of the business. . . . Of the teachers, administrators, parents, and guidance counselors who believe that science has shown that boys are better at math than girls, how many know the predictiveness of this fact?"[27]

Suppose, therefore, that we move away from the narrow and limited question of "Do men and women differ, and if so, who's better?" and ask instead: Why is everyone so interested in differences? Why are differences regarded as deficiencies? What functions does the *belief* in differences serve? The answers begin to emerge in the following story from the halls of science, where we can see how even "pure" biological research is besmirched by the dusty fingerprints of those who conduct it.

BRAIN: DISSECTING THE DIFFERENCES

> It must be stated boldly that conceptual thought is exclusive to the masculine intellect . . . [but] it is no deprecation of a woman to state that she is more sensitive in her emotions and less ruled by her intellect. We are merely stating a difference, a difference which equips her for the special part for which she was cast . . . Her skull is also smaller than man's; and so, of course, is her brain.[28]
>
> — T. Lang, *The Difference Between a Man and a Woman*

In recent years the sexiest body part far and away, has become the brain. Magazines with cover stories on the brain fly off the newsstands, and countless seminars, tapes, books, and classes teach people how to use "all" of their brains. New technologies, such as PET scans, produce gorgeous photographs of the brain at work and play. Weekly we hear new discoveries about this miraculous organ, and it seems that scientists will soon be able to pinpoint the very neuron, the very neurotransmitter, responsible for joy, sadness, rage, and suffering. At last we will know the reasons for all the differences between women and men that fascinate and infuriate, such as why men won't stop and ask directions and why women won't stop asking men what they are feeling.

In all this excitement, it seems curmudgeonly to sound words of caution, but the history of brain research does not exactly reveal a noble and impartial quest for truth, particularly on sensitive matters such as sex and race differences. Typically, when scientists haven't found the differences they were seeking, they haven't abandoned the goal or their belief that such differences exist; they just moved to another part of the anatomy or a different corner of the brain.

A century ago, for example, scientists tried to prove that women had smaller brains than men did, which accounted for women's alleged intellectual failings and emotional weaknesses. Dozens of studies purported to show that men had larger brains, making them smarter than women. When scientists realized that men's greater height and weight offset their brain-size advantage, however, they dropped this line of research like a shot. The scientists next tried to argue that women had smaller frontal lobes and larger parietal lobes than men did, another brain pattern thought to account for women's intellectual inferiority. Then it was reported that the parietal lobes might be associated with intellect. Panic in the labs—until anatomists suddenly found that women's parietal lobes were *smaller* than they had originally believed. Wherever they looked, scientists conveniently found evidence of female inferiority, as Gustave Le Bon, a Parisian, wrote in 1879:

> In the most intelligent races, as among the Parisians, there are a large number of women whose brains are closer in size to those of gorillas than to the most developed male brains. This inferiority is so obvious that no one can contest it for a moment; only its degree is worth discussion.[29]

We look back with amusement at the obvious biases of research a century ago, research designed to prove the obvious inferiority of women and minorities (and non-Parisians). Today, many researchers are splitting brains instead of weighing them, but they are no less determined to find sex differences. Nevertheless, skeptical neuroscientists are showing that biases and values are just as embedded in current research—old prejudices in new technologies.

The brain, like a walnut, consists of two hemispheres of equal size, connected by a bundle of fibers called the corpus callosum. The left hemisphere has been associated with verbal and reasoning ability, whereas the right hemisphere is associated with spatial reasoning and artistic ability. Yet by the time these findings reached the public, they had been vastly oversimplified and diluted. Even the great neuroscientist Roger Sperry, the grandfather of hemispheric research, felt obliged to warn that the "left-right dichotomy . . . is an idea with which it is very easy to run wild."[30] And many people have run wild with it: Stores are filled with manuals, cassettes, and handbooks that promise to help people become fluent in "whole-brain thinking," to beef up the unused part of their right brain, and to learn to use the intuitive right brain for business, painting, and inventing.

The fact that the brain consists of two hemispheres, each characterized by different specialties, provides a neat analogy to the fact that human beings consist of two genders, each characterized by different specialties. The analogy is so tempting that scientists keep trying to show that it is grounded in physical reality. Modern theories of gender and the brain are based on the idea that the left and right hemispheres develop differently in boys and girls, as does the corpus callosum that links the halves of the brain.

According to one major theory, the male brain is more "lateralized," that is, its hemispheres are specialized in their abilities, whereas females use both hemispheres more symmetrically because their corpus callosum is allegedly larger and contains more fibers. Two eminent scientists, Normal Geschwind and Peter Behan, maintained that this sex difference begins in the womb, when the male fetus begins to secrete testosterone—the hormone that will further its physical development as a male. Geschwind and Behan argued that testosterone in male fetuses washes over the brain, selectively attacking parts of the left hemisphere, briefly slowing its development, and producing right-hemisphere dominance in men. Geschwind speculated that the effects of testosterone on the prenatal brain produce "superior right hemisphere talents, such as artistic, musical, or mathematical talent."[31]

Right-hemisphere dominance is also thought to explain men's excellence in some tests of "visual-spatial ability"—the ability to imagine objects in three-dimensional space (the skill you need for mastering geometry, concocting football formations, and reading maps). This is apparently the reason that some men won't stop and ask directions when they are lost; they prefer to rely on their right brains, whereas women prefer to rely on a local informant. It is also supposed to be the reason that men can't talk about their feelings and would rather watch television or wax the car. Women have interconnected hemispheres, which explains why they excel in talk, feelings, intuition, and quick judgments. Geschwind and Behan's theory had tremendous scientific appeal, and it is cited frequently in research papers and textbooks. *Science* hailed it with the headline "Math Genius May Have Hormonal Basis."[32]

The theory also has had enormous popular appeal. It fits snugly, for example, with the Christian fundamentalist belief that men and women are innately different and thus innately designed for different roles. For his radio show "Focus on the Family," James Dobson interviewed Donald Joy, a professor of "human development in Christian education" at Asbury Theological Seminary, who explained Geschwind and Behan's theory this way:

> Joy: . . . this marvelous female brain, is a brain that's not damaged during fetal development as the male brain is, but the damage gives a specialization to the male brain which we don't get in the female.
>
> Dobson: I want to pick up on that concept of us brain-damaged males. [laugher, chuckling]
>
> Joy: . . . It's giving a chemical bath to the left hemisphere and this connecting link between the two hemispheres that reduced to the size and number of transmission passages that exist here . . . So males simply can't talk to themselves across the hemispheres in a way that a woman does.
>
> Dobson: So some of the sex differences that we see in personality can be tracked back to that moment.
>
> Joy: Oh, absolutely. And when we're talking about this now, we're talking about a glorious phenomenon because these are intrinsic sex differences . . . this is glorious because we are fearfully and wonderfully differentiated from each other.
>
> Dobson: Let's look at 'em, name 'em.
>
> Joy: We're, we're mutually interdependent. Every household needs both a male brain and a female brain, for example. The woman's brain works much like a computer . . . lateral transmission in her brain allows her to consult all of her past experience and give you an instant response. She can make a judgment more quickly than a male can. . . . [but how she arrives at it is] hidden even from her, because it is like a computer, all it gives is the answer, it doesn't give you the process.[33]

The male brain, Joy added, is more like an "adding machine," in which facts are totaled and a logical solution presents itself. So males are good at logical reasoning, and females at intuitive judgments, because of the prenatal "chemical bath" that affects the male brain.

The same explanation and language—down to the same joke that men are "brain-damaged"—turns up in a book by two Christian fundamentalists, *The Language of Love,* published by Dobson's organization. The authors, Gary Smalley and John Trent, write:

> Specifically, medical studies have shown that between the eighteenth and twenty-sixth week of pregnancy, something happens that forever separates the sexes. . . . researchers have actually observed a chemical bath of testosterone and other sex-related hormones wash over a baby boy's brain. This causes changes that

> never happen to the brain of a baby girl.... The sex-related hormones and chemicals that flood a baby boy's brain cause the right side to recede slightly, destroying some of the connecting fibers [*sic* the authors have it backward; the theory actually says that the left side is affected]. One result is that, in most cases, a boy starts life more *left*-brain oriented [*sic*]. Because little girls don't experience this chemical bath, they leave the starting blocks much more two-sided in their thinking....
>
> *Now wait a minute,* you may be thinking. *Does this mean that men are basically brain-damaged?*
>
> Well, not exactly. What occurs in the womb merely sets the stage for men and women to "specialize" in two different ways of thinking. And this is one major reason men and women need each other so much.[34] (Emphases in original.)

Now it may be true that men and women, on the average, differ in the physiology of their brains. It may even be true that this difference explains why James Dobson's wife Shirley can sum up a person's character right away, while he, with his slower, adding-machine brain, takes weeks or months to come to the same impressions. But given the disgraceful history of bias and sloppy research designed more to confirm prejudices than to enlighten humanity, I think we would all do well to be suspicious and to evaluate the evidence for these assertions closely.

This is difficult for those of us who are not expert in physiology, neuroanatomy, or medicine. We are easily dazzled by words like "lateralization" and "corpus callosum." Besides, physiology seems so *solid;* if one study finds a difference between three male brains and three female brains, that must apply to all men and women. How do I know what my corpus callosum looks like? Is it bigger than a man's? Should I care?

For some answers, I turned to researchers in biology and neuroscience who have critically examined the research and the assumptions underlying theories of sex differences in the brain.[35] The first discovery of note was that, just like the nineteenth-century researchers who kept changing their minds about which *lobe* of the brain accounted for male superiority, twentieth-century researchers keep changing their minds about which *hemisphere* of the brain accounts for male superiority. Originally, the left hemisphere was considered the repository of intellect and reason. The right hemisphere was the sick, bad, crazy side, the side of passion, instincts, criminality, and irrationality. Guess which sex was thought to have left-brain intellectual superiority? (Answer: males.) In the 1960s and 1970s, however, the right brain was resuscitated and brought into the limelight. Scientists began to suspect that it was the source of genius and inspiration, creativity and imagination, mysticism and mathematical brilliance. Guess which sex was now thought to have right-brain specialization? (Answer: males.)

It's all very confusing. Today we hear arguments that men have greater left-brain specialization (which explains their intellectual advantage) *and* that they have greater right-brain specialization (which explains their mathematical and artistic advantage). *Newsweek* recently asserted as fact, for instance, that "women's language and other skills are more evenly divided between left and right hemisphere; in men, such functions are concentrated in the left brain."[36]

But fundamentalists Smalley and Trent asserted that:

> most women spend the majority of their days and nights camped out on the right side of the brain [which] harbors the center for feelings, as well as the primary relational, language, and communication skills . . . and makes an afternoon devoted to art and fine music actually enjoyable.[37]

You can hear the chuckling from men who regard art museums and concert halls as something akin to medieval torture chambers, but I'm sure that the many men who enjoy art and fine music, indeed who create art and fine music, would not find that last remark so funny. Geschwind and Behan, of course, had argued that male specialization of the right hemisphere explained why men *excel* in art and fine music. But since Smalley and Trent apparently do not share these prissy female interests, they relegate them to women–to women's brains.

The two hemispheres of the brain do have different specialties, but it is far too simple-minded (so to speak) to assume that human abilities clump up in opposing bunches. Most brain researchers today believe that the two hemispheres complement one another, to the extent that one side can sometimes take over the functions of a side that has been damaged. Moreover, specific skills often involve components from both hemispheres: one side has the ability to tell a joke, and the other has the ability to laugh at one. Math abilities include both visual-spatial skills and reasoning skills. The right hemisphere is involved in creating art, but the left hemisphere is involved in appreciating and analyzing art. As neuropsychologist Jerre Levy once said, "Could the eons of human evolution have left half of the brain witless? Could a bird whose existence is dependent on flying have evolved only a single wing?"[38]

These qualifications about the interdependence of brain hemispheres have not, however, deterred those who believe that there are basic psychological differences between the sexes that can be accounted for in the brain. So let's consider their argument more closely.

The neuroscientist Ruth Bleier, who at her untimely death was Professor of Neurophysiology at the University of Wisconsin, carefully examined Geschwind and Behan's data, going back to many of their original references.[39] In one such study of 507 fetal brains of 10 to 44 weeks gestation, the researchers had actually stated that they found *no significant sex differences* in these brains. If testosterone had an effect on the developing brain, it would surely have been apparent in this large sample. Yet Geschwind and Behan cited this study for other purposes and utterly ignored its findings of no sex differences.

Instead, Geschwind and Behan cited as evidence for their hypothesis a study of *rats'* brains. The authors of the rat study reported that in male rats, two areas of the cortex that are believed to be involved in processing visual information were 3 percent thicker on the right side than on the left. In one of the better examples of academic gobbledygook yet to reach the printed page, the researchers interpreted their findings to mean that "in the male rat it is necessary to have greater spatial orientation to interact with a female rat during estrus and to integrate that input into a meaningful output." Translation: When having sex with a female, the male needs to be able to look around in case a dangerous predator, such as her husband, walks in on them.

Bleier found more holes in this argument than in a screen door. No one knows, she said, what the slightly greater thickness in the male rat's cortex means for the rat, let alone what it means for human beings. There is at present no evidence that spatial orientation is related to asymmetry of the cortex, or that female rats have a lesser or deficient ability in this regard. And although Geschwind and Behan unabashedly used their limited findings to account for male "superiority" in math and art, they did not specifically study the incidence of genius, talent, or even modest giftedness in their sample, nor did they demonstrate a difference between the brains of geniuses and the brains of average people.

Gleier wrote to *Science,* offering a scholarly paper detailing these criticisms. *Science* did not publish it, on the grounds, as one reviewer put it, that Bleier "tends to err in the opposite direction from the researchers whose results and conclusions she criticizes" and because "she argues very strongly for the predominant role of environmental influences."[40] Apparently, said Bleier, one is allowed to err in only one direction if one wants to be published in *Science.* The journal did not even publish her critical Letter to the Editor.

At about the same time, however, *Science* saw fit to publish a study by two researchers who claimed to have found solid evidence of gender differences in the splenium (posterior end) of the corpus callosum.[41] In particular, they said, the splenium was larger and more bulbous in the five female brains than in the nine male brains they examined, which had been obtained at autopsy. The researchers speculated that "the female brain is less well lateralized—that is, manifests less hemispheric specialization—than the male brain for visuospatial functions." Notice the language: The female brain is *less specialized* than, and by implication inferior to, the male brain. They did not say, as they might have, that the female brain was *more integrated* than the male's. The male brain is the norm, and specialization, in the brain as in academia, is considered a good thing. Generalists in any business are out of favor these days.

This article, which also met professional acclaim, had a number of major flaws that, had they been part of any other research paper, would have been fatal to its publication. The study was based on a small sample of only fourteen brains. The researchers did not describe their methods of selecting the brains in that sample, so it is possible that some of the brains were diseased or otherwise abnormal. The article contained numerous unsupported assumptions and leaps of faith. For example, there is at present absolutely no evidence that the number of fibers in the corpus callosum is even related to hemispheric specialization. Indeed, no one knows what role, if any, the callosum plays in determining a person's mental abilities. Most damaging of all, the sex differences that the researchers claimed to have found in the size of the corpus callosum were not statistically significant, according to the scientific conventions for accepting an article for publication.

Bleier again wrote to *Science,* delineating these criticisms and also citing four subsequent studies, by her and by others, that independently failed to find gender differences of any kind in the corpus callosum. *Science* failed to publish this criticism, as it has failed to publish all studies that find no gender differences in the brain.

Ultimately, the most damning blow to all of these brain-hemisphere theories is that the formerly significant sex differences that brain theories are attempting to account for—in verbal, spatial, and math abilities—are fading rapidly. Let's start with the famed female superiority of verbal ability. Janet Hyde, a professor of psychology at the University of Wisconsin, and her colleague Marcia Linn reviewed 165 studies of verbal ability (including skills in vocabulary, writing, anagrams, and reading comprehension), which represented tests of 1, 418,899 people. Hyde and Linn reported that at present in America, there simply are no gender differences in these verbal skills. They noted: "Thus our research pulls out one of the two wobbly legs on which the brain lateralization theories have rested."[42]

Hyde recently went on to kick the other leg, the assumption of overall male superiority in mathematics and spatial ability. No one disputes that males do surpass females at the highly gifted end of the math spectrum. But when Hyde and her colleagues analyzed 100 studies of mathematics performance, representing the testing of 3,985,682 students, they found that gender differences were smallest and favored *females* in samples of the general population, and grew larger, favoring males, only in selected samples of precocious individuals.[43]

What about spatial abilities, another area thought to reveal a continuing male superiority? When psychologists put the dozens of existing studies on spatial ability into a giant hopper and looked at the overall results, this was what they reported: Many studies show no sex differences. Of the studies that do report sex differences, the magnitude of the difference is often small. And finally, there is greater variation *within* each sex than *between* them. As one psychologist who reviewed these studies summarized: "The observed differences are very small, the overlap [between men and women] large, and abundant biological theories are supported with very slender or no evidence."[44]

Sometimes scientists and science writers put themselves through contortions in order to reconcile the slim evidence with their belief in sex differences in the brain. The authors of a popular textbook on sexuality, published in 1990, acknowledge that "sex differences in cognitive skills have declined significantly in recent years. Then they add: "Notwithstanding this finding, theories continue to debate why these differences exist." Pardon? Notwithstanding the fact that there are few differences of any magnitude, let's discuss why there are differences? Even more mysteriously, they conclude: "If Geschwind's theory is ultimately supported by further research, we will have hard evidence of a biological basis for alleged sex differences in verbal and spatial skills."[45] "Hard evidence" for *alleged* sex differences—the ones that don't exist!

It is sobering to read, over and over and over again in scholarly papers, the conclusions of eminent scientists who have cautioned their colleagues against generalizing about sex differences from poor data. One leader in brain-hemisphere research, Marcel Kinsbourne, observing that the evidence for sex differences "fails to convince on logical, methodological, and empirical grounds," then asked:

> Why then do reputable investigators persist in ignoring [this evidence]? Because the study of sex differences is not like the rest of psychology. Under pressure from the gathering momentum of feminism, and perhaps in backlash to it, many investigators seem determined to discover that men and women "really" are different. It seems that if sex differences (e.g., in lateralization) do not exist, then they have to be invented.[46]

These warnings have, for the most part, gone unheeded. Poor research continues to be published in reputable journals, and from there it is disseminated to the public. Many scientists and science writers continue to rely on weak data to support their speculations, like using pebbles as foundation for a castle. Because these speculations fit the dominant beliefs about gender, however, they receive far more attention and credibility than they warrant. Worse, the far better evidence that fails to conform to the dominant experience, remains unpublished.

As a result, the ideas enter the common vocabulary as proven facts when they should be encumbered with "maybes," "sometimes," and "we-don't-know-yets." Scientists Hugh Fairweather, reviewing the history of sex differences research in cognition, concluded: "What had before been a possibility at best slenderly evidenced, was widely taken for a fact; and 'fact' hardened into a 'biological' dogma."[47]

Now, it is possible that reliable sex differences in the brain will eventually be discovered. Will it then be all right for Dobson to go on the air to celebrate how delightfully but innately different men and women are? Should we then all make sure we have a male brain and a female brain in every household? Should we then worry about the abnormality of households like mine, in which the male is better at intuitive judgments and the female has the adding-machine mentality?

The answers are no, for three reasons. First, theories of sex differences in the brain cannot account for the complexities of people's everyday behavior. They cannot explain, for instance, why, if women are better than men in verbal ability, so few women are auctioneers or diplomats, or why, if women have the advantage in making rapid judgments, so few women are air-traffic controllers or umpires. Nor can brain theories explain why abilities and ambitions change when people are given opportunities previously denied to them. Two decades ago, theorists postulated biological limitations that were keeping women out of men's work like medicine and bartending. When the external barriers to these professions fell, the speed with which women entered them was dizzying. Did everybody's brain change? Today we would be amused to think that women have a brain-lateralization deficiency that is keeping them out of law school. But we continue to hear about the biological reasons that keep women out of science, math, and politics. For sex differences in cognitive abilities to wax and wane so rapidly, they must be largely a result of education, motivation, and opportunity, not of innate differences between male and female brains.

Second, the meanings of terms like "verbal ability" and "spatial reasoning" keep changing too, depending on who is using them and for what purpose. For example, when conservatives like Dobson speak of women's verbal abilities, they usually mean women's interest in and willingness to talk about relationships and feelings. But in studies of total talking time in the workplace, men far exceed women in the talk department. In everyday life, men interrupt women more than vice versa, dominate the conversation, and are more successful at introducing new topics and having their comments remembered in group discussions.[48] What does this mean for judgments of which sex has the better "verbal ability"?

Third, the major key problem with biological theories of sex differences is that they deflect attention from the far more substantial evidence for sex similarity. The finding that men and women are more alike in their abilities and brains than different almost never makes the news. Researchers and the public commit the error of focusing on the small differences—usually of the magnitude of a few percentage points—rather than on the fact that the majority of women and men overlap. For example, this is what the author of a scientific paper that has been widely quoted as *supporting* sex differences in brain hemispheres actually concluded:

> Thus, one must not overlook perhaps the most obvious conclusion, which is that basic patterns of male and female brain asymmetry seem to be more similar than they are different.[49]

Everyone, nevertheless, promptly overlooked it.

The habit of seeing women and men as two opposite categories also leads us to avoid the practical question: How much ability does it take to do well in a particular career? When people hear that men are better than women in spatial ability, many are quick to conclude that perhaps women, with their deficient brains, should not try to become architects or engineers. This reaction is not merely unfortunate; it is cruel to the women who *do* excel in architectural or engineering ability. The fields of math and science are losing countless capable women because girls keep hearing that women aren't as good as men in these fields.

None of this means that biology is irrelevant to human behavior. But whenever the news trumpets some version of "biology affects behavior," it obscures the fact that biology and behavior form a two-way street. Hormones affect sexual drive, for instance, but sexual activity affects hormone levels. An active brain seeks a stimulating environment, but living in a stimulating environment literally changes and enriches the brain. Fatigue and boredom cause poor performance on the job, but stultifying job conditions produce fatigue and boredom. Scientists and writers who reduce our personalities, problems, and abilities to biology thereby tell only half the story, and miss half the miracle of how human biology works.

Ruth Bleier, who after all was herself a neuroscientists, put the whole matter in perspective this way:

> Such efforts directed at the callosum (or any other particular structure in the brain, for that matter) are today's equivalent of 19th-century craniology: if you can't find a bigger bump here or a smaller one there on a person's skull, if you can find a more bulbous splenium here or a more slender one there . . . you will know something significant about their intelligence, their personality, their aspirations, their astrological sign, their gender and race, and their status in society. We are still mired in the naive hope that we can find something that we can *see* and *measure* and it will explain everything. It is silly science and it serves us badly.[50]

Once defined as fundamentally different from—and inferior to—men in body, psyche, and brain, women have tried various ways of coping with being "the other." The most common approach, the one that most women today have adopted, has been to try to prove that they are as good as, as competent as, as intelligent as, as valued as, the men who set the norm. Of course, after a while all the efforts to be "as something as" men get tiring. In 1991, after twenty-five years of trying to be accepted by her male colleagues, Dr. Frances K. Conley, a tenured professor in the department of medicine at Stanford and one of the few female neurosurgeons in the country, resigned her post. She had had enough of being called "hon," of having other surgeons fondle her in the operating room, of the relentlessly "hostile" environment, of having her opinions dismissed as evidence of her "PMS." Dr. Conley resigned because, she wrote, "I was tired of being treated as less than an equal person."[51] (She has since returned to her job at Stanford, with renewed conviction in the importance of persistence.)

And so, weary of the seemingly fruitless struggle to be like men and repeatedly having to demonstrate their human competence, many women have set off in a separatist direction to define their own standards of excellence and to redeem qualities and experiences that had long been disparaged. This approach has offered a beguiling, exhilarating, luminous alternative to the impossibility of measuring up. Yet it too has its perils, as we shall see next.

NOTES

1. Donovan and Sanford, 1986, p. 33.

2. Sample findings on women's "problems": Self-esteem, Donovan and Sanford, 1986; on value of work, Major, 1987, hurt rather than angry, Mary K. Biaggio, "Sex Differences in Anger: Are they real?", paper presented at the annual meeting of the American Psychological Association, Atlanta, 1988; separate sense of self, Aries and Olver, 1985.

3. Cheryl B. Olson, "The Influence of Context on Gender Differences in Performance Attributions: Further evidence of a 'feminine modesty' effect." Paper presented at the annual meeting of the Western Psychological Association, San Francisco, 1988.

4. Silverstein, Peterson, and Purdue, 1986; Silverstein et al., 1988, 1990.

5. Garner et al., 1980.

6. Adam Drewnowski and Doris K. Yee, "Adolescent Dieting: Fear of fatness and the role of puberty." Paper presented at the annual meeting of the American Psychological Association, Atlanta, 1988. See also Striegel-Moore, Silberstein, and Rodin, 1986.

7. Joan S. Girgus, Susan Nolen-Hoeksema, and Martin E. P. Seligman, "Why Do Sex Differences in Depression Emerge During Adolescence?" Paper presented at the annual meeting of the American Psychological Association, New Orleans, 1989; Attie and Brooks-Gunn, 1987.

8. Silverstein, personal interview with author, quoted in Carol Tavris, "Is Thin Still In?" *Woman's Day,* March 3, 1987, p. 35.

9. Susan Wooley and O Wayne Wooley, "Thinness Mania," *American Health,* October 1986, pp. 68–74. Quote, p. 72.

10. For statistics on the prevalence and risks of breast implants, see Wolfe, 1991. See also Doug Podolsky, "Breast Implants: What price vanity?" *American Health,* March 1991, pp. 70–75. In 1991 the head of the Food and Drug Administration, Dr. David Kessler, observing that too many women were being lulled into believing that breast implants were risk free, urges physicians to inform potential clients of the risk involved. (*The New York Times,* August 1, 1991.)

11. Betty Goodwin, "Soft Sell: Leading ladies throw moviegoers a curve," *Los Angeles Times,* February 1, 1991, p. E3. This article also contains the quotes by Gale Hayman and Margaret Sharley, deputy general manager of Lancôme. See also Amy Louise Kazmin, "The Voluptuous

Woman Makes a Comeback," *Los Angeles Times,* February 22, 1991, pp. E1 and E7, for interviews with designers.

12. Paddy Calistro, "For Good Measure," *Los Angeles Times Magazine,* April 8, 1990, p. 32.
13. Source: National Osteoporosis Foundation, Washington, D.C.
14. See Bennett and Gurin, 1982.
15. Ernsberger and Nelson, 1988.
16. Attie and Brooks-Gunn, 1987; Striegel-Moore, Silberstein, and Rodin, 1986.
17. Wooley, personal interview with author, quoted in Carol Tavris, "Is This Still In?" *Woman's Day,* March 3, 1987, p. 114.
18. Quoted in Kazmin, p. E7. (See Note 11.)
19. Gilligan, 1982, p. 6.
20. Ibid., pp. 12–13. See also Gilligan, Ward, and Taylor, 1988; Josselson, 1987.
21. Offer and Sabshin, 1984.
22. Apter, 1990, pp. 2–3.
23. Ibid., p. 71.
24. Baruch, Barnett, and Rivers, 1982.
25. See, for example, Mary Crawford, "The Discourse of Humor: Two levels," paper presented at the annual meeting of the American Psychological Association, Boston, 1990; see also Crawford and Gressley, 1991, and Wade, 1986.
26. Robert Sapolsky, "The Case of the Falling Nightwatchmen," *Discover,* July 1987, pp. 42–45.
27. Ibid., p. 44. The data that Sapolsky reanalyzed come from Benbow and Stanley, 1980.
28. T. Lang, *The Difference Between a Man and a Woman* (New York: The John Day Co., 1971), pp. 203–204.
29. Le Bon quoted in Gould, 1981, pp. 104–105.
30. Sperry, 1982.
31. Quoted in Gina Kolata, "Math Genius May Have Hormonal Basis," *Science,* 222 (December 23, 1983), p. 1312.

32. Ibid., p. 1312.

33. Transcript from radio show "Focus on the Family: 'Dr. James Dobson interviews Dr. Donald Joy–The innate differences between males and females.'" 1984, 1986, CS-099, pp. 4, 78.

34. Gary Smalley and John Trent, *The Language of Love* (Pomona, CA: Focus on the Family Publishing, 1988). Quote, pp. 35–36.

35. See Bleier, 1988; Fausto-Sterling, 1985; Harrington, 1987; Hubbard, 1990. For an excellent history of psychological revisionism in the study of the brain, see Shields, 1975.

36. *Newsweek*, "Guns and Dolls," May 28, 1990, p. 59.

37. Smalley and Trent, p. 36. (See Note 34.)

38. Levy, 1983.

39. The discussion and critique of Geschwind and Behan, 1982, is from Bleier, 1988.

40. Ruth Bleier, "Sex Differences Research in the Neurosciences." Paper presented at the annual meeting of the American Association for the Advancement of Science, Chicago, 1987.

41. The study of the corpus callosum is from de Lacoste-Utamsing and Holloway, 1982.

42. Hyde and Linn, 1986, 1988. Males are more likely to have speech problems, such as stuttering, and to be referred for treatment for dyslexia—though not more likely to actually be dyslexic (see Shaywitz et al., 1990). See also Feingold (1988), who found that gender differences in SAT scores have "declined precipitously" in the last forty years. In 1950, school-age boys and girls differed markedly in verbal ability (girls excelled), abstract reasoning (boys excelled),and "clerical ability" (girls excelled). By 1980, boys had completely caught up with girls in verbal ability. Girls had completely caught up in verbal and abstract reasoning and numerical ability, and halved the difference in mechanical reasoning and space relations. The only exception to the rule of "vanishing gender differences," Feingold found, was the gender gap at the highest levels of math performance.

43. Hyde, Fennema, and Lamon, 1990.

44. Caplan, MacPherson, and Tobin, 1985. Researcher quoted on p. 786.

45. Robert Crooks and Karla Baur, *Our Sexuality*, 4th edition (Redmond City, CA: Benjamin Cummings, 1990), p. 64. To see how easy it is to slip from describing gender "differences" to speaking of one gender's "superiority," regard this statement by the authors: "Because the right

hemisphere is the primary repository of spatial abilities, it is not surprising that male rats, with *quantitatively superior right hemispheres,* perform better than do their female counterparts on maze-learning tasks that require skill with spatial relationships. . . ." (My emphasis.)

46. Kinsbourne, 1980, p. 242.

47. Fairweather quoted in Bleier, 1988, p. 154.

48. Fishman, 1983; Lakoff, 1990, McConnell-Ginet, 1983, 1984; Tannen, 1990 (esp. pp. 75–76).

49. McGlone, 1980, p. 226.

50. Bleier, 1987, pp. 11–12. (See Note 40.)

51. Frances K. Conley, "Why I'm Leaving Stanford: I Wanted My Dignity Back," *Los Angeles Times,* June 9, 1991, pp. M1, M6.

Questions

1. What evidence does Tavris offer that "the universal man is buried deep within the habits of thought"? According to Tavris, what consequences result from viewing men's bodies and psychology as the norm? How have women sometimes unconsciously internalized these standards?

2. What languages do researchers often use to describe their findings and how does this reveal androcentrism? How would we conceptualize women and men differently if we viewed "women" as the norm? Why does Tavris veiw this reversal as problematic as well? What are the dangers in generalizing results of research performed on animals to humans?

3. What differences does Tavris leave unexplored in this essay? What are the consequences of viewing women as a universal group? Why are sex differences so fascinating to our culture? What does this preoccupation with differences between men and women obscure?

Carol Gilligan: Leader for a Different Kind of Future (1984)

Lindsy Van Gelder

Carol Gilligan is a Psychologist, a Professor of Education, and the chair of the Gender Studies Doctoral Program at Harvard University. She has contributed over 20 years of research on adolescence and women's moral reasoning to the field of psychology, including the groundbreaking text In a Different Voice *(1982). Interviewed by journalist Lindsy Van Gelder shortly after the publication of that influential work, Gilligan describes her realization that psychological and moral development studies had primarily been done on men and their results generalized to women—often with the result that women were judged as "inferior" or "less well developed" than men on morality scales. Arguing that focusing on a single gender distorts our understanding of the human experience, Gilligan claimed that women "speak in a different voice" based on relations and connections rather than individual-*

"Carol Gilligan: Leader for a Different Kind of Future" by Lindsy Van Gelder, from *Ms.*, January 1984. Reprinted by permission.

ism and autonomy. A controversial belief at the time, her work has been essential to rethinking "what we have been missing by not listening to half of the human population." Gilligan's most recent book is Between Voice and Silence: Women and Girls, Race and Relationship *(1995).*

At the time we're writing this—and certainly by the time you're reading this—the popular imagination is becoming obsessed with George Orwell's "1984," and, more broadly, with The Future. Few of these futuristic scenarios are serene. Most combine the power of nascent technology with all the horrors of the past—war, plagues, poverty, repression. If this imagined Future has a texture, it's metallic: as convoluted as a circuit board, as icy and unswerving as the cone of a missile. We seem to be plunging headlong into helplessness, toward a revolution of machines that do our very thinking. At best, we seem to be telling ourselves, we can only hope for machines that won't enslave us, won't destroy us.

But the Future is also a revolution of values. If anything can change the uses to which our technology is put, it can be found here, in the realm of how we view ourselves and one another. Such revolutions are subtle, and their leaders often more easily picked out in hindsight. Educator and psychologist Carol Gilligan, author of "In a Different Voice" (published in 1982 by the Harvard University Press) is one of our future leaders. A study of contrasting ways of defining and developing morality, her book (and subsequent work) are predicated on finding that men in this culture tend to see the world in terms of their autonomy (and are overthreatened by intimacy), whereas women tend to see the world in terms of connectedness (and are overthreatened by isolation). The male view, for obvious reasons, has been seen as the correct one. Gilligan's work has created a new appreciation for a previously uncatalogued female sensibility, as well as possibilities for new understanding between the genders. But her contributions go beyond these. Because we live in a world where our survival may depend on our sense of connection, Gilligan's work has implications for a rather different kind of future—one in which humanity takes its cues not from Big Brother, but from sisters, mothers, and daughters.

"The spirit in which I wrote the book was to raise questions," according to Carol Gilligan, who as she speaks is gathering up papers from the table and replacing them with stoneware mugs of freshly brewed coffee. We are in her large, sunny kitchen in Cambridge, Massachusetts, a few blocks from the Harvard Graduate School of Education, where she is an associate professor. A ginger-dappled pork roast is in the oven, and calendar photographs of French chateaux are on the wall. Everything radiates a certain well-put-together warmth, including Gilligan herself, who chooses her words carefully, but isn't above an occasional giggle. She is a mature woman—one of her grown sons is playing the piano in another part of the house—but one who appears obviously comfortable in the undergraduate uniform of jeans, an old green sweater, and long hair parted pristinely down the middle. She pauses to think before she adds: "And in some sense, I very straightforwardly wanted to ask men to *listen* to women's voices—and to say to women that if men hadn't listened in the past, it wasn't simply a matter of being narrow-minded or biased. They simply didn't know what to do with these voices. They did not fit."

That Gilligan's theories don't blame men, and—in her words—"speak about the differential access of the genders to certain kinds of understanding, not the superiority of one gender over the other" may account in part for their popularity. Still, Gilligan has clearly served as something of a much-needed healer, particularly within the academic community. "There's been a sort of coming forward from other researchers, for example, who've told me about studies where women were dropped from the sample because their responses were complicating the situation. Again, this wasn't done out of small-mindedness, so much as genuine confusion and the normal scholarly impulse to make sense of one's data." Post-Gilligan, it will be much harder for researchers to equate "human" with male and to see female experience as simply an aberrant substratum. More than that, she has, she hopes, pointed the way for other researchers to pick up where she left off.

"I would really like to remap the whole domain of human development—the story we tell ourselves about the Nature of Man, as it's phrased," *she* explains. "For example, the word 'defense'—as in 'defense mechanisms'—is absolutely unquestioned in the psychological parlance, which reflects the state of nature as a state of war. Why do we have the notion of offense and defense as the main dynamic of human psychology? I mean, who's attacking?

"Then we have this group here—women—who seem less warlike, and we say that 'they're having a problem with aggression.' What if instead you *took* these seemingly peace-loving souls and before you so readily attribute their behavior to biology you asked in all seriousness, 'What is it about the way women deal with conflict that makes it less likely to erupt in violence?' And what if you said, 'Our notions of winning and losing have been rendered obsolete by nuclear technology, so we need a new set of rules, and you in fact have this microcosm of little girls who've been saying all along that they don't like to play games where people win and lose and get their feelings hurt and feel bad—I mean, instead of ignoring them or thinking that there's something wrong with them, why aren't we out there *studying* them?'

Little girls are, in many ways, Gilligan's key to the future. One of the most striking sections of *In a Different Voice* involved a study in which children were told a story about a man who can't afford to pay for a drug to save his dying wife. Boys often see the story in terms of the man's individual moral choice, and conclude that the man should choose life over property and steal the drug. Girls, on the other hand, often take an overview: they wonder what will happen to the relationship if the man gets caught and goes to jail, or they fix on the morality of the druggist, seeing the problem as one of communication—persuading the druggist to do the right thing. Although the approaches to the problem are simply different, the girls' responses have, in the past, been considered *wrong*. What interests Gilligan now is the connection between that research and the self-effacement typical of girls from puberty on up.

"Something happens to girls when they're about twelve. The eleven-year-old who's asked the story about the man and the druggist will hold out for her point of view, whereas the fifteen-year-old will yield. In some ways, a crucial question for the future will be: how do we get females not to abandon what they know at eleven?" Gilligan suspects the root is the change in the school curriculum at that level from subjects based on facts to those based on "interpretation—whether it's literature or history or psychology or even biology. And because male values are considered the norm, girls begin to see their own experience disappear from the representation of human experience. Girls begin to become aware that bringing in their own values is going to make trouble. So they start waiting and watching for other people to give them their cues as to what their, values should be. And of course, the irony is, that since they're very tuned in to other people, they're very good at this."

For the rest of her life, according to Gilligan, the girl who goes ethically underground at 11 will retain the female view of the connectedness of humanity, but she will regard that view as appropriate only within the "interpersonal sphere"—not the big world. For girls and women to have the confidence to trust their own ethical perspectives, Gilligan added, the educational system will have to learn to stop thinking of female input as troublesome. "Why not label it creativity? Or research, or progress, or knowledge?" she asks.

More is at stake here, of course, than women's self-esteem, as important as that may be. "I could argue—although I hold back on doing so, because I know this kind of argument is so readily misconstrued—that as long as females get pregnant and give birth to children, and therefore all female children know they have within themselves at least that possibility, that there will be easier access for women to the fact of human connection," she said. "It doesn't mean there's no access for men, just that it's easier for them to forget how connected people's lives are. And at a time when to remember connection and to see autonomy as an illusion are important, then it becomes important to hear women's voices." The crucial question, to Gilligan, is whether women have arrived at the point where they're willing to use their voices in public.

"The disappointment of suffrage was that women yielded their votes—they tended to vote as their husbands told them. I'm now watching the Gender Gap with great interest. Women do see war in terms of waste and in terms of what it means to raise a child—they're less willing to abstract that into a body count. Women do see so-called acceptable levels of unemployment in terms of what's going on in those households. The question is whether we finally take ourselves seriously enough to realize that if we see something differently, maybe we're not wrong. I hope we'll act on that in the next election, but I'm still not convinced. I think it could go either way."

Another key to the future for Gilligan is what might be called sisterhood. Since we each harbor the uncertainty that our perceptions are in fact valid, she suggests, it becomes imperative for each of us to speak out and make her perceptions known—in the classroom, at the office, at the polls. "Women are tremendously sensitive to abandonment. It's very critical to all of us not to feel isolated. So one of the issues right now, I think, is do we abandon each other? Do the women faculty in the universities abandon the support staff? Do the women physicians abandon the women nurses? If you're a corporate woman or a lawyer and you see that the structure leaves no one with any time to deal with sick children, do you put pressure on the system and stand with each other—do you say, 'You're not crazy, I know what you're talking about'—or do you fall into a competitive stance?"

Gilligan is not a figure on the *People* magazine/"Good Morning America" circuit, but within academic and feminist circles, she (along with such thinkers as Jean Baker Miller, Nancy Chodorow, and Dorothy Dinnerstein) has provided a vocabulary and a context for women (and men) to envision new worlds. "It's the most significant work to come out in years," according to Dr. Margaret Hennig of the Simmons College Graduate School of Management and coauthor with Anne Jardim of *The Managerial Woman* (Doubleday/Anchor). "She's given us the only hope for a future of decency within organizations."

Like many, Hennig sees Gilligan's work as a jumping-off point, a foundation on which to build concepts in areas that Gilligan herself hasn't touched upon. In business, for example, Hennig says that Gilligan's theories helped her understand certain stereotypical female behavior. "Gilligan points out that women feel guilty about making a rupture in human connectedness. It occured to me that this is what's behind the 'bitch behavior' that's complained about in some executive women. What's going on is that the woman behaving nastily is so threatened by having to hurt someone's feelings that she freezes up and turns off inside; she's confusing maturity with being self-sacrificing, so she can't just say to someone, 'Listen, I like you and I like working with you, but this particular piece of work is terrible.'"

Hennig also reports getting an insight into another common problem of corporate women: "Gilligan talks about women who are embedded in their personal relationships, and who derive their identity from being a part of relationships. What I think she's getting at is that as long as one sees oneself that way, it's difficult to separate oneself without pain. A lot of working women wait to be *told* things—even in middle managment—because women still fear that if we open our mouths, we'll rupture the social fabric and be abandoned. They don't say 'I have to tell people what I want.' It's 'They'll come to me.' They're embedded in the work relationship in that same self-sacrificing way." At the same time, Hennig wonders how Gilligan's insights about women will intersect with other trends in the corporate world, such as the introduction of computers ("Will men latch onto them because they see them as distancing and nonintimate?") and of cooperation-centered Japanese management styles ("Will American women be more predisposed than men to taking them on?").

"When I first heard Gilligan," said Dr. Charlotte Jacobsen, dean of students at Rosemont College in Pennsylvania, "I thought *Aha*!" Gilligan's work gave her a new conceptual framework within her own area, the study of individual differences in cognitive style, which has particular relevance to her work in counseling women. One of the primary theories in the discipline, she explained, is "field dependence/independence." "Field independence"—characterized by the ability to look at a visual pattern and identify its discrete parts—is the learning style into which the majority of male test subjects fit. Those who are "field dependent"—mostly women—look at the same pattern and, according to Jacobsen, "they see it holistically—as a whole." What bothered Jacobsen was that "the whole vocabulary used to describe the field dependent style came across as negative. Why call it 'dependent'? Why not 'global' or 'sensitive'?" Also, "It was always implied that this style was over-influenced by external things, that it was unanalytic, a weakness. Why not look at it as a different way of being strong?"

Gilligan has been critiqued by some feminists for giving aid and comfort to those who welcome the news that men and women are so different. Jacobsen disagrees: "She's liberating us all to be fully human." One professor noticed that Gilligan's work was especially liberating for profeminist male students. It gives them affirmation that you can change behavior, that it doesn't just spring naturally from your genes.

Trudy J. Hanmer is associate principal of the Emma Willard School, a private girls' high school in Troy, New York, where Gilligan has been studying the values of female adolescents for several years—the *only* ongoing study of its kind. "What Carol is doing," according to Hanmer, "is giving us the tools to learn how to help girls develop intellectually—on their own terms." In the future, girls might be stimulated by seeing the pursuit of knowledge as an enterprise in which everyone wins and no one loses. "For instance, we might think about whether math is best taught in the traditional hierarchical setting, in which the individual is pitted against the discipline. We might try a group setting instead. By the same token, we might emphasize to girls the little-publicized truth that most Nobel Prizes and Pulitzer Prizes are the result of many people's work, even if only one is named."

Dorothy Austin, a psychologist who lectures in psychiatry at the Cambridge Hospital/Harvard Medical School, is part of a research program studying the effects of nuclear threat on daily life and psyches and the difference in men's and women's attitudes toward nuclear weapons. "Gilligan's work provides a psychological frame that enables us to understand the psychology of this gender gap," she says. By defining a distinctly different mode of moral reasoning, Gilligan allows us to rethink the male notion of patriotic sacrifice, and the notion of the "other" as enemy. Women have always been willing to sacrifice themselves to preserve the lives of their children, for example, whereas men have been willing to sacrifice themselves in the act of war—in what is referred to as moral killing. As the threat of nuclear war brings male leadership close to "the limits of its adaptive imagination," as Erik Erikson writes, Gilligan's work offers another track of moral imagination. "No longer is woman's style of moral reasoning and the desire to preserve context viewed as less developed," argues Austin, "it has become a political necessity for the preservation of the world."

Dr. Julia Wood, associate professor of speech communication at the University of North Carolina at Chapel Hill, uses Gilligan's book in several of her courses. "Her credentials are flawless, which makes it fun to hear people try to be critical of her," she noted. "More importantly, she has questioned the whole assumptive base of male values. You read her, and it's like having a veil lifted."

One Gilligan spin-off that Wood has been considering is the seemingly "liberated" trend of the last decade for women to enter the corporate life. "A lot of the advice given to young women is based on a set of male assumptions, learn about hierarchies, play hardball, even wear a necktie. Whatever else that may do, it really reinforces a sense of female inadequacy. We're being asked to fit into this structure that we had no part in creating, and we're being told that what we could bring to it of our own is worthless." Perhaps, Wood added, some of the "Superwoman" stresses so common to modern middle-class working mothers are a function of trying (like Gilligan's 15-year olds) to perform the schizophrenic task of living in the world of male values while inwardly clinging to the need to connect.

"What's great about Gilligan," Wood added, "is that her work is so heuristic—you start thinking of all the possible research you could do and all the questions you could ask, and you find yourself thinking that it's too bad you have only, say, fifty years left."

If Gilligan herself has a 1984 message for us, it is to find our own different voices and use them. "We have to separate our sense of connection from our sense of self-sacrifice, our sense that the most noble thing we can do is keep silent," she said. "For example, adolescent girls often operate on the assumption that disagreement is a disaster. They so fear isolation that they believe that if men were to see them as they really are, they would turn away. The temptation is to become interested in the way the boy experiences the world, and—as one of my students puts it—to 'float' in the relationship: you know, 'Tell me what you want me to be and I'll be it.' We may all do this to some extent. What we have to realize, however, is that if you do that, and you win, you lose. If you don't bring *yourself* into that relationship--that scholarship, that politics, that tradition, that international arena, you won't be heard."

Questions

1. How do women "speak in a different voice," according to Gilligan? On what is this voice based and how is it different from men's? How does this thinking manifest itself in the workplace and in personal relationships?
2. Why have women's ways of thinking been considered "wrong"? How does the language used in research findings reflect perceptions about women and men?

3. How does Gilligan see women's tendency toward self-effacement connected to school curriculum? What other factors might also contribute to the change in girl's self-esteem and willingness to speak publicly around age 12? How might Gilligan's notion of "sisterhood" help reverse this tendency?

4. How do Gilligan's findings expand the way we think about the "nature of man"? What does Gilligan mean when she says, "our notions of winning and losing have been rendered obsolete by nuclear technology"? How do Van Gelder, Gilligan and other researchers see women's conceptual framework as essential to the future?

The Body Politic (1995)

Abra Fortune Chernik

Body hatred is something many women share in what Abra Chernik terms a "diet culture," but the life-threatening aspects of anorexia and bulimia are sometimes dismissed. In the following narrative from Listen Up! Voices From the Next Feminist Generation, *screenwriter and activist Abra Chernik describes her hospitalization for anorexia and her struggle to overcome the illusion of power and control that she felt in her anorexic world.*

My body possesses solidness and curve, like the ocean. My weight mingles with Earth's pull, drawing me onto the sand. I have not always sent waves into the world. I flew off once, for five years, and swirled madly like a cracking brown leaf in the salty autumn wind. I wafted, dried out, apathetic.

I had no weight in the world during my years of anorexia. Curled up inside my thinness, a refugee in a cocoon of hunger, I lost the capacity to care about myself or others. I starved my body and twitched in place as those around me danced in the energy of shared existence and progressed in their lives. When I graduated from college crowned with academic honors, professors praised my potential. I wanted only to vanish.

It took three months of hospitalization and two years of outpatient psychotherapy for me to learn to nourish myself and to live in a body that expresses strength and honesty in its shape. I accepted my right and my obligation to take up room with my figure, voice and spirit. I remembered how to tumble forward and touch the world that holds me. I chose the ocean as my guide.

Who disputes the ocean's fullness?

Growing up in New York City, I did not care about the feminist movement. Although I attended an all-girls high school, we read mostly male authors and studied the history of men. Embracing mainstream culture without question, I learned about womanhood from fashion magazines, Madison Avenue and Hollywood. I dismissed feminist alternatives as foreign and offensive, swathed as they were in stereotypes that threatened my adolescent need for conformity.

Puberty hit late; I did not complain. I enjoyed living in the lanky body of a tall child and insisted on the title of "girl." If anyone referred to me as a "young woman," I would cry out, horrified, "Do not call me the W word!" But at sixteen years old, I could no longer deny my fate. My stomach and breasts rounded. Curly black hair sprouted in the most embarrassing places. Hips swelled from a once-flat plane. Interpreting maturation as an unacceptable lapse into fleshiness, I resolved to eradicate the physical symptoms of my impending womanhood.

Magazine articles, television commercials, lunchroom conversation, gymnastics coaches and write-ups on models had saturated me with diet savvy. Once I decided to lose weight, I quickly turned expert. I dropped hot chocolate from my regular breakfast order at the Skyline Diner. I replaced lunches of peanut butter and Marshmallow Fluff sandwiches with small platters of cottage cheese and cantaloupe. I eliminated dinner altogether and blunted my appetite with Tab, Camel Lights, and Carefree bubble gum. When furious craving overwhelmed my resolve and I swallowed an extra something, I would flee to the nearest bathroom to purge my mistake.

Within three months, I had returned my body to its preadolescent proportions and had manipulated my monthly period into drying up. Over the next five years, I devoted my life to losing my weight. I came to resent the body in which I lived, the body that threatened to develop, the body whose hunger I despised but could not extinguish. If I neglected a workout or added a pound or ate a bite too many, I would stare in the mirror and drown myself in a tidal wave of criticism. Hatred of my body generalized to hatred of myself as a person, and self-referential labels such as "pig," "failure" and "glutton" allowed me to believe that I deserved punishment. My self-hatred became fuel for the self-mutilating behaviors of the eating disorder.

As my body shrank, so did my world. I starved away my power and vision, my energy and inclinations. Obsessed with dieting, I allowed relationships, passions and identity to wither. I pulled back from the world, off of the beach, out of the sand. The waves of my existence ceased to roll beyond the inside of my skin.

And society applauded my shrinking. Pound after pound the applause continued, like the pounding ocean outside the door of my beach house.

The word "anorexia" literally means "loss of appetite." But as an anorexic, I felt hunger thrashing inside my body. I denied my appetite, ignored it, but never lost it. Sometimes the pangs twisted so sharply, I feared they would consume the meat of my heart. On desperate nights I rose in a flannel nightgown and allowed myself to eat an unplanned something.

No matter how much I ate, I could not soothe the pangs. Standing in the kitchen at midnight, spotlighted by the blue-white light of the open refrigerator, I would frantically feed my neglected appetite: the Chinese food I had not touched at dinner; ice cream and whipped cream; microwaved bread; cereal and chocolate milk; doughnuts and bananas. Then, solid sadness inside my gut, swelling agitation, a too-big meal I would not digest. In the bathroom I would rip off my shirt, tie up my hair, and prepare to execute the desperate ritual, again. I would ram the back of my throat with a toothbrush handle, crying, impatient, until the food rushed up. I would vomit until the toilet filled and I emptied, until I forgave myself, until I felt ready to try my life again. Standing up from my position over the toilet, wiping my mouth, I would believe that I was safe. Looking in the mirror through puffy eyes in a tumescent face, I would promise to take care of myself. Kept awake by the fast, confused beating of my heart and the ache in my chest, I would swear I did not miss the world outside. Lost within myself, I almost died.

By the time I entered the hospital, a mess of protruding bones defined my body, and the bones of my emaciated life rattled me crazy. I carried a pillow around because it hurt to sit down, and I shivered with cold in sultry July. Clumps of brittle hair clogged the drain when I showered, and blackened eyes appeared to sink into my head. My vision of reality wrinkled and my disposition turned mercurial as I slipped into starvation psychosis, a condition associated with severe malnutrition. People told me that I resembled a concentration camp prisoner, a chemotherapy patient, a famine victim or a fashion model.

In the hospital, I examined my eating disorder under the lenses of various therapies. I dissected my childhood, my family structure, my intimate relationships, my belief systems. I participated in experiential therapies of movement, art and psychodrama. I learned to use words instead of eating patterns to communicate my feelings. And still I refused to gain more than a minimal amount of weight.

I felt powerful as an anorexic. Controlling my body yielded an illusion of control over my life; I received incessant praise for my figure despite my sickly mien, and my frailty manipulated family and friends into protecting me from conflict. I had reduced my world to a plate of steamed carrots, and over this tiny kingdom I proudly crowned myself queen.

I sat cross-legged on my hospital bed for nearly two months before I earned an afternoon pass to go to the mall with my mother. The privilege came just in time; I felt unbearably large and desperately wanted a new outfit under which to hide gained weight. At the mall, I searched for two hours before finally discovering, in the maternity section at Macy's, a shirt large enough to cover what I perceived as my enormous body.

With an hour left on my pass, I spotted a sign on a shop window: "Body Fat Testing, $3.00." I suggested to my mother that we split up for ten minutes; she headed to Barnes & Noble, and I snuck into the fitness store.

I sat down in front of a machine hooked up to a computer, and a burly young body builder fired questions at me:

"Age?"

"Twenty-one."

"Height?"

"Five nine."

"Weight?"

"Ninety-nine."

The young man punched my statistics into his keyboard and pinched my arm with clippers wired to the testing machine. In a moment, the computer spit out my results. "Only ten percent body fat! Unbelievably healthy. The average for a woman your age is twenty-five percent. Fantastic! You're this week's blue ribbon winner."

I stared at him in disbelief. *Winner? Healthy? Fantastic?* I glanced around at the other customers in the store, some of whom had congregated to watch my testing, and I felt embarrassed by his praise. And then I felt furious. Furious at this man and at the society that programmed him for their ignorant approbation of my illness and my suffering.

"I am dying of anorexia," I whispered. "Don't congratulate me."

I spent my remaining month in the hospital supplementing psychotherapy with an independent examination of eating disorders from a social and political point of view. I needed to understand why society would reward my starvation and encourage my vanishing. In the bathroom, a mirror on the open door behind me reflected my backside in a mirror over the sink. Vertebrae poked at my skin, ribs hung like wings over chiseled hip bones, the two sides of my buttocks did not touch. I had not seen this view of myself before.

In writing, I recorded instances in which my eating disorder had tangled the progress of my life and thwarted my relationships. I filled three and a half Mead marble notebooks. Five years' worth of: *I wouldn't sit with Daddy when he was alone in the hospital because I needed to go jogging; I told Derek not to visit me because I couldn't throw up when he was there; I almost failed my comprehensive exams because I was so hungry; I spent my year at Oxford with my head in the toilet bowl; I wouldn't eat the dinner my friends cooked me for my nineteenth birthday because I knew they had used oil in the recipe; I told my family not to come to my college graduation because I didn't want to miss a day at the gym or have to eat a restaurant meal.* And on and on for hundreds of pages.

This honest account of my life dissolved the illusion of

anorexic power. I saw myself naked in the truth of my pain, my loneliness, my obsessions, my craziness, my selfishness, my defeat. I also recognized the social and political implications of consuming myself with the trivialities of calories and weight. At college, I had watched as classmates involved themselves in extracurricular clubs, volunteer work, politics and applications for jobs and graduate schools. Obsessed with exercising and exhausted by starvation, I did not even consider joining in such pursuits. Despite my love of writing and painting and literature, despite ranking at the top of my class, I wanted only to teach aerobics. Despite my adolescent days as a loud-mouthed, rambunctious class leader, I had grown into a silent, hungry young woman.

And society preferred me this way: hungry, fragile, crazy. *Winner! Healthy! Fantastic!* I began reading feminist literature to further understand the disempowerment of women in our culture. I digested the connection between a nation of starving, self-obsessed women and the continued success of the patriarchy. I also cultivated an awareness of alternative models of womanhood. In the stillness of the hospital library, new voices in my life rose from printed pages to echo my rage and provide the conception of my feminist consciousness.

I had been willing to accept self-sabotage, but now I refused to sacrifice myself to a society that profited from my pain. I finally understood that my eating disorder symbolized more than "personal psychodynamic trauma." Gazing in the mirror at my emaciated body, I observed a woman held up by her culture as the physical ideal because she was starving, self-obsessed and powerless, a woman called beautiful because she threatened no one except herself. Despite my intelligence, my education, and my supposed Manhattan sophistication, I had believed all the lies; I had almost given my life in order to achieve the sickly impotence that this culture aggressively links with female happiness, love and success. And everything I had to offer to the world, every tumbling wave, every thought and every passion, nearly died inside me.

As long as society resists female power, fashion will call healthy women physically flawed. As long as society accepts the physical, sexual and economic abuse of women, popular culture will prefer women who resemble little girls. Sitting in the hospital the summer after my college graduation, I grasped the absurdity of a nation of adult women dying to grow small.

Armed with this insight, I loosened the grip of the starvation disease on my body. I determined to recreate myself based on an image of a woman warrior. I remembered my ocean, and I took my first bite.

Gaining weight and getting my head out of the toilet bowl was the most political act I have ever committed.

I left the hospital and returned home to Fire Island. Living at the shore in those wintry days of my new life, I wrapped myself in feminism as I hunted sea shells and role models. I wanted to feel proud of my womanhood. I longed to accept and honor my body's fullness.

During the process of my healing, I had hoped that I would be able to skip the memory of anorexia like a cold pebble into the dark winter sea. I had dreamed that in relinquishing my obsessive chase after a smaller body, I would be able to come home to rejoin those whom I had left in order to starve, rejoin them to live together as healthy, powerful women. But as my body has grown full, I have sensed a hollowness in the lives of women all around me that I had not noticed when I myself stood hollow. I have made it home only to find myself alone.

Out in the world again, I hear the furious thumping dance of body hatred echoing every place I go. Friends who once appeared wonderfully carefree in ordering late-night french fries turn out not to eat breakfast or lunch. Smart, talented, creative women talk about dieting and overeating and hating the beach because they look terrible in bathing suits. Famous women give interviews insulting their bodies and bragging about bicycling twenty-four miles the day they gave birth.

I had looked forward to rejoining society after my years of anorexic exile. Ironically, in order to preserve my health, my recovery has included the development of a consciousness that actively challenges the images and ideas that define this culture. Walking down Madison Avenue and passing emaciated women, I say to myself, *those women are sick*. When smacked with a diet commercial, I remind myself, *I don't do that anymore*. I decline invitations to movies that feature anorexic actors, I will not participate in discussions about dieting, and I refuse to shop in stores that cater to women with eating-disordered figures.

Though I am critical of diet culture, I find it nearly impossible to escape. Eating disorders have woven their way into the fabric of my society. On television, in print, on food packaging, in casual conversation and in windows of clothing stores populated by ridiculously gaunt mannequins, messages to lose my weight and control my appetite challenge my recovered fullness. Finally at home in my body, I recognize myself as an island in a sea of eating disorders, a sea populated predominantly by young women.

A perversion of nature by society has resulted in a phenomenon whereby women feel safer when starving than when eating. Losing our weight boosts self-esteem, while nourishing our bodies evokes feelings of self-doubt and self-loathing.

When our bodies take up more space than a size eight (as most of our bodies do), we say, *too big*. When our appetites demand more than a Lean Cuisine, we say, *too much*. When we want a piece of a friend's birthday cake, we say, *too bad*. Don't eat too much, don't talk too loudly, don't take up too much space, don't take from the world. Be pleasant or crazy, but don't seem hungry. Remember, a new study shows that men prefer women who eat salad for dinner over women who eat burgers and fries.

So we keep on shrinking, starving away our wildness, our power, our truth.

Hiding our curves under long T-shirts at the beach, sitting silently and fidgeting while others eat dessert, sneaking back into the kitchen late at night to binge and hating ourselves the next day, skipping breakfast, existing on diet soda and cigarettes, adding up calories and subtracting everything else. We accept what is horribly wrong in our lives and fight what is beautiful and right.

Over the past three years, feminism has taught me to honor the fullness of my womanhood and the solidness of the body that hosts my life. In feminist circles I have found mentors, strong women who live with power, passion and purpose. And yet, even in groups of feminists, my love and acceptance of my body remains unusual.

Eating disorders affect us all on both a personal and a political level. The majority of my peers—including my feminist peers—still measure their beauty against anorexic ideals. Even among feminists, body hatred and chronic dieting continue to consume lives. Friends of anorexics beg them to please start eating; then these friends go home and continue their own diets. Who can deny that the millions of young women caught in the net of disordered eating will frustrate the potential of the next wave of feminism?

Sometimes my empathy dissolves into frustration and rage at our situation. For the first time in history, young women have the opportunity to create a world in our image. But many of us concentrate instead on recreating the shape of our thighs.

As young feminists, we must place unconditional acceptance of our bodies at the top of our political agenda. We must claim our bodies as our own to love and honor in their infinite shapes and sizes. Fat, thin, soft, hard, puckered, smooth, our bodies are our homes. By nourishing our bodies, we care for and love ourselves on the most basic level. When we deny ourselves physical food, we go hungry emotionally, psychologically, spiritually and politically. We must challenge ourselves to eat and digest, and allow society to call us too big. We will understand their message to mean too powerful.

Time goes by quickly. One day we will blink and open our eyes as old women. If we spend all our energy keeping our bodies small, what will we have to show for our lives when we reach the end? I hope we have more than a group of fashionably skinny figures.

QUESTIONS

1. How can individual eating problems actually be considered political problems? What factors contribute to the existence of eating problems?
2. What is the meaning and significance of "body hatred"? What are the effects of body hatred for both the individual and society?
3. How does Chernik change through the course of her narrative? What issues does Chernik face in her struggle for personal growth as a woman? How does she feel about her experiences?

I am Not Your Princess (1988)

Chrystos

Chrystos' rhythmic, fragmented poem "I am Not Your Princess" protests the persistent stereotyping of Native American people. The narrator expresses her frustration that distinct individuals with diverse heritages are often lumped into a generic category, and her weariness at having to battle the constant romanticization and commercialization of complex and rich cultural traditions. A woman of Menominee heritage, Chrystos is a poet and a political activist for Native American land rights. She has contributed to numerous anthologies and published a collection of her poetry entitled Not Vanishing *in 1988.*

Sandpaper between two cultures which tear
one another apart I'm not
a means by which you can reach spiritual understanding or even
learn to do beadwork
I'm only willing to tell you how to make fry bread
1 cup flour, spoon of salt, spoon of baking powder

Stir   Add milk or water or beer until it holds together
Slap each piece into rounds   Let rest
Fry in hot grease until golden
This is Indian food
only if you know that Indian is a government word
which has nothing to do with our names for ourselves
I won't chant for you
I admit no spirituality to you
I will not sweat with you or ease your guilt with fine turtle tales
I will not wear dancing clothes to read poetry or
explain hardly anything at all
I don't think your attempts to understand us are going to work so
I'd rather you left us in whatever peace we can still
scramble up   after all you continue to do
If you send me one more damn flyer about how to heal myself
for $300 with special feminist counseling
I'll probably set fire to something
If you tell me one more time that I'm wise I'll throw up on you
Look at me
See my confusion   loneliness   fear   worrying about
all our struggles to keep   what little is left for us
Look at my heart   not your fantasies   Please don't ever
again tell me about your Cherokee great-great grandmother
Don't assume I know every other Native Activist
in the world personally That I even know names of all the tribes
or can pronounce names I've never heard
or that I'm expert at the peyote stitch
If   you ever
again tell me
how strong I am
I'll lay down on the ground & moan so you'll see
at last   my human weakness   like your own
I'm not strong   I'm scraped
I'm blessed with life while so many I've known are dead
I have work to do   dishes to wash   a house to clean
There is no magic
See my simple cracked hands which have washed the same things
you wash   See my eyes dark with fear in a house by myself
late at night   See that to pity me or to adore me
are the same
1 cup flour, spoon of salt, spoon of baking powder, liquid to hold

Remember this is only my recipe   There are many others
Let me rest
here
at least

especially for Dee Johnson

QUESTIONS

1. What emotions are expressed in this poem? Refer to specific language in the text for evidence.
2. What stereotypes and misconceptions about Native Americans are introduced in this poem? What are the effects of these stereotypes and misconceptions? What does the narrator mean when she says "Indian" is a government word? What does the title of this selection mean? What does it mean when she states, "to pity me and adore me are the same"? How can the romanticization of "difference" be damaging?
3. What does the narrator clarify about Native people? What characteristics does she emphasize as acultural, that is, common elements among people regardless of culture? What does the narrator believe Native people need to preserve their energy for?
4. What is the narrator trying to accomplish? Describe the form and style of Chrystos' poem. How do they emphasize the narrator's message?

Homage to My Hips, Homage to My Hair (1980)

Lucille Clifton

In each of the following two poems, Lucille Clifton challenges Euro-American traditional standards of beauty, celebrating that which is culturally defined as falling outside of beauty norms—big hips and nappy hair. Clifton is the author of several poetry books including good woman: poems and a memoir 1969–1980, *as well as a number of children's books. She currently lives in Maryland and California, and she teaches at the University of Santa Cruz.*

Homage to My Hips

these hips are big hips
they need space to
move around in.
they don't fit into little
petty places. these hips
are free hips.

they don't like to be held back.
these hips have never been enslaved,
they go where they want to go
they do what they want to do.
these hips are mighty hips.
these hips are magic hips.
I have known them
to put a spell on a man and
spin him like a top!

Homage to My Hair

when i feel her jump up and dance
i hear the music! my God
i'm talking about my nappy hair!
she is a challenge to your hand
black man,
she is as tasty on your tongue as good greens
black man,
she can touch your mind
with her electric fingers and
the grayer she do get, good God,
the blacker she do be!

Questions

1. What do the poems indicate about specific problems Black women face in their confrontation with beauty norms?
2. In what ways are U.S. beauty norms racist? Think of some examples of how this racism is reflected in our culture.
3. Why do you think Clifton celebrates her hips and hair in these poems?

Arroz Con Pollo vs. Slim Fast (1992)

Linda Delgado

Female body norms and the meanings of food differ according to culture. This can be confusing for young women who must negotiate the gender ideals of several different cultures. In this brief essay, Linda Delgado explains the conflicting messages she encountered about beauty and body size as a Latina woman in the United States.

To many white American women, thinness and tallness are essential parts of beauty. Yet in Spanish, the words *delgada* and *flaca* have a different connotation. Both words mean thin. *Delgada* connotes thin and weak, while *flaca* connotes thin as in skinny. Neither is very flattering. In fact, the question that usually follows after someone notices you are looking rather *delgada* is whether you have been ill.

Weight problems, aside from their health implications, are not seen as important in Latino culture as they are in mainstream American culture. There is a ceremonial importance to food and many rituals assigned to the sharing of food with others. Recently during a warm-up exercise in a new class, students were asked to introduce themselves by identifying with a particular food. A young Dominican woman said she was like *arroz con pollo* (rice with chicken). Her reason for picking this dish was that rice with chicken symbolized warmth, love, and acceptance. It is a dish made for new neighbors, new in-laws, and new friends to celebrate important events. It means welcome and good luck.

The breaking of bread with family, friends, and strangers is part of Latino hospitality. "*Mi casa, su casa*" is an unaltered tradition. When you visit my aunt's house, for example, go there hungry! The variety and amounts of food are quite extraordinary. I get full just looking at the table! Not only must you partake of everything there, you must also keep in mind that there are at least three or four desserts to follow. On special occasions, such as Easter, Christmas, and Mother's Day, everyone has a signature dish, and part of the celebration is sharing these delicacies. Failure to eat the right amount will cause personal distress to the hostess. What did she do wrong? At my aunt's house, usually my grandmother will ask if you have been sick or if your children have been giving you a hard time. There must be some explanation why you have not eaten your share of food. By "your share of food" they mean enough to feed a small army! The word "diet" or "calories" is never mentioned. For the current generations, these messages can be confusing.

Putting weight on your bones, as my grandmother explains it, is necessary for many reasons. First of all, how else can you carry the burdens of being a woman? You have to eat in order to have the strength to deal with a husband and/or children (regardless of the fact that, at present, you may be 11 years old). You have to eat to have the strength to deal with *lo que Dios te mande,* whatever God sends you because *uno nunca sabe lo de mañana, so uno tierne que aprobechar lo de hoy*, we never know what tomorrow may bring, so we have to enjoy what we have today. Living in New York, you also have to eat in order to deal with the cold, wintry weather. There is always a good reason for a second or third helping of food. In the film *Acting Our Age*, an African-American woman about the age of 65 expresses her concern for the next generation of young women. She says, "Now that black women are being used as models and thought of as beautiful, they will pick up the same false notions about beauty as white women." I think this is also true for Latinas in the United States.

One of my childhood memories was an episode involving my grandmother when I was in the fifth grade. She picked me up at school and told my mother we were going shopping. Well, we did, but first she had someplace to take me. For as long as I could remember, I was a tall and very skinny child. That day, my grandmother and I took a bus ride into Manhattan to a nutrition clinic. She swore I was undernourished and that something was wrong. The doctor said I was healthy and of a good weight. My grandmother was quite surprised and, in fact, didn't believe him.

Having a "good set of hips" means not only that you can carry a child well but also that you can manage whatever your husband has in store for you. "You have to eat in order to have strength." So, from the time you are an infant, chubbiness is applauded as healthy. As you grow older, mental and physical well-being are assessed by your outer appearance. Thin is not sexy. It is unhealthy, unappealing, and sad. My grandmother told me that I didn't look strong enough to carry my bookbag and asked how was I going to carry whatever God sent my way. I learned early in life to expect to bear something! That was part of the gender-role experience.

Interestingly, flabbiness is not acceptable, either. Flabbiness is a sign of laziness and overindulgence. Formal exercise is not part of the Latino culture for women, while men often play softball, handball, or paddle ball. It is generally accepted that women who are flabby and out of shape must not be taking care of their homes, themselves, or their children. They must be watching *novelas*. Women's exercise happens in the course of cleaning, cooking, and caring for children.

In the dating game, life gets really confusing for young Latinas. If women look too much like the models, they will be considered the kind of women men play with but don't necessarily marry. A man brings a woman who is a size 10 or 12 home to mother and a family dinner, but a woman who is size 5 or 6, you have to keep away from your brother! A 16-year-old Puerto Rican student recently told me that her boyfriend wanted her to put on some weight before the summer. She said that he was not pleased at the fact that other men were watching her on the beach last summer. The other side of the problem was that her mother had taught her that if she gained weight, she would not have any boyfriends. When I heard this story, it reminded me of the African-American woman in the film and her description of "false notions about beauty."

Some of my fondest memories are wrapped in the warmth of mealtimes. Special foods are part of special holidays. Watching generations of women cook and exchange recipes, taking in all the wonderful aromas and feeling their sense of pride and accomplishment as they fulfilled their understood role, was positive for me. Although their place of power was in the kitchen, I learned how that power worked. Being in the kitchen did not mean being passive or subservient. It meant doing your share of the business of parenting and partnering, since the kitchen is the center of family activity. It is a place of importance in the Latino household. Feeding those whom you care about is nurturing the entire unit, and eating all of your *arroz con pollo* means you are loved for your efforts in return.

There are many mixed messages to negotiate in a cross-cultural environment. Immigrants, like everyone else, want to belong. They find themselves trapped somewhere between the cultural values of their home and their host country. Although some can negotiate the conflict better than others, it nevertheless distorts views of the self. Reconciliation of different cultural repertoires is quite a challenge, especially for young Latinas who are trying to "fit in."

QUESTIONS

1. What is the ideal body size for women within Latino culture? How is this ideal different from the dominant U.S. cultural definition of beauty?

2. How "natural" and universal are beauty norms? Why are they so powerful? What effect do these powerful standards have on women who are exposed to multiple and differing cultural messages?

3. What meanings are attached to food in different communities? What experiences did Delgado have with food in her childhood?

ABUSING WOMEN (1995)

Lesley Doyal

Women threaten their own health by using substances such as alcohol, nicotine, tranquillisers, or illicit drugs to alter mind and mood. While women engage in such practices less than men, evidence suggests more women are engaging in addictive practices almost everywhere in the world. Lesley Doyal, professor of health studies in England, relates addiction to global, political, and economic patterns in this chapter from What Makes Women Sick *(1995).*

Introduction

Millions of women consume legal but potentially hazardous substances every day in an attempt to ensure their own well-being and that of their families. In this chapter we explore some of the reasons behind this paradox. In particular we look at women's use of food, alcohol, cigarettes and tranquillisers, linking this with patterns of inequality and discrimination that have already emerged in earlier chapters.

Blowing Her Mind

All societies have devised a variety of artificial means for reducing stress and promoting feelings of well-being. These usually include the ingestion of mood-altering substances that may or may not be damaging to health. Traditionally it is men who have had easiest access to these resources, because of their superior purchasing power. In addition there is usually a gender bias in the social codes regulating the use of intoxicating substances. In the case of alcohol for instance, some societies condemn drunken women much more heavily than their male counterparts (Heath, 1991). This 'double standard' reflects the fact that women are often regarded not only as the caretakers of dependent children but also as the guardians of public morality (Lisansky Gomberg, 1982; Morgan, 1987). Any loss of control is perceived as either a symbolic or a real threat to the social order, and is punished accordingly.

During the postwar period many of these traditional constraints on female behaviour have begun to break down, while many women have had more income to spend on themselves. The effect of these trends on their health has been contradictory. On the one hand some women are now able to indulge in harmless pleasures that were previously monopolised by men. Moderate drinking, for example, can be pleasurable and possibly health promoting. On the other hand there is evidence that growing numbers of women are using or abusing substances in ways that pose a serious threat to their health (Ettore, 1992). The reality of their lives as workers and carers has put many women under increasing strain. In the absence of other socially accepted mechanisms for resolving tension and conflict, many are turning to addictive substances in an attempt to sustain themselves in an otherwise unsupportable environment.

Detailed evidence of these changing patterns of consumption is difficult to obtain. However, it is clear that the pattern is a complex one. While women's intake of some potentially addictive substances is certainly increasing, their consumption of others remains stable, or is even declining. There is little sign of a significant increase in social problems caused by women's use of addictive substances, but there is considerable evidence of a growing health risk to women themselves.

Women's rates of alcohol abuse are not approaching those of men in any of the countries for which data are available (Wilsnack and Wilsnack, 1991). But research does show that younger women in many parts of the world are now drinking more than was the case in the past, and in Scandinavia this pattern is evident among older women too (Hammer and Vaglum, 1989). This does appear to have led to a slight increase in alcohol-related health problems in some of the developed countries and many commentators have expressed concern about the effects as this cohort of younger women get older. However men are still three or four times more likely than women to experience physical or psychological problems from drinking. They are also, of course, much more likely to hurt others as a result of their own alcohol consumption (Christensen, 1989).

Female patterns of tobacco use are very different. In many of the developed countries the gap between male and female smoking rates is rapidly diminishing as more girls than boys take up the habit (Chollat-Traquet, 1992). Current estimates suggest that by the end of the century women will outnumber men in the population of smokers in many of the developed countries, and women in the third world are also taking up the habit in increasing numbers. Unlike alcohol, there is no safe level for tobacco consumption, and it is clear that smoking will constitute a major threat to women's health over the coming decades.

Tranquillisers differ from both alcohol and cigarettes in that they have always been taken in greater quantities by women than by men. The introduction of the benzodiazepines in the early 1960s offered for the first time a socially acceptable means for millions of women to alter their consciousness—often on a daily basis over long periods. Though access was controlled by doctors, the medical profession responded enthusiastically, prescribing drugs such as valium and librium in huge quantities—twice as often for women as for men. These drugs do appear to cause less physical damage than cigarettes or heavy alcohol consumption, but by the 1980s there was growing concern about dependency in long-term users. As a result there has been a decline in their consumption, but women continue to be the major recipients (Ashton, 1991).

Thus the pattern of women's use of legal mood-altering substances is a complex one. In order to make it clearer, we will disentangle the potential effects of each in turn, assessing their meaning and significance in the lives of different groups of women. However it is important to begin by acknowledging that women can also damage their health through the use of a wide range of substances not normally recognised as addictive. Many appear to be dependent on coffee or over-the-counter analgesics, for instance, while food can be a source of both psychological and physical problems.

Eating Her Heart Out

Food is clearly very different from the psychoactive substances usually associated with dependence. For both men and women it can be a source of intense pleasure as well as an essential element in maintaining their health. It is a basic necessity for survival and is not addictive in the orthodox medical sense. However many women have a problematic relationship with food throughout their lives. For some this can amount to an 'abuse' of food, causing significant damage to both physical and mental health.

. . . Millions of women in third world countries and some in the developed world struggle to remain healthy without adequate nutrition. Viewed on a global scale this is certainly the most serious aspect of the problematic relationship between women and food. However we also need to consider the plight of those relatively affluent women who are obsessed with food, caught in a never-ending cycle of dieting and over-eating which makes them feel humiliated and self-destructive (Lawrence, 1987). For some this can become a significant threat to health, with clinically diagnosed eating disorders being ten times more common among women than among men (Krahn, 1991).

The factors influencing women's relationship with food are complex (Chernin, 1983; Lawrence, 1987; Orbach, 1978, 1986). Social pressures to conform to an idealised body-image mean that many are doomed to feel like constant failures. Paradoxically only the rich can afford to be healthy and thin while poor women are often both overweight and badly nourished. If women cannot control their weight, many believe that they cannot control the rest of their lives, and their sense of their own powerlessness is reinforced. Women also report using food as a way of controlling their emotions, of eating to suppress anger or hostility (Epstein, 1987).

For many, these contradictory pressures lead not just to unhappiness and low self-esteem, but to the more extreme symptoms associated with anorexia, bulimia and compulsive eating. These are especially common among girls and young women facing what is sometimes a painful process of adolescence. One US study estimated that anywhere between 8 and 20 percent of female high school and college students in the United States are now bulimic (Pope *et al.*, 1983). A 1984 national poll of American women found that only 25 percent were 'overweight' by orthodox standards but more than 40 percent were unhappy with their bodies and 80 percent felt that they needed to be thin to attract men. Many had started to feel this way when they were very young. They often expressed a desperate desire to control their weight with more than 50 percent having tried diet pills, 27 percent liquid formula diets and 18 percent diuretics (Anderson, 1988, p. 197).

Not surprisingly there is growing evidence of a link between these eating disorders and more traditional forms of substance use. Female patients seeking medical help with bulimia and anorexia have high rates of alcohol and other drug abuse (Krahn, 1991, p. 241). Just over a third of one group of bulimic women in the United States reported that they had a history of problems with alcohol or other drugs (Mitchell *et al.*, 1985), while half of another bulimic group had significant alcohol abuse problems (Beary *et al.*, 1986). Conversely there is a high prevalence of eating disorders among women presenting with other forms of substance abuse (Beary *et al.*, 1986; Krahn, 1991). Often these overlapping problems are related to a history of violence in women's lives.

It would appear then that many women use food along with or instead of more traditional 'drugs' to deal with complex feelings for which they have few alternative means of expression. In the following sections we explore this theme in more detail by looking at the 'big three'—alcohol, tranquillisers and cigarettes. As we shall see, all are promoted by multinational corporations with a vested interest in maintaining women's dependence. Yet many women would find it difficult to manage without them. Far from being a sign of their liberation, substance abuse is, for many, a symptom of the inequality and disadvantage that continues to characterise their daily lives.

Fallen Angels: Alcohol

Until the early 1980s the predominance of men in the population of problem drinkers meant that both research and treatment were heavily male-oriented. Most studies either excluded women from their sample or failed to use gender as a variable in the analysis (Vannicelli and Nash, 1984). Where gender issues were raised, women were simply compared with men rather than being studied in their own right. As a result the specificity of female alcohol abuse remained unexplored and those women having the courage to seek treatment were offered therapies geared to male needs (Ettore, 1992).

Over the past decade or so this pattern has begun to change, as women with drinking problems have become increasingly visible (Wilsnack and Wilsnack, 1991). Male stereotypes have been challenged both by problem drinkers themselves and by some researchers, and preliminary studies have identified a number of factors frequently associated with female alcohol abuse. It appears that many women drink heavily to relieve feelings of helplessness, powerlessness, ineffectiveness and lack of self-esteem in the face of stressful life events (Beckman, 1980; Reed, 1985; Snell *et al.*, 1987). More research is needed to relate these characteristics to the concrete reality of women's lives, but certain important clues are beginning to emerge.

First we know that in most societies women are more likely than men to abuse alcohol at home (Corrigan and Butler, 1991). This may indicate a continuation of the double standard whereby women drinkers are more severely stigmatised than their male counterparts as well as reflecting women's lack of transport and other factors necessary for access to the public domain. We also know that their responsibilities continue to confine many women within a stressful domestic environment which may in itself contribute to their alcohol abuse. True, an American woman attributed her problem drinking to her home circumstances:

> I took to buying a bottle of wine at the 7-Eleven every day, then drinking the whole thing all by myself in the evening. It made me feel less empty and less lonely. The loneliness was really beginning to get to me. I had gotten married to escape from loneliness and here I was lonelier than ever (Sandmaier, 1992, p. 116).

Many women have their drinking reinforced by a male partner who is himself an alcohol abuser (Hammer and Vaglum, 1989; Jacob and Bremer, 1986; Wilsnack and Wilsnack, 1991, pp. 149–50). Drinking then becomes an important and sometimes immutable part of the central relationship in their lives. It is also increasingly clear that a significant proportion of women with drinking problems have experienced incest or sexual abuse at some point in their lives (Rohsenow *et al.*, 1988; Swett *et al.*, 1991). One survey in the United States found that twice as many problem drinkers (23 percent) as non-problem drinkers (10 percent) reported having been sexually abused before the age of 18 (Wilsnack and Wilsnack, 1991, p. 149).

A number of different factors in women's domestic lives may therefore contribute to their unhealthy drinking. For many, these problems will be relieved by the companionship and greater independence offered by waged work (Wilsnack and Cheloha, 1987). However employment may increase the likelihood of alcohol-related problems for others (Wilsnack *et al.*, 1984). Those who work in male-dominated occupations are especially likely to drink heavily (Hammer and Vaglum, 1989; La Rosa, 1990).

The need to understand the specificity of the female route to alcohol abuse is made more urgent by the recognition that women are more susceptible than men to psychological and physical damage from drinking (Dunne, 1988). Since women's bodies are, on average, smaller than men's and have a higher proportion of fat to water, alcohol becomes more concentrated in their bodily fluids. They are more prone than men to liver disease, digestive and nutritional problems, and brain damage, and appear to develop alcohol-related disease earlier than men with the same levels of intake. Hence women who are dependent on alcohol may be putting their health at greater risk than their male counterparts, especially if they combine drinking with the use of tranquillisers. Though the risk is sometimes overemphasised, women also have to face the possibility that drinking during pregnancy may damage their unborn child. Each year in the United States at least 300,000 infants are born with alcohol-related defects of some degree of severity (Little and Wendt, 1991, p. 187).

Despite these obvious problems women often find it difficult to get help with alcohol abuse. They are less likely than men to receive encouragement from their families to seek counselling. This may be due in part to the stigma still attached to female drinkers and by extension to their families. However it may also reflect the relatively low level of disruption female drinkers cause. Many women with drinking problems remain largely invisible and hence are unlikely to be offered help.

The structure of the services themselves may also contribute to women's reluctance to use them (Beckman, 1984; Duckert, 1989). For those with dependants, residential programmes may be inappropriate and some will not have the money to pay. Many will not feel confident in a male-dominated environment and they are often pressed into traditional female roles with their treatment needs subordinated to those of men (Duckert, 1989). Research in the United States has identified particular problems faced by black women seeking help in predominantly white environments (Amaro *et al.*, 1987). Similarly, many Native American and Australian Aboriginal women have been damaged by alcohol but there are very few services designed to meet their needs (Asetoyer, 1993).

This brief exploration of female patterns of alcohol abuse has shown that women may drink in different ways and for different reasons than men, and the effects on their health may be different. Hence their treatment needs may also be gender-specific. It has also indicated that female drinkers are themselves a heterogeneous group and more research is needed to identify the complex reality of their use and abuse of alcohol. As we shall see, detailed information on women's consumption of tranquillisers also remains to be collected, but similar themes can already be observed.

A Pill for Every Ill

Chlordiazepoxide (or librium), the first of the new breed of minor tranquillisers, was introduced in 1960, followed by diazepam (or valium) in 1963. Since they were more effective and less dangerous than their predecessors, the barbiturates, both were soon prescribed on a huge scale. Throughout the 1970s librium and valium were the most widely prescribed drugs in the world (Ray, 1991, p. 140).

During this 'benzodiazepine era' one in every ten US adults was using valium or librium at any given moment, with the volume of tranquilliser prescriptions rising by 78 percent between 1964 and 1970 (Silverman and Lee, 1974, p. 293). A similar increase occurred in the United Kingdom. By 1975 one in five of all National Health Service prescriptions were for minor tranquillisers, of which 70 percent were for librium or valium (Ray, 1991, p. 140). Though consumption fell markedly during the 1980s, the number of people taking tranquillisers remains high. Long-term users form a 'hard core' and many are now dependent on a regular supply of drugs from their doctor.

Throughout this period it is women who have been the major consumers of benzodiazepines. In Europe and North America women are about twice as likely as men to be prescribed tranquillisers (Ashton, 1991). One cross-national study carried out in 1980 found the highest rate of psychotropic drug use in Belgium, where about 13 percent of men and 21 percent of women used them regularly to sleep or to control anxiety (Balter *et al.*, 1984). Use is especially high among older women (Glantz and Backenheimer, 1988; Harding, 1986). In the United Kingdom 60 percent of benzadiazepine prescriptions are written for women over 40, and 40 percent go to those over 65 (Glantz and Backenheimer, 1988; Taylor, 1987).

Why are women so consistently overrepresented among the recipients of minor tranquillisers? We can begin to answer this question by looking at the gender issues inherent in those medical consultations where tranquillisers are prescribed. First we examine the basis upon which doctors appear to make their treatment decisions and then we explore women's own accounts of their use of tranquillisers.

The Politics of Prescribing

Most critics of the 'tranquilliser epidemic' have focused on the actions of individual doctors as the cause of the problem. They emphasise the role of medical practice in the control of women, arguing that doctors prescribe tranquillisers for women they see as 'neurotic' rather than attempting to resolve the underlying cause of any distress (Edwards, 1988, Ch. 6; Illich, 1977; Zola, 1975). As a result doctors are able to demonstrate their competence, docile women continue to perform their daily tasks and the profits of the pharmaceutical industry are maintained.

There is certainly some evidence to confirm the belief that doctors operate with stereotypes of appropriate 'male' and 'female' behaviour. In this, they are of course no different from most of their fellow citizens, but their beliefs are particularly important since their actions can help to maintain a woman in a situation that is ultimately damaging to her health. We know from a classic study carried out in the late 1960s that many clinicians in the United States have very different conceptions of a 'normal healthy woman' and a 'normal healthy man.' The 'male' characteristics approximate to the social stereotype of a healthy person and the 'female' ones reflect sickness and instability (Broverman *et al.*, 1970). Other research has shown that when doctors are confronted with similar 'cases', they are more likely to attribute symptoms in women to psychological causes and those in men to physical problems (Bernstein and Kane, 1981; Miles, 1991, pp. 151–61; Verbrugge and Steiner, 1981; Verbrugge, 1984).

There is also evidence that despite doctors' inclination to attribute more psychosomatic problems to female patients, women who consult a general physician tend to receive more tests and treatment than their male counterparts (Verbrugge and Steiner, 1981). Women may represent their problems as more serious, doctors may feel less able to deny treatment to the 'weaker sex', or they may simply want to get rid of them. Whatever the factors involved, both participants will feel pressured to find a cure, and if mental distress is the presenting problem, a pill may seem to be the only solution.

Such decisions will often be reinforced by the techniques used to sell tranquillisers. During the late 1960s and early 1970s women were featured in the majority of advertisements and were consistently represented as the most suitable recipients of psychotropic drugs (Prather and Fidell, 1986). They were presented as less serious than men, they were sometimes pictured in alluring poses and were often defined as irritating in their distress—as a problem for doctor and family alike. While the style of these advertisements has changed over the past decade, women are still used more often than men to sell tranquillisers (Prather, 1991, pp. 121–2).

The precise effect of this advertising on doctors' prescribing habits is difficult to assess. However it appears to play a significant part in alerting some physicians to new products on the market while at the same time suggesting women as the most appropriate recipients. In one recent study of the marketing of a new tranquilliser, 68 percent of doctors who prescribed the drug said that they had first heard about it from commercial sources, and 59 percent said promotional materials were the most important influence on their decision (Peay and Peay, 1988, p. 1185). The impact of drug advertising appears to be especially great in third world countries, where there are few alternative sources of information.

The growing criticism of tranquillisers does appear to have influenced a number of doctors. A recent study in the United Kingdom showed that younger doctors in particular were increasingly reluctant to prescribe them, preferring other approaches, such as counselling, when they were available (Gabe and Lipshitz-Phillips, 1986, p. 280). However doctors around the world continue to be exposed to huge quantities of promotional material, and often have few alternative treatments to offer.

Clinical decisions are therefore shaped by a variety of factors, including broad gender stereotypes, the curative and technological orientation of the biomedical model, and the specific promotional activities of the pharmaceutical industry. However these factors alone cannot explain prescribing patterns. We also need to look at what women themselves bring to the medical encounter.

Women living in developed countries make more visits to their doctors than their male counterparts (Miles, 1991, p. 63). In part this reflects their greater longevity, since tranquillisers and anti-depressants are often prescribed to help with the anxiety associated with the chronic illnesses of old age. However it is women's higher consultation rates for psychological problems that are most often associated with gender differences in psychotropic drug prescribing.

In most of the developed countries the ratio of female to male consultations for what doctors would class as neurotic or psychosocial problems varies between 2:1 and 4:1 (Weissman and Klerman, 1977). This may not of course mean that more women than men actually experience mental distress. It may also reflect an apparently greater willingness among women than among men to admit their difficulties and seek medical help. They may be encouraged to go to their doctor by the general perception of women as more 'sickly' or be driven to do so by the lack of alternative sources of support. These different factors are extremely difficult to disentangle, making it impossible to obtain any precise comparison of the 'real' levels of psychological distress experienced by men and women. However the end result is that women are more likely than men to receive a tranquilliser prescription.

Pharmacology and Social Control

According to some commentators, many of these women are given psychotropic drugs to help them continue with an otherwise intolerable life, while their labour continues to benefit those around them. In Cecil Helman's study in North London, he described the feelings of 'Mrs B', a 'housewife' aged 70 and a long-term Mogadon user:

> Without the drug she gets 'bad-tempered' with her husband—very 'snappy' with him and 'all groans and moans'. With the drug she is 'nice and calm' in relation to him. Both he and her daughter know of her taking the drug: he very much approves, though her daughter is against it (Helman, 1986, p. 219).

Ruth Cooperstock and Henry Lennard heard similar stories from the Canadian women they interviewed in the late 1970s. One mother with four teenagers reported:

> I take it to protect the family from my irritability because the kids are kids. I don't think it's fair for me to start yelling at them because their normal activity is bothering me. My husband says I over-react . . . I'm an emotional person, more so than my husband, who's an engineer and very calm and logical—he thinks (Cooperstock and Lennard, 1986, p. 232).

Quotes such as these suggest that tranquillisers can be a means of keeping women in their place. As Cooperstock and Lennard point out, the few men in their study tended to use tranquillisers to cope with employment problems while the women emphasised domestic concerns, thus reinforcing a gendered division of labour. However we cannot simply write off these drugs as a 'top down' method used by doctors to control helpless patients.

Tranquillisers as a Coping Strategy

Qualitative research in this area is rare, but it does appear that not all women are passive victims. Though many are extremely ambivalent about tranquillisers they choose to go on using them as an active strategy to sustain themselves in a situation they know to be damaging, but which they also believe they cannot change. In an attempt to explore these issues further, Jonathan Gabe and Nicki Thorogood interviewed a racially mixed group of working-class women in East London (Gabe and Thorogood, 1986). Their aim was to understand the use of tranquillisers within the context of the other 'resources' available to these women in the management of their everyday tasks and problems.

The women themselves identified the major resources at their disposal as paid work, housing, social supports, leisure activities, cigarettes, alcohol and religion. Each woman's access to these resources depended on her circumstances, and in this context at least the black women tended to have more at their disposal. More had full-time jobs that they enjoyed, more had children still living at home, especially daughters whom they found particularly supportive, and more were regular churchgoers. As a group the white women had fewer of these resources. They were also significantly more likely to be users of benzodiazepines (ibid., pp. 260–1).

Among the white women, those most likely to be long-term users were divorced and did not have children living at home. Few had any opportunity for leisure, few were regular churchgoers, and those who had jobs found them unrewarding. Thus the more 'positive' resources were rarely available to long-term users. Instead many used cigarettes as well as tranquillisers to manage the stresses in their lives.

In a linked study, a group of white women using tranquillisers were asked about their attitude to the drugs. Some saw them as a lifeline without which they would be unable to carry on: 'Well the valium I've got to take haven't I really because there's no doubt I do need something. I think even you would recognise . . .' (ibid., p. 252). Others saw them as a 'standby' to be used only intermittently when problems were acute:

> Valium does help if you're that desperate but I tend if I can to do without it—I do without it as long as I can and I only take it if it's absolutely necessary. I can go three or four weeks without and then I suddenly feel this need. That's why I keep some in my bag just in case I need it (ibid., p. 252).

Few users were uncritical of tranquillisers. Most of those who saw them as a standby, and some of those who saw them as a lifeline, were ambivalent about using them. However the benefits were seen to outweigh the risks, at least at that point in their lives.

Assessing Risks and Benefits of Drug Use

In the initial euphoria after their introduction, the benzodiazepines were hailed as risk-free and non-addictive, but problems have now emerged, mostly among long-term users. Small-scale studies indicate that about 5–10 percent of users experience significant withdrawal symptoms after six months' continuous use, 25–45 percent after two to four years, and 75 percent after six to eight years (Williams and Bellantuono, 1991, p. 79). These effects include sleep disturbance and anxiety, irritability, muscle pain, headaches, tremors, nausea and intolerance of sound and light. Some women have reported appalling experiences in their attempts to get off large doses of tranquillisers.

> The first two weeks I stuck to the programme, so I cut down quite drastically: from 20mg down to 15mg and then from 15mg down to 10mg, and that two weeks was awful, physically and mentally—it was frightening. Some of the worst things were the changes in perception that happened. I'd be in a room and it felt like the walls were coming in and out; I couldn't see straight and everything looked distorted . . . I was shaking and sweating and had terrible muscle tension and lots of pains in different parts of my body (Wolfson and Murray, 1986).

Others have had little or no physical problems in kicking the habit, though psychological dependence can be severe.

Women's use of tranquillisers therefore remains a complex and contradictory phenomenon. On the one hand there are conditions of acute anxiety and distress in which few would argue that the short-term use of benzodiazepines would be inappropriate

(Clare, 1991, p. 184). However long-term use is clearly more complicated. Some women choose to continue using the drugs as a resource for dealing with very real distress and appear to obtain some benefit. But others find that the drugs themselves become a problem, causing physical and/or psychological dependence, sometimes greater than the distress they were originally designed to alleviate. Many of the women using tranquillisers do so in response to emotional problems directly caused by their social circumstances. While the drugs may help to alleviate some of the pain, they may also perpetuate the damaging situation itself. But without them the distress may be intolerable and the situation still unchangeable. As we shall see in the next section, very similar contradictions arise in understanding women's consumption of cigarettes.

A Smoking Epidemic

Cigarettes are the single most important cause of premature death in the world today. In most of the developed countries a growing recognition of this danger has contributed to a marked decline in consumption among both sexes. However men have been quicker to abandon the habit than women, and in some countries teenage girls are taking up the habit in greater numbers than their male counterparts. In 1991, 27 percent of 15-year-old girls in the United Kingdom were smokers compared with only 18 percent of boys (Chollat-Traquet, 1992, p. 16). Recent estimates from the United States suggest that if current trends continue, the majority of US smokers will be women by the year 2000. In most third world countries the gap between male and female smoking rates remains wide. However there are certain notable exceptions, including Nepal, Papua New Guinea, Uruguay and Brazil, where women's rates are catching up with those of men (Crofton, 1990, p. 165).

As women make up a growing proportion of the smoking population, cigarettes are increasingly linked with poverty and social disadvantage. In most of the developed countries female smokers are much more likely than non-smokers to have received little education and to have a low income. In the United States this association between smoking and social disadvantage is also reflected in racial differences in smoking patterns, with black women having very high rates of tobacco consumption. In Canada too, racial differences are marked, with an astonishing 78 percent of Inuit women being smokers (Greaves, 1987, p. 28).

In most third world countries, the proportion of women who smoke is still less than 10 percent. However in some this figure is rising rapidly, especially among women in towns who start smoking as part of their transition to a 'modern' way of life (Chollat-Traquet, 1992). It is this group who are the major targets of the tobacco industry. In 1988 cigarette consumption fell by 1 percent in the developed countries, but rose by 2.3 percent in the third world, largely as a result of these promotional efforts (Crofton, 1990, p. 164). Their impact can be seen with particular clarity in urban areas of Brazil, where the rate of female smoking is rapidly overtaking that in the United States.

Thus the effects of cigarette smoking seem set to cause further damage to some of the world's unhealthiest women. In developed countries the overall decline in smoking has led to its concentration among women whose rates of morbidity and mortality are already higher than those of their compatriots. In the third world rising cigarette consumption means that many more women will be burdened with the 'diseases of affluence' while the diseases of poverty remain unresolved.

Smoking and the Diseases of Equal Opportunity

In the developed countries, smoking now kills about 300,000 women every year (Chollat-Traquet, 1992, p. 34). Millions more suffer from tobacco-related illness and disability including impairment of their reproductive potential. More and more women are succumbing to what have traditionally been regarded as 'male' problems—heart disease and lung cancer in particular. Over the next thirty years tobacco-related deaths among women will more than double, and by the year 2020 well over a million women across the world will die each year from smoking-related illness (Chollat-Traquet, 1992, p. 3). Thus women smokers are achieving an equality in death that they never attained in life (Jacobson, 1981, p. vi).

Lung cancer has traditionally been rare among women, but many of the developed countries are now witnessing a sharp rise.

Most of the victims are women who took up smoking some thirty or forty years ago in the aftermath of the Second World War. In most of the EU countries, deaths of women from cancer of the lung rose by at least 15 percent in every five-year period between 1955 and 1988. In Japan, Scotland and the United States lung cancer now kills more women than breast cancer, and a similar pattern is emerging in England and Wales, Australia and Denmark (Chollat-Traquet, 1992, p. 42).

This represents a major increase in the cancer toll among women and it is concentrated among the underprivileged. Data from the United Kingdom confirm that class differentials in female lung cancer deaths have widened markedly since the 1970s, with the least prosperous being more than twice as likely to be affected as their more affluent counterparts (Pugh *et al.*, 1991, p. 1106). While lung cancer remains an uncommon cause of death for women in most of the third world, Brazil again provides an important exception. Brazilian women already rank fourteenth in the world in the league table of female lung cancer deaths and they are moving up rapidly.

India is the third largest producer of tobacco in the world. Consumption is increasing by about 2 percent per year and it is estimated that about 20 percent of all cancer morbidity in women is related to tobacco (Stanley *et al.*, 1987, p. 276). While few can afford cigarettes, many smoke water pipes, bidis or chuttas, while others chew betel quid. In some regions women practise 'reverse smoking', where the lit end of a chutta or cheroot is turned around and kept burning inside the mouth (Jacobson, 1986, p. 33; Stanley *et al.*, 1987). This is considered more 'feminine' but it is extremely dangerous. The riskiest habit of all is pan chewing combined with smoking which gives a risk of mouth cancer thirty-six times greater than that of someone who does not use tobacco at all (International Agency for Research on Cancer, 1985; Jacobson, 1986, p. 34). In the Indian cities of Madras and Bangalore the rate of oral cancer among women is the highest in the world (Stanley *et al.*, 1987, p. 276).

The health hazards faced by smokers are also evident in their high levels of respiratory disease. These effects are often exacerbated by occupational hazards and in parts of the third world by smoke from domestic fires, which affects women in particular. About 60 percent of women in Nepal smoke, usually cupping their hands around bidis to prevent the smoke escaping

(Jacobson, 1986, p. 35). Most live in tiny houses filled with smoke and as a result more than half of Nepalese men and women are afflicted with 'cigarette lung'. Thus female smokers face the same hazards as their male counterparts, and global mortality and morbidity rates are beginning to reflect this symmetry.

However women also face additional risks associated with reproduction. Smokers who use the contraceptive pill significantly increase their chance of developing cardiovascular disease. There is also an association between smoking and reduced fertility (US Department of Health and Human Services, 1989). Those who do conceive have an increased risk of spontaneous abortion, of producing low-birth-weight babies, of stillbirth, premature rupture of the membranes and preterm delivery (Berman and Gritz, 1991; Chollat-Traquet, 1992, pp. 48–9). Maternal smoking may also be linked with sudden infant death syndrome (Berman and Gritz, 1991). When their childbearing years are over, women smokers are more likely than non-smokers to have an early menopause and health problems associated with osteoporosis (Chollat-Traquet, 1992, p. 49).

Seduced into Smoking

Any attempt to understand these trends in female smoking must look at two different processes—women's initiation into the habit, and its reinforcement and maintenance. In some countries female smoking has a long history embedded in particular cultural traditions. In others recent developments may have contributed to an increase in the number of women smokers. However it is evident that whatever their circumstances women smokers have a great deal in common, and it is this shared experience that we explore here.

Most immediately, they are all targets of a very powerful industry concerned to maintain or expand the world population of smokers. Over the past sixty years or so the style and content of the industry's appeal has varied, but women have frequently been in their sights (Davis, 1987; Ernster, 1985). As existing smokers give up or die off, new recruits have always been sought and women's lower levels of smoking have made them natural targets for cigarette advertisers.

During the Victorian period women's temperance movements campaigned against cigarettes as well as alcohol, and women smokers were looked on with considerable disapproval. By the early

1920s this pattern was changing as advertisements were first directed specifically at women, presenting cigarettes as a symbol of female emancipation (Greaves, 1990, p. 5). Smoking rates continued to rise during the 1930s as advertisements portrayed cigarettes as glamorous and sophisticated, and the Second World War gave a further boost as women took on male jobs as well as some traditionally male habits. This was temporarily reflected in androgynous and egalitarian advertising images, but the postwar period saw a shift back to the themes of glamour and sexual attractiveness as women were pushed back into their homes.

As the health evidence against cigarettes began to pile up in the 1960s, women were again entering the labour force in large numbers. In this changing environment, advertisements represented smoking as a source of relaxation in a stressful world as well as a sign of independence and freedom from male dominance. Yet at the same time they also continued to associate them with 'thinness' and conformity to cultural stereotypes of female beauty. In the United States the 'targeting' of women of colour has caused particular concern. Thus tobacco companies have attempted to mould their advertisements to reflect the changing aspirations and circumstances of women, but always with the ultimate aim of turning them into smokers.

Until recently women in third world countries had largely escaped the attentions of the industry. However this is beginning to change as the number of smokers declines in developed countries and some third world women have increased their disposable income. While the first wave of advertising was directed at men, women are now being drawn in behind them (Stebbins, 1991). In 1973 less than 2 percent of Nigerian female university students smoked, but by 1982 this figure had reached 21 percent, with much of the increase resulting from specially targeted advertising (Jacobson, 1986, p. 36). Virginia Slims Light—the first specifically 'female' brand directed at women in the third world—was launched in Hong Kong in 1984 (Jacobson, 1986).

The companies themselves claim that these advertisements are designed only to ensure brand loyalty or to attract existing smokers to their particular product. However research suggests that they have a major influence on the behaviour of young people, who form the majority of new smokers. Teenage girls in particular are encouraged by enticing images of smoking to experiment with cigarettes, and many continue the habit into adulthood (ASH Women and Smoking Group, 1990a). Many read youth publications or women's magazines that contain glossy smoking advertisements and give little information on the health risks of cigarettes. Thus potential young smokers receive mainly positive messages (ASH Women and Smoking Group, 1990b).

Why are so many young women enticed by these commercial blandishments into becoming smokers? The reasons are complex, but we can identify a number of key factors. Social acceptability makes it much more likely that a girl will take up smoking, and both family and peers can be important role models. An adolescent girl is much more likely to start smoking if one or both parents is a smoker or if older siblings smoke (ASH Women and Smoking Group, 1990a).

Psychological factors too are important. Girls with low self-esteem are more likely to start smoking than their more confident peers, using cigarettes to generate a feeling of greater maturity and a stronger sense of identity (Piepe *et al.*, 1988). Rebellion, excitement, curiosity and a desire to be 'one of the gang' are also mentioned frequently by girls explaining their initiation into the smoking culture. In more affluent parts of the world a desire to be slim also appears to be a central feature in many girls' induction into smoking (Charlton, 1989).

Smoking for Life

Once the smoking habit has been established a complex mixture of psychological, pharmacological, physical and social factors combine to maintain it. Nicotine dependence plays a major part in preventing the majority of women who would like to quit from doing so. For some the appetite suppressant effect of cigarettes also continues to be important as they strive to be thin. However it is increasingly clear that for many the major benefit of smoking is an enhanced capacity to manage the difficulties they face in their daily lives. This appears to be especially true for those disadvantaged women who now make up the majority of female smokers.

A number of studies have shown that women are more likely than men to use cigarettes to cope with negative feelings (Greaves, 1987; Wells and Batten, 1990). Instead of focusing on the pleasures of smoking they frequently describe cigarettes as a means of keeping loneliness, sadness, anger and frustration under control. As one British woman explained:

> I think smoking stops me getting so irritable. I can cope with things better. If I was economising, I'd cut down on cigarettes but I wouldn't give up. I'd stop eating . . . food just isn't that important to me but having a cigarette is the only thing I do just for myself (Graham, 1987, p. 55).

Poor women have to face more stressful life events than their affluent counterparts and often have fewer resources to deal with them. As a result many who have to manage multiple responsibilities on a low income become dependent on cigarettes as a source of support. Hilary Graham's research in the United Kingdom showed that full-time child care on a low income is especially conducive to smoking. Stopping for a cigarette seems to offer a space and a reward in a life otherwise devoted mainly to the needs and demands of others (Graham, 1987). As one young mother put it:

> A cigarette is the only pleasure you can indulge in without the kids pestering you for their share—especially if you've had no break from them for hours or days and couldn't afford to go out even if you did have a babysitter. You're tired, they're whiny, bored and awful. Ten fags may be the only pleasure you can (just) afford. They are your substitute for leisure, pleasure and ordinary adult activities (Jacobson, 1986, p. 95).

Lorraine Greaves identified similar feelings in a sample of Canadian women (Greaves, 1990). Very few of the women 'liked' smoking and most used it to organise social relationships. Some smoke to create a self-image and a sense of identity as well as a feeling of bonding with others. However the most common experience was the use of cigarettes to cope with a variety of oppressions or intrusions into their bodies or lives (Greaves, 1990, p. 906).

Many of Greaves' respondents used smoking as a distancing strategy, designed to repel interaction with others and also to defuse situations of tension or disagreement. Some stated quite clearly that they would rather blunt their feelings than experience the effects of releasing their emotions (Greaves, 1990, p. 906). Some described 'smoking back their anger' for example. Very often this internalisation of emotions reflected the powerlessness these women felt in their most intimate relationships. Cigarettes were controllable, reliable and 'always there'. Significantly, these feelings were especially important for women with abusive partners, whose lives were often insecure and unpredictable.

Not surprisingly women appear to have much less confidence than men in their ability to give up smoking. Most claim to be addicted, reflecting the lack of control they experience in so many areas of their lives. Fewer women than men get support in their efforts to give up. Indeed some report encouragement from their families to carry on smoking.

More research is needed in a variety of cultures to explore the way smoking is closely integrated into so many women's lives. But it is already evident that cigarettes represent a paradox for all women smokers. They undoubtedly pose a serious threat to their physical health, yet they are a central plank in the strategy that many have devised to maintain themselves in their roles as carers and workers. Like tranquillisers, they offer women the illusion of power over their emotions. But too often they end up controlling them—or even killing them.

Conclusion

This chapter has presented a preliminary exploration of women's use of 'drugs of solace'. It has not offered a unitary explanation of all women's use of all drugs, or even all women's use of a particular drug. However, it has demonstrated that a gendered understanding of women's substance use and misuse is essential if their health is to be protected.

The last few decades have seen the convergence of a number of trends. The greater purchasing power of some women and their increased access to medication has given them more opportunity to acquire a wider range of legal but potentially hazardous substances. At the same time many find themselves in circumstances that are increasingly difficult to manage without traditional networks and sources of social support. These developments have led large numbers of women to abuse one or more substances in an attempt to manage in the here-and-now—a tactic encouraged by those industries who stand to make a massive profit from women's distress.

The need to interrupt this process is urgent, as more third world women are drawn into the trap. Short-term strategies would include more culturally aware and gender-sensitive education strategies and support and treatment services, as well as tougher regulation of advertising and promotion policies. However, the long-term solution will clearly involve more fundamental change in the social and economic position of women.

FURTHER READINGS

Ashton, H. (1991) 'Psychotropic drug prescribing for women', *British Journal of Psychiatry*, vol. 158, supplement 10, pp. 30–35. A summary of current trends in the prescribing of psychotropic drugs for women in Europe and North America. It includes a useful discussion of the reasons why women are prescribed these drugs so much more often than men, and highlights the problems that follow from this.

Chollat-Traquet, C. (1992) *Women and Tobacco* (Geneva: WHO). A global overview of current trends in female smoking. Produced with the support of WHO, this book highlights the growing number of women smokers around the world and documents the likely health effects.

Gabe, J. and Thorogood, N. (1986) 'Tranquillisers as a resource', in J. Gabe and P. Williams (eds), *Tranquillisers: social, psychological and clinical perspectives* (London: Tavistock). An important study challenging the notion that all women taking psychotropic drugs are passive victims. Through interviews with a group of working-class women in London, it illustrates their use of tranquillisers as a resource for coping with the contradictions of everyday life.

Jacobson, B. (1986) *Beating the Ladykillers: women and smoking* (London: Pluto Press). A campaigning book designed to reduce the female death toll from tobacco. It explores in depth the reasons why girls and women are drawn into the smoking habit and offers a guide to women who want to quit smoking themselves or to help others to do so.

Journal of Substance Abuse, vol. 3 (1991) Special issue on women and substance abuse: A wide-ranging collection describing women's use and misuse of a number of different substances. Two survey articles are especially useful: Berman, B. and Gritz, E., 'Women and smoking: current trends and issues for the 1990s'; and Wilsnack, S. and Wilsnack, R., 'Epidemiology of women's drinking'.

QUESTIONS

1. Does living in a sexist society affect women's rates of alcohol, nicotine, or drug use? Do factors that influence women and girls differ from those that influence men and boys? Do changes in women's social power affect women's substance abuse?
2. Why are women over-represented as licit pharmaceutical drug users? Why would physicians prescribe more tranquilizers or antidepressants to women than men?

African-American Women Are for Reproductive Freedom

Marcia Ann Gillespie

This conference handout from the National Black Women's Self-help Project asserts that reproductive rights are essential for freedom. Women's control over their own bodies has never been absolute or universal, but has been determined by law, economic class, and race. The fate of one's body is particularly important for some African-Americans given the long history of colonization and slavery that have denied them personal power and deprived them of legal rights.

Choice is the essence of freedom. It's what we African-Americans have struggled for all these years. The right to choose where we would sit on a bus. The right to vote. The right for each of us to select our own paths, to dream and reach for our dreams. The right to choose how we would or would not live our lives.

"African-American Women Are for Reproductive Freedom: We Remember," by Marcia Ann Gillespie, a conference handout Compliments of the National Black Women's Health Project, Atlanta, Georgia. Reprinted by permission of the author.

This freedom—to choose and to exercise our choices—is what we've fought and died for. Brought here in chains, worked like mules, bred like beasts, whipped one day, sold the next—for 244 years we were held in bondage. Somebody said that we were less than human and not fit for freedom. Somebody said we were like children and could not be trusted to think for ourselves. Somebody owned our flesh, and decided if and when and with whom and how our bodies were to be used. Somebody said that Black women could be raped, held in concubinage, forced to bear children year in and year out, but often not raise them. Oh yes, we have known how painful it is to be without choice in this land.

Those of us who remember the bad old days when Jim Crow ruled and segregation was the way of things, know the hardships and indignities we faced. We were free, but few or none were our choices. Somebody said where we could live and couldn't, where we could work, what schools we could go to, where we could eat, how we could travel. Somebody prevented us from voting. Somebody said we could be paid less than other workers. Somebody burned crosses, harassed and terrorized us in order to keep us down.

Now once again somebody is trying to say that we can't handle the freedom of choice. Only this time they're saying African-American women can't think for themselves and, therefore, can't be allowed to make serious decisions. Somebody's saying that we should not have the freedom to take charge of our personal lives and protect our health, that we only have limited rights over our bodies. Somebody's once again forcing women to acts of desperation, because somebody's saying that if women have unintended pregnancies, it's too bad, but they must pay the price.

Somebody's saying that we must have babies whether we choose to or not. Doesn't matter what we say, doesn't matter how we feel. Some say that abortion under any circumstance is wrong, others that rape and incest and danger to the life of the woman are the only exceptions. Doesn't matter that nobody's saying who decides if it was rape or incest; if a woman's word is good enough; if she must go into court and prove it. Doesn't matter that she may not be able to take care of a baby; that the problem also affects girls barely out of adolescence; that our children are having children. Doesn't matter if you're poor and pregnant—go on welfare, or walk away.

What does matter is that we know abortions will still be done, legal or not. We know the consequences when women are forced to make choices without protection—the coat hangers and knitting needles that punctured the wombs of women forced to seek back-alley abortions on kitchen tables at the hands of butchers. The women who died screaming in agony, awash in their own blood. The women who were made sterile. All the women who endured the pain of makeshift surgery with no anesthetics, risked fatal infection.

We understand why African-American women risked their lives then, and why they seek safe legal abortion now. It's been a matter of survival. Hunger and homelessness. Inadequate housing and income to properly provide for themselves and their children. Family instability. Rape. Incest. Abuse. Too young, too old, too sick, too tired. Emotional, physical, mental, economic, social—the reasons for not carrying a pregnancy to term are endless and varied, personal, urgent, and private. And for all these pressing reasons, African-American women once again will be among the first forced to risk their lives if abortion is made illegal.

There have always been those who have stood in the way of our exercising our rights, who tried to restrict our choices. There probably always will be. But we who have been oppressed should not be swayed in our opposition to tyranny, of any kind, especially attempts to take away our reproductive freedom. You may believe abortion is wrong. We respect your belief and we will do all in our power to protect that choice for you. You may decide that abortion is not an option you would choose. Reproductive freedom guarantees your right not to. All that we ask is that no one deny another human being the right to make her own choice. That no one condemn her to exercising her choices in ways that endanger her health, her life. And that no one prevent others from creating safe, affordable, legal conditions to accommodate women, whatever the choices they make. Reproductive freedom gives each of us the right to make our own choices, and guarantees us a safe, legal, affordable support system. It's the right to choose.

We are still an embattled people beset with life-and-death issues. Black America is under siege. Drugs, the scourge of our community, are wiping out one, two, three generations. We are killing ourselves and each other. Rape and other unspeakable acts of violence are becoming sickeningly commonplace. Babies linger on death's door, at risk at birth: born addicted to crack and cocaine; born underweight and undernourished; born AIDS-infected. An ever-growing number of our children are being abandoned, being mentally, physically, spiritually abused. Homelessness, hunger, unemployment run rife. Poverty grows. Our people cry out in desperation, anger, and need.

Meanwhile, those somebodies who claim they're "pro-life" aren't moved to help the living. They're not out there fighting to break the stranglehold of drugs and violence in our communities, trying to save our children, or moving to provide infant and maternal nutrition and health programs. Eradicating our poverty isn't on their agenda. No—somebody's too busy picketing, vandalizing and sometimes bombing family-planning clinics, harassing women, and denying funds to poor women seeking abortions.

So when somebody denouncing abortion claims that they're "pro-life," remind them of an old saying that our grandmothers often used: "It's not important what people say, it's what they do." And remember who we are, remember our history, our continuing struggle for freedom. Remember to tell them that We Remember!

QUESTIONS

1. Why do the authors use the term reproductive "freedom" in place of reproductive "rights"? How do the meanings of the terms differ? Does "freedom" capture something that "rights" does not? How does the defense of reproductive rights presented in this handout differ from others you have heard or read? How does placing "choice" and "control" in historical perspective expand your thinking about these terms and their significance?

2. What arguments in defense of reproductive rights are offered in this handout? How does the handout respond to the arguments of abortion opponents? How could limiting reproductive rights complicate the issues African-American communities face? Where do the authors of this handout believe attention should be focused?

3. How does the restriction of reproductive freedom affect women's development and potential differently than men? How might the restriction of reproductive rights affect individuals and communities differently based on their race or class?

"A Way Outa No Way": Eating Problems Among African American, Latina, and White Women (1996)

Becky W. Thompson

Although researchers have long recognized that women experience eating problems more often than men, studies have mainly been directed at only one female demographic—those who are white and middle-class. In the following selection, social researcher Becky Thompson, author of a book-length study entitled A Hunger So Wide and So Deep, *presents interviews with women of color and working-class women who have experienced eating problems to understand how race, ethnicity, class and sexuality shape their experiences. Moving beyond the "culture of thinness" model to explain eating problems, Thompson suggests other factors that may contribute to their development.*

"'A Way Outa No Way': Eating Problems Among African American, Latina, and White Women," by Becky W. Thompson, reprinted from *Race, Class, and Gender*, edited by Esther Ngan-ling Chow, Doris Wilkinson, and Maxine Baca Zinn, 1996, by permission of Sage Publications, Inc.

Bulimia, anorexia nervosa, binging, and extensive dieting are among the many health issues women have been confronting in the last twenty years. Until recently, however, there has been almost no research about eating problems among African American, Latina, Asian American, or Native American women, working-class women, or lesbians.[1] In fact, according to the normative epidemiological portrait, eating problems are largely a white, middle-, and upper-class heterosexual phenomenon. Further, while feminist research has documented how eating problems are fueled by sexism, there has been almost no attention paid to how other systems of oppression may also be implicated in the development of eating problems.

In this chapter, I reevaluate the portrayal of eating problems as issues of appearance based on the "culture of thinness." I propose that eating problems begin as ways women cope with various traumas including sexual abuse, racism, classism, sexism, heterosexism, and poverty. Showing the interface between these traumas and the onset of eating problems explains why women may use eating to numb pain and cope with violations to their bodies. This theoretical shift also permits an understanding of the economic, political, social, educational, and cultural resources that women need to change their relationship to food and their bodies.

Existing Research on Eating Problems

There are three theoretical models used to explain the epidemiology, etiology, and treatment of eating problems. The biomedical model offers important scientific research about possible physiological causes of eating problems and the physiological dangers of purging and starvation (Copeland 1985; Spack 1985). However, this model adopts medical treatment strategies that may disempower and traumatize women (Garner 1985; Orbach 1985). In addition, this model ignores many social, historical, and cultural factors that influence women's eating patterns. The psychological model identifies eating problems as "multidimensional disorders" that are influenced by biological, psychological, and cultural factors (Garfinkel and Garner 1982). While useful in its exploration of effective therapeutic treatments, this model, like the biomedical one, tends to neglect women of color, lesbians, and working-class women.

The third model, offered by feminists, asserts that eating problems are gendered. This model explains why the vast majority of people with eating problems are women, how gender socialization and sexism may relate to eating problems, and how masculine models of psychological development have shaped theoretical interpretations. Feminists offer the *culture of thinness model* as a key reason why eating problems predominate among women. According to this model, thinness is a culturally, socially, and economically enforced requirement for female beauty. This imperative makes women vulnerable to cycles of dieting, weight loss, and subsequent weight gain, which may lead to anorexia nervosa and bulimia (Chernin 1981; Orbach 1978, 1985; Smead 1984).

Feminists have rescued eating problems from the realm of individual psychopathology by showing how the difficulties are rooted in systematic and pervasive attempts to control women's body sizes and appetites. However, researchers have yet to give significant attention to how race, class, and sexuality influence women's understanding of their bodies and appetites. The handful of epidemiological studies that include African American women and Latinas casts doubt on the accuracy of the normative epidemiological portrait. The studies suggest that this portrait reflects which particular populations of women have been studied rather than actual prevalence (Andersen and Hay 1985; Gray, Ford, and Kelly 1987; Hsu 1987; Nevo 1985; Silber 1986).

More important, this research shows that bias in research has consequences for women of color. Tomas Silber (1986) asserts that many well-trained professionals have either misdiagnosed or delayed their diagnoses of eating problems among African American and Latina women due to stereotypical thinking that these problems are restricted to white women. As a consequence, when African American women or Latinas are diagnosed, their eating problems tend to be more severe due to extended processes of starvation prior to intervention. In her autobiographical account of her eating problems, Retha Powers (1989), an African American woman, describes being told not to worry about her eating problems since "fat is more acceptable in the Black community" (p. 78). Stereotypical perceptions held by her peers and teachers of the "maternal Black woman" and the "persistent mammy-brickhouse Black woman image" (p. 134) made it difficult for Powers to find people who took her problems with food seriously.

Recent work by African American women reveals that eating problems often relate to women's struggles against a "simultaneity of oppressions" (Clarke 1982; Naylor 1985; White 1991). Byllye Avery (1990), the founder of the National Black Women's Health Project, links the origins of eating problems among African American women to the daily stress of being undervalued and overburdened at home and at work. In Evelyn C. White's (1990) anthology, *The Black Women's Health Book: Speaking for Ourselves,* Georgiana Arnold (1990) links her eating problems partly to racism and racial isolation during childhood.

Recent feminist research also identifies factors that are related to eating problems among lesbians (Brown 1987; Dworkin 1989; Iazzetto 1989; Schoenfielder and Wieser 1983). In her clinical work, Brown (1987) found that lesbians who have internalized a high degree of homophobia are more likely to accept negative attitudes about fat than are lesbians who have examined their internalized homophobia. Autobiographical accounts by lesbians have also indicated that secrecy about eating problems among lesbians partly reflects their fear of being associated with a stigmatized illness ("What's Important" 1988).

Attention to African American women, Latinas, and lesbians paves the way for further research that explores the possible interface between facing multiple oppressions and the development of eating problems. In this way, this study is part of a larger feminist and sociological research agenda that seeks to understand how race, class, gender, nationality, and sexuality inform women's experiences and influence theory production.

Methodology

I conducted eighteen life history interviews and administered lengthy questionnaires to explore eating problems among African American, Latina, and white women. I employed a snowball sample, a method in which potential respondents often first learn about the study from people who have already participated. This method was well suited for the study since it enabled women to get information about me and the interview process from people they already knew. Typically, I had much contact with the respondents prior to the interview. This was particularly important given the secrecy associated with this topic (Russell 1986;

Silberstein, Striegel-Moore, and Rodin 1987), the necessity of women of color and lesbians to be discriminating about how their lives are studied, and the fact that I was conducting across-race research.

To create analytical notes and conceptual categories from the data, I adopted Glaser and Strauss's (1967) technique of theoretical sampling, which directs the researcher to collect, analyze, and test hypotheses during the sampling process (rather than imposing theoretical categories onto the data). After completing each interview transcription, I gave a copy to each woman who wanted one. After reading their interviews, some of the women clarified or made additions to the interview text.

Demographics of the Women in the Study

The 18 women I interviewed included 5 African American women, 5 Latinas, and 8 white women. Of these women, 12 are lesbian and 6 are heterosexual. Five women are Jewish, 8 are Catholic, and 5 are Protestant. Three women grew up outside of the United States. The women represented a range of class backgrounds (both in terms of origin and current class status) and ranged in age from 19 to 46 years old (with a median age of 33.5 years).

The majority of the women reported having had a combination of eating problems (at least two of the following: bulimia, compulsive eating, anorexia nervosa, and/or extensive dieting). In addition, the particular types of eating problems often changed during a woman's life span. (For example, a woman might have been bulimic during adolescence and anorexic as an adult.) Among the women, 28 percent had been bulimic, 17 percent had been bulimic and anorexic, and 5 percent had been anorexic. All of the women who had been anorexic or bulimic also had a history of compulsive eating and extensive dieting. Of the women, 50 percent were either compulsive eaters and dieters (39 percent) or compulsive eaters (11 percent) but had not been bulimic or anorexic.

Two-thirds of the women have had eating problems for more than half of their lives, a finding that contradicts the stereotype of eating problems as transitory. The weight fluctuation among the women varied from 16 to 160 pounds, with an average fluctuation of 74 pounds. This drastic weight change illustrates the degree to which the women adjusted to major changes in body size at least once during their lives as they lost, gained, and lost weight again.

The average age of onset was 11 years old, meaning that most of the women developed eating problems prior to puberty. Almost all of the women (88 percent) considered themselves as still having a problem with eating, although the majority believed they were well on the way to recovery.

The Interface of Trauma and Eating Problems

One of the most striking findings in this study was the range of traumas the women associated with the origins of their eating problems, including racism, sexual abuse, poverty, sexism, emotional or physical abuse, heterosexism, class injuries, and acculturation.[2] The particular constellation of eating problems among the women did not vary with race, class, sexuality, or nationality. Women from various race and class backgrounds attributed the origins of their eating problems to sexual abuse, sexism, and emotional and/or physical abuse. Among some of the African American and Latina women, eating problems were also associated with poverty, racism, and class injuries. Heterosexism was a key factor in the onset of bulimia, compulsive eating, and extensive dieting among some of the lesbians. These oppressions are not the same nor are the injuries caused by them. And certainly, there are a variety of potentially harmful ways that women respond to oppression (such as using drugs, becoming a workaholic, or committing suicide). However, for all these women, eating was a way of coping with trauma.

Sexual Abuse

Sexual abuse was the most common trauma that the women related to the origins of their eating problems. Until recently, there has been virtually no research exploring the possible relationship between these two phenomena. Since the mid-1980s, however, researchers have begun identifying connections between the two, a task that is part of a larger feminist critique of traditional psychoanalytic symptomatology (DeSalvo 1989; Herman 1981; Masson 1984). Results of a number of incidence studies indicate that between one-third and two-thirds of women who have eating problems have been abused (Oppenheimer et al. 1985; Root and Fallon 1988). In addition, a growing number of therapists and researchers have offered interpretations of the meaning and impact of eating problems for survivors of sexual abuse (Bass and Davis 1988; Goldfarb 1987; Iazzetto 1989; Swink and Leveille 1986). Kearney-Cooke (1988) identifies dieting and binging as common ways in which women cope with frequent psychological consequences of sexual abuse (such as body image disturbances, distrust of people and one's own experiences, and confusion about one's feelings). Root and Fallon (1989) specify ways that victimized women cope with assaults by binging and purging: bulimia serves many functions, including anesthetizing the negative feelings associated with victimization. Iazzetto's innovative study (1989), based on in-depth interviews and art therapy sessions, examines how a woman's relationship to her body changes as a consequence of sexual abuse. Iazzetto discovered that the process of leaving the body (through progressive phases of numbing, dissociating, and denying) that often occurs during sexual abuse parallels the process of leaving the body made possible through binging.

Among the women I interviewed, 61 percent were survivors of sexual abuse (11 of the 18 women), most of whom made connections between sexual abuse and the beginning of their eating problems. Binging was the most common method of coping identified by the survivors. Binging helped women "numb out" or anesthetize their feelings. Eating sedated, alleviated anxiety, and combated loneliness. Food was something that they could trust and was accessible whenever they needed it. Antonia (a pseudonym) is an Italian American woman who was first sexually abused by a male relative when she was four years old. Retrospectively, she knows that binging was a way she coped with the abuse. When the abuse began, and for many years subsequently, Antonia often woke up during the middle of the night with anxiety attacks or nightmares and would go straight to the kitchen cupboards to get food. Binging helped her block painful feelings because it put her back to sleep.

Like other women in the study who began binging when they were very young, Antonia was not always fully conscious as she binged. She described eating during the night as "sleep walking. It was mostly desperate—like I had to have it." Describing why she ate after waking up with nightmares, Antonia said, "What else do you do? If you don't have any coping mechanisms, you eat." She said that binging made her "disappear," which made her feel protected. Like Antonia, most of the women were sexually abused before puberty; four of them before they were five years old. Given their youth, food was the most accessible and socially acceptable drug available to them. Because all of the women endured the psychological consequences alone, it is logical that they coped with tactics they could use alone as well.

One reason Antonia binged (rather than dieted) to cope with sexual abuse is that she saw little reason to try to be the small size girls were supposed to be. Growing up as one of the only Italian Americans in what she described as a "very WASP town," Antonia felt that everything from her weight and size to having dark hair on her upper lip were physical characteristics she was supposed to hide. From a young age she knew she "never embodied the essence of the good girl. I don't like her. I have never acted like her. I can't be her. I sort of gave up." For Antonia, her body was the physical entity that signified her outsider status. When the sexual abuse occurred, Antonia felt she had lost her body. In her mind, the body she lived in after the abuse was not really hers. By the time Antonia was 11, her mother put her on diet pills. Antonia began to eat behind closed doors as she continued to cope with the psychological consequences of sexual abuse and feeling like a cultural outsider.

Extensive dieting and bulimia were also ways in which women responded to sexual abuse. Some women thought that the men had abused them because of their weight. They believed that if they were smaller, they might not have been abused. For example, when Elsa, an Argentine woman, was sexually abused at the age of 11, she thought her chubby size was the reason the man was abusing her. Elsa said, "I had this notion that these old perverts liked these plump girls. You heard adults say this too. Sex and flesh being associated." Looking back on her childhood, Elsa believes she made fat the enemy partly due to the shame and guilt she felt about the incest. Her belief that fat was the source of her problems was also supported by her socialization. Raised by strict German governesses in an upper-class family, Elsa was taught that a woman's weight was a primary criterion for judging her worth. Her mother "was socially conscious of walking into places with a fat daughter and maybe people staring at her." Her father often referred to Elsa's body as "shot to hell." When asked to describe how she felt about her body when growing up, Elsa described being completely alienated from her body. She explained,

> Remember in school when they talk about the difference between body and soul? I always felt like my soul was skinny. My soul was free. My soul sort of flew. I was tied down by this big bag of rocks that was my body. I had to drag it around. It did pretty much what it wanted and I had a lot of trouble controlling it. It kept me from doing all the things that I dreamed of.

As is true for many women who have been abused, the split that Elsa described between her body and soul was an attempt to protect herself from the pain she believed her body caused her. In her mind, her fat body was what had "bashed in her dreams." Dieting became her solution but, as is true for many women in the study, this strategy soon led to cycles of binging and weight fluctuation.

Ruthie, a Puerto Rican woman who was sexually abused from 12 until 16 years of age, described bulimia as a way she responded to sexual abuse. As a child, Ruthie liked her body. Like many Puerto Rican women of her mother's generation, Ruthie's mother did not want skinny children, interpreting that as a sign that they were sick or being fed improperly. Despite her mother's attempts to make her gain weight, Ruthie remained thin through puberty. When a male relative began sexually abusing her, Ruthie's sense of her body changed dramatically. Although she weighed only 100 pounds, she began to feel fat and thought her size was causing the abuse. She had seen a movie on television about Romans who made themselves throw up and so she began doing it, in hopes that she could look like the "little kid" she was before the abuse began. Her symbolic attempt to protect herself by purging stands in stark contrast to the psychoanalytic explanation of eating problems as an "abnormal" repudiation of sexuality. In fact, her actions and those of many other survivors indicate a girl's logical attempt to protect herself (including her sexuality) by being a size and shape that does not seem as vulnerable to sexual assault.

These women's experiences suggest many reasons why women develop eating problems as a consequence of sexual abuse. Most of the survivors "forgot" the sexual abuse after its onset and were unable to retrieve the abuse memories until many years later. With these gaps in memory, frequently they did not know why they felt ashamed, fearful, or depressed. When sexual abuse memories resurfaced in dreams, they often woke feeling upset but could not remember what they had dreamed. These free-floating, unexplained feelings left the women feeling out of control and confused. Binging or focusing on maintaining a new diet were ways women distracted or appeased themselves, in turn, helping them regain a sense of control. As they grew older, they became more conscious of the consequences of these actions. Becoming angry at themselves for binging or promising themselves they would not purge again was a way to direct feelings of shame and self-hate that often accompanied the trauma.

Integral to this occurrence was a transference process in which the women displaced onto their bodies painful feelings and memories that actually derived from or were directed toward the persons who caused the abuse. Dieting became a method of trying to change the parts of their bodies they hated, a strategy that at least initially brought success as they lost weight. Purging was a way women tried to reject the body size they thought was responsible for the abuse. Throwing up in order to lose the weight they thought was making them vulnerable to the abuse was a way to try to find the body they had lost when the abuse began.

Poverty

Like sexual abuse, poverty is another injury that may make women vulnerable to eating problems. One woman I interviewed attributed her eating problems directly to the stress caused by poverty. Yolanda is a Black Cape Verdean mother who began eating compulsively when she was twenty-seven years old. After leaving an abusive husband in her early twenties, Yolanda was forced to go on welfare. As a single mother with small children and few financial resources, she tried to support herself and her children on $539 a month. Yolanda began binging in the evenings after putting her children to bed. Eating was something she could do alone. It would calm her, help her deal with loneliness, and make her feel safe. Food was an accessible commodity that was cheap. She ate three boxes of macaroni and cheese when nothing else was available. As a single mother with little money, Yolanda felt as if her body was the only thing she had left. As she described it,

> I am here [in my body] 'cause there is nowhere else for me to go. Where am I going to go? This is all I got . . . that probably contributes to putting on so much weight 'cause staying in your body, in your home, in yourself, you don't go out. You aren't around other people. . . . You hide and

> as long as you hide you don't have to face . . . nobody can see you eat. You are safe.

When she was eating, Yolanda felt a momentary reprieve from her worries. Binging not only became a logical solution because it was cheap and easy but also because she had grown up amid positive messages about eating. In her family, eating was a celebrated and joyful act. However, in adulthood, eating became a double-edged sword. While comforting her, binging also led to weight gain. During the three years Yolanda was on welfare, she gained seventy pounds.

Yolanda's story captures how poverty can be a precipitating factor in eating problems and highlights the value of understanding how class inequalities may shape women's eating problems. As a single mother, her financial constraints mirrored those of most female heads of households. The dual hazards of a race- and sex-stratified labor market further limited her options (Higginbotham 1986). In an article about Black women's health, Byllye Avery (1990) quotes a Black woman's explanation about why she eats compulsively. The woman told Avery,

> I work for General Electric making batteries, and, I know it's killing me. My old man is an alcoholic. My kids got babies. Things are not well with me. And one thing I know I can do when I come home is cook me a pot of food and sit down in front of the TV and eat it. And you can't take that away from me until you're ready to give me something in its place. (p. 7)

Like Yolanda, this woman identifies eating compulsively as a quick, accessible, and immediately satisfying way of coping with the daily stress caused by conditions she could not control. Connections between poverty and eating problems also show the limits of portraying eating problems as maladies of upper-class adolescent women.

The fact that many women use food to anesthetize themselves, rather than other drugs (even when they gained access to alcohol, marijuana, and other illegal drugs), is partly a function of gender socialization and the competing demands that women face. One of the physiological consequences of binge eating is a numbed state similar to that experienced by drinking. Troubles and tensions are covered over as a consequence of the body's defensive response to massive food intake. When food is eaten in that way, it effectively works like a drug with immediate and predictable effects. Yolanda said she binged late at night rather than getting drunk because she could still get up in the morning, get her children ready for school, and be clearheaded for the college classes she attended. By binging, she avoided the hang-over or sickness that results from alcohol or illegal drugs. In this way, food was her drug of choice since it was possible for her to eat while she continued to care for her children, drive, cook, and study. Binging is also less expensive than drinking, a factor that is especially significant for poor women. Another woman I interviewed said that when her compulsive eating was at its height, she ate breakfast after rising in the morning, stopped for a snack on her way to work, ate lunch at three different cafeterias, and snacked at her desk throughout the afternoon. Yet even when her eating had become constant, she was still able to remain employed. While her patterns of eating no doubt slowed her productivity, being drunk may have slowed her to a dead stop.

Heterosexism

The life history interviews also uncovered new connections between heterosexism and eating problems. One of the most important recent feminist contributions has been identifying compulsory heterosexuality as an institution which truncates opportunities for heterosexual and lesbian women (Rich 1986). All of the women interviewed for this study, both lesbian and heterosexual, were taught that heterosexuality was compulsory, although the versions of this enforcement were shaped by race and class. Expectations about heterosexuality were partly taught through messages that girls learned about eating and their bodies. In some homes, boys were given more food than girls, especially as teenagers, based on the rationale that girls need to be thin to attract boys. As the girls approached puberty, many were told to stop being athletic, begin wearing dresses, and watch their weight. For the women who weighed more than was considered acceptable, threats about their need to diet were laced with admonitions that being fat would ensure becoming an "old maid."

While compulsory heterosexuality influenced all of the women's emerging sense of their bodies and eating patterns, the women who linked heterosexism directly to the beginning of their eating problems were those who knew they were lesbians when very young and actively resisted heterosexual norms. One working-class Jewish woman, Martha, began compulsively eating when she was 11 years old, the same year she started getting clues of her lesbian identity. In junior high school, as many of her female peers began dating boys, Martha began fantasizing about girls, which made her feel utterly alone. Confused and ashamed about her fantasies, Martha came home every day from school and binged. Binging was a way she drugged herself so that being alone was tolerable. Describing binging, she said, "It was the only thing I knew. I was looking for a comfort." Like many women, Martha binged because it softened painful feelings. Binging sedated her, lessened her anxiety, and induced sleep.

Martha's story also reveals ways that trauma can influence women's experience of their bodies. Like many other women, Martha had no sense of herself as connected to her body. When I asked Martha whether she saw herself as fat when she was growing up, she said, "I didn't see myself as fat. I didn't see myself. I wasn't there. I get so sad about that because I missed so much." In the literature on eating problems, *body image* is the term that is typically used to describe a woman's experience of her body. This term connotes the act of imagining one's physical appearance. Typically, women with eating problems are assumed to have difficulties with their body image. However, the term *body image* does not adequately capture the complexity and range of bodily responses to trauma experienced by the women. Exposure to trauma did much more than distort the women's visual image of themselves. These traumas often jeopardized their capacity to consider themselves as having bodies at all.

Given the limited connotations of the term body image, I use the term *body consciousness* as a more useful way to understand the range of bodily responses to trauma.[3] By body consciousness I mean the ability to reside comfortably in one's body (to see oneself as embodied) and to consider one's body as connected to oneself. The disruptions to their body consciousness that the women described included leaving their bodies, making a split between their body and mind, experiencing being "in" their bodies as painful, feeling unable to control what went in and out of their bodies, hiding in one part of their bodies, or simply not seeing themselves as having bodies. Binging, dieting, or purging were common ways women responded to disruptions to their body consciousness.

Racism and Class Injuries

For some of the Latinas and African American women, racism coupled with the stress resulting from class mobility related to the onset of their eating problems. Joselyn, an African American woman, remembered her white grandmother telling her she would never be as pretty as her cousins because they were lighter skinned. Her grandmother often humiliated Joselyn in front of others, as she made fun of Joselyn's body while she was naked and told her she was fat. As a young child, Joselyn began to think that although she could not change her skin color, she could at least try to be thin. When Joselyn was young, her grandmother was the only family member who objected to Joselyn's weight. However, her father also began encouraging his wife and daughter to be thin as the family's class standing began to change. When the family was working class, serving big meals, having chubby children, and keeping plenty of food in the house was a sign the family was doing well. But, as the family became mobile, Joselyn's father began insisting that Joselyn be thin. She remembered, "When my father's business began to bloom and my father was interacting more with white businessmen and seeing how they did business, suddenly thin became important. If you were a truly well-to-do family, then your family was slim and elegant."

As Joselyn's grandmother used Joselyn's body as territory for enforcing her own racism and prejudice about size, Joselyn's father used her body as the territory through which he channeled the demands he faced in the white-dominated business world. However, as Joselyn was pressured to diet, her father still served her large portions and bought treats for her and the neighborhood children. These contradictory messages made her feel confused about her body. As was true for many women in this study, Joselyn was told she was fat beginning when she was very young even though she was not overweight. And, like most of the women, Joselyn was put on diet pills and diets before even reaching puberty, beginning the cycles of dieting, compulsive eating, and bulimia.

The confusion about body size expectations that Joselyn associated with changes in class paralleled one Puerto Rican woman's association between her eating problems and the stress of assimilation as her family's class standing moved from poverty to working class. When Vera was very young, she was so thin that her mother took her to a doctor who prescribed appetite stimulants.

However, by the time Vera was eight years old, her mother began trying to shame Vera into dieting. Looking back on it, Vera attributed her mother's change of heart to competition among extended family members that centered on "being white, being successful, being middle class, . . . and it was always, 'Ay Bendito. She is so fat. What happened?'"

The fact that some of the African American and Latina women associated the ambivalent messages about food and eating to their family's class mobility and/or the demands of assimilation while none of the eight white women expressed this (including those whose class was stable and changing) suggests that the added dimension of racism was connected to the imperative to be thin. In fact, the class expectations that their parents experienced exacerbated standards about weight that they inflicted on their daughters.

Eating Problems as Survival Strategies

Feminist Theoretical Shifts

My research permits a reevaluation of many assumptions about eating problems. First, this work challenges the theoretical reliance on the culture-of-thinness model. Although all of the women I interviewed were manipulated and hurt by this imperative at some point in their lives, it is not the primary source of their problems. Even in the instances in which a culture of thinness was a precipitating factor in anorexia, bulimia, or binging, this influence occurred in concert with other oppressions.

Attributing the etiology of eating problems primarily to a woman's striving to attain a certain beauty ideal is also problematic because it labels a common way that women cope with pain as essentially appearance-based disorders. One blatant example of sexism is the notion that women's foremost worry is about their appearance. By focusing on the emphasis on slenderness, the eating problems literature falls into the same trap of assuming that the problems reflect women's "obsession" with appearance. Some women were raised in families and communities in which thinness was not considered a criterion for beauty. Yet they still developed eating problems. Other women were taught that women should be thin but their eating problems were not primarily in reaction to this imperative. Their eating strategies began as logical solutions to problems rather than problems themselves as they tried to cope with a variety of traumas.

Establishing links between eating problems and a range of oppressions invites a rethinking of both the groups of women who have been excluded from research and those whose lives have been the basis of theory formation. The construction of bulimia and anorexia nervosa as appearance-based disorders is rooted in a notion of femininity in which white middle- and upper-class women are portrayed as frivolous, obsessed with their bodies, and overly accepting of narrow gender roles. This portrayal fuels women's tremendous shame and guilt about eating problems—as signs of self-centered vanity. This construction of white middle- and upper-class women is intimately linked to the portrayal of working-class white women and women of color as their opposite: as somehow exempt from accepting the dominant standards of beauty or as one step away from being hungry and therefore not susceptible to eating problems. Identifying that women may binge to cope with poverty contrasts the notion that eating problems are class bound. Attending to the intricacies of race, class, sexuality, and gender pushes us to rethink the demeaning construction of middle-class femininity and establishes bulimia and anorexia nervosa as serious responses to injustices.

Understanding the link between eating problems and trauma also suggests much about treatment and prevention. Ultimately, their prevention depends not simply on individual healing but also on changing the social conditions that underlie their etiology. As Bernice Johnson Reagon sings in Sweet Honey in the Rock's song "Oughta Be a Woman," "A way outa no way is too much to ask/too much of a task for any one woman" (Reagon 1980).[4] Making it possible for women to have healthy relationships with their bodies and eating is a comprehensive task. Beginning steps in this direction include ensuring that (1) girls can grow up without being sexually abused, (2) parents have adequate resources to raise their children, (3) children of color grow up free of racism, and (4) young lesbians have the chance to see their reflection in their teachers and community leaders. Ultimately, the prevention of eating problems depends on women's access to economic, cultural, racial, political, social, and sexual justice.

NOTES

1. I use the term *eating problems* as an umbrella term for one or more of the following: anorexia nervosa, bulimia, extensive dieting, or binging. I avoid using the term *eating disorder* because it categorizes the problems as individual pathologies, which deflects attention away from the social inequalities underlying them (Brown 1985). However, by using the term *problem* I do not wish to imply blame. In fact, throughout, I argue that the eating strategies that women develop begin as logical solutions to problems, not problems themselves.

2. By trauma I mean a violating experience that has long-term emotional, physical, and/or spiritual consequences that may have immediate or delayed effects. One reason the term *trauma* is useful conceptually is its association with the diagnostic label Post Traumatic Stress Disorder (PTSD) (American Psychological Association 1987). PTSD is one of the few clinical diagnostic categories that recognizes social problems (such as war or the Holocaust) as responsible for the symptoms identified (Trimble 1985). This concept adapts well to the feminist assertion that a woman's symptoms cannot be understood as solely individual, considered outside of her social context, or prevented without significant changes in social conditions.

3. One reason the term *consciousness* is applicable is its intellectual history as an entity that is shaped by social context and social structures (Delphy 1984; Marx 1964). This link aptly applies to how the women described their bodies because their perceptions of themselves as embodied (or not embodied) directly relate to their material conditions (living situations, financial resources, and access to social and political power).

4. Copyright © 1980. Used by permission of Songtalk Publishing.

REFERENCES

American Psychological Association. 1987. *Diagnostic and statistical manual of mental disorders*. 3rd ed. rev. Washington, DC: American Psychological Association.

Andersen, Arnold, and Andy Hay. 1985. Racial and socioeconomic influences in anorexia nervosa and bulimia. *International Journal of Eating Disorders* 4:479–87.

Arnold, Georgiana. 1990. Coming home: One Black woman's journey to health and fitness. In *The Black women's health book: Speaking for ourselves*, edited by Evelyn C. White. Seattle, WA: Seal.

Avery, Byllye Y. 1990. Breathing life into ourselves: The evolution of the National Black Women's Health Project. In *The Black women's health book: Speaking for ourselves*, edited by Evelyn C. White. Seattle, WA: Seal.

Bass, Ellen, and Laura Davis. 1988. *The courage to heal: A guide for women survivors of child sexual abuse*. New York: Harper & Row.

Brown, Laura S. 1985. Women, weight and power: Feminist theoretical and therapeutic issues. *Women and Therapy* 4:61–71.

_____. 1987. Lesbians, weight and eating: New analyses and perspectives. In *Lesbian psychologies*, edited by the Boston Lesbian Psychologies Collective. Champaign: University of Illinois Press.

Chernin, Kim. 1981. *The obsession: Reflections on the tyranny of slenderness*. New York: Harper & Row.

Clarke, Cheryl. 1982. *Narratives*. New Brunswick, NJ: Sister Books.

Copeland, Paul M. 1985. Neuroendocrine aspects of eating disorders. In *Theory and treatment of anorexia nervosa and bulimia: Biomedical sociocultural and psychological perspectives*, edited by Steven Wiley Emmett. New York: Brunner/Mazel.

Delphy, Christine. 1984. *Close to home: A materialist analysis of women's oppression*. Amherst: University of Massachusetts Press.

DeSalvo, Louise. 1989. *Virginia Woolf: The impact of childhood sexual abuse on her life and work*. Boston: Beacon.

Dworkin, Sari H. 1989. Not in man's image: Lesbians and the cultural oppression of body image. In *Loving boldly: Issues facing lesbians*, edited by Ester D. Rothblum and Ellen Cole. New York: Harrington Park.

Garfinkel, Paul E., and David M. Garner. 1982. *Anorexia nervosa: A multidimensional perspective*. New York: Brunner/Mazel.

Garner, David. 1985. Iatrogenesis in anorexia nervosa and bulimia nervosa. *International Journal of Eating Disorders* 4:701–26.

Glaser, Barney G., and Anselm L. Strauss. 1967. *The discovery of grounded theory: Strategies for qualitative research*. New York: Aldine DeGruyter.

Goldfarb, Lori. 1987. Sexual abuse antecedent to anorexia nervosa, bulimia and compulsive overeating: Three case reports. *International Journal of Eating Disorders* 6:675–80.

Gray, James, Kathryn Ford, and Lily M. Kelly. 1987. The prevalence of bulimia in a Black college population. *International Journal of Eating Disorders* 6:733–40.

Herman, Judith. 1981. *Father-daughter incest*. Cambridge, MA: Harvard University Press.

Higginbotham, Elizabeth. 1986. We were never on a pedestal: Women of color continue to struggle with poverty, racism and sexism. In *For crying out loud*, edited by Rochelle Lefkowitz and Ann Withorn. Boston: Pilgrim.

Hsu, George. 1987. Are eating disorders becoming more common in Blacks? *International Journal of Eating Disorders* 6:113–24.

Iazzetto, Demetria. 1989. When the body is not an easy place to be: Women's sexual abuse and eating problems. Ph.D. diss., Union for Experimenting Colleges and Universities, Cincinnati, OH.

Kearney-Cooke, Ann. 1988. Group treatment of sexual abuse among women with eating disorders. *Women and Therapy* 7:5–21.

Marx, Karl. 1964. *The economic and philosophic manuscripts of 1844*. New York: International.

Masson, Jeffrey. 1984. *The assault on the truth: Freud's suppression of the seduction theory*. New York: Farrar, Strauss & Giroux.

Naylor, Gloria. 1985. *Linden Hills*. New York: Ticknor & Fields.

Nevo, Shoshana. 1985. Bulimic symptoms: Prevalence and ethnic differences among college women. *International Journal of Eating Disorders* 4:151–68.

Oppenheimer, R., K. Howells, R. L. Palmer, and D. A. Chaloner. 1985. Adverse sexual experience in childhood and clinical eating disorders: A preliminary description. *Journal of Psychiatric Research* 19:357–61.

Orbach, Susie. 1978. *Fat is a feminist issue*. New York: Paddington.

_____. 1985. Accepting the symptom: A feminist psychoanalytic treatment of anorexia nervosa. In *Handbook of psychotherapy for anorexia nervosa and bulimia*, edited by David M. Garner and Paul E. Garfinkel. New York: Guilford.

Powers, Retha. 1989. Fat is a Black women's issue. *Essence*, Oct., 75, 78, 134, 136.

Reagon, Bernice Johnson. 1980. Oughta be a woman. On Sweet Honey in the Rock's album, *Good News*. Music by Bernice Johnson Reagon; lyrics by June Jordan. Washington, DC: Songtalk.

Rich, Adrienne. 1986. Compulsory heterosexuality and lesbian existence. In *Blood, bread and poetry*. New York: Norton.

Root, Maria P. P., and Patricia Fallon. 1988. The incidence of victimization experiences in a bulimic sample. *Journal of Interpersonal Violence* 3:161–73.

_____. 1989. Treating the victimized bulimic: The functions of binge-purge behavior. *Journal of Interpersonal Violence* 4:90–100.

Russell, Diana E. 1986. *The secret trauma: Incest in the lives of girls and women*. New York: Basic Books.

Schoenfielder, Lisa, and Barbara Wieser, eds. 1983. *Shadow on a tightrope: Writings by women about fat liberation*. Iowa City, IA: Aunt Lute Book Co.

Silber, Tomas. 1986. Anorexia nervosa in Blacks and Hispanics. *International Journal of Eating Disorders* 5:121–28.

Silberstein, Lisa, Ruth Striegel-Moore, and Judith Rodin. 1987. Feeling fat: A woman's shame. In *The role of shame in symptom formation*, edited by Helen Block Lewis. Hillsdale, NJ: Lawrence Erlbaum.

Smead, Valerie. 1984. Eating behaviors which may lead to and perpetuate anorexia nervosa, bulimarexia, and bulimia. *Women and Therapy* 3:3 7–49.

Spack, Norman. 1985. Medical complications of anorexia nervosa and bulimia. In *Theory and treatment of anorexia nervosa and bulimia: Biomedical sociocultural and psychological perspectives*, edited by Steven Wiley Emmett. New York: Brunner/Mazel.

Swink, Kathy, and Antoinette E. Leveille. 1986. From victim to survivor: A new look at the issues and recovery process for adult incest survivors. *Women and Therapy* 5:119–43.

Trimble, Michael. 1985. Post-traumatic stress disorder: History of a concept. In *Trauma and its wake: The study and treatment of post-traumatic stress disorder*, edited by C. R. Figley. New York: Brunner/Mazel.

What's important is what you look like. 1988. *Gay Community News*, July, 24–30.

White, Evelyn C., ed. 1990. *The Black women's health book: Speaking for ourselves*. Seattle, WA: Seal Press.

_____. 1991. Unhealthy appetites. *Essence*, Sept., 28, 30.

QUESTIONS

1. What is the "culture of thinness" model for eating problems? In what ways is this a "feminist" model?
2. How does Thompson challenge the "culture of thinness" model for explaining eating problems? Why is this model inappropriate for all women? What other models does she advance?
3. According to Thompson, what other factors lead to eating problems? On what evidence does she base her argument? What steps did the author find might prevent the development of eating problems?
4. What meanings are attached to food in different communities? How can a woman grow up in a family that does not equate beauty with thinness, yet still develop an eating problem?

Coming Out (1991)

Linda Villarosa and Clara Villarosa

Linda Villarosa is the author of Body & Soul: The Black Woman's Guide to Physical Health and Emotional Well-Being, *and the co-author of* Finding Our Way: The Teen Girls' Survival Guide *(1995). She is also the executive editor of* Essence, *the first general magazine directed at African-American women, which as been in circulation since 1970. In this 1991 Mother's Day special edition essay, Linda and her mother Clara, a Denver bookstore owner, share their feelings about Linda's lesbian identity. Mother and daughter describe the coming out process and the effects it has had on their relationship.*

The Model Daughter

Linda—Growing up, I was what you'd call a "good girl." I minded my parents, sent Hallmark cards to all my great-aunts on

"Coming Out," by Linda Villarosa and Clara Villarosa, reprinted from *Essence*, Vol. 22, No. 1, May 1991. Reprinted by permission of Linda Villarosa.

their birthdays, said the Pledge of Allegiance and never got into trouble. Other kids probably thought I was nauseating.

In high school I was a cheerleader, the president of the senior class, captain of the track team, an honor student and a prom-queen candidate, and I still managed to work evenings and weekends. I had a nice boyfriend, and I wanted to marry him, have two children, live near my parents and have a career as a lawyer or writer, or maybe even a social worker like my mother.

I seemed just like all the other girls I knew who were my age—only more of a goody-goody. But somehow deep inside I suspected I was different.

Becoming a Mother

Clara—At 3 P.M. on January 9, 1959, the doctor smiled at me and said, "You have a beautiful baby girl." And beautiful my baby was, dainty and small, a cute little thing I could dress up, play with and read to. Her father and I named her Linda, which in Spanish means pretty. In my life, all was well. I had completed my master's in psychiatric social work. I had worked for five years before having the baby, so that I could stay at home with her once I had her. Three years later, just as we'd planned, I had another baby.

As Linda grew up she remained petite and feminine. Whenever we went out, people remarked on her beauty and grace. She had large hazel eyes that stared both knowingly and inquisitively, and I enjoyed dressing her up in frilly dresses and fixing her hair in two bouncy ponytails. She loved little-girl activities, like having tea parties and playing house with real chores. When she was older she modeled in fashion shows, demonstrating poise and confidence.

Linda dated in high school, and by that time I was back at work, surrounded by friends. The highlight of those years for me was Linda's senior prom. I made her a beautiful peach-colored dress, and that prom night, when her steady boyfriend picked her up, I was so proud of my beautiful daughter. As I watched her leave, I fantasized about her being happily married, a mother, with me a happy grandmother.

I used to think of Linda as my "normal" child. That turned out to be totally unrealistic, because all the other parents were having problems with their adolescents. But Linda was so good.

Facing Up to It

Linda—Even in high school I was attracted to other girls. I loved slumber parties, cheerleading practice, basketball and track workouts and other all-girl activities. Sometimes I assumed my feelings were normal, just another one of those adolescent things you don't really understand, you're ashamed of and don't tell a soul.

By the time I reached my sophomore year in college, my high-school boyfriend and I had broken up. It was very difficult for me for a few months because he had been my first love, and we had been—and remain—good friends. We had also fumbled through losing our virginity together, and he was a loving, caring and creative sexual partner and I liked having sex with him. I continued to date men. The men I dated were handsome and outgoing and my parents approved of them. I felt that I was sleepwalking, though, going through the motions. One of my boyfriends was really cute but he was boring. All he talked about was his fraternity. But I wanted to have a boyfriend so I could be like everybody else. I wasn't very attentive, I didn't dress up or wear makeup and I wasn't particularly excited about sex. And of course this lackadaisical attitude made me more attractive because guys thought I was a challenge.

Then everything changed. I became increasingly attracted to Laura, one of my female instructors. She was bright and funny and she listened with interest to everything I said. Eventually I admitted to myself that I was attracted to this woman. Finally, after I had spent five months worshiping her in the classroom, we spent a day together. After that I realized I was in love. That realization was all at once frightening, horrifying, gratifying and relieving. At that point I began to think of myself as bisexual, something that seemed cool and hip. I didn't think about what this might mean to my life, I didn't wonder why I was this way, I didn't contemplate whether gay people were good or bad or would go to heaven or be sweating it out in hell. All I could think of was how nice it felt to truly love someone and admit it.

Suspicion

Clara—Once Linda got to college, I began to notice that she didn't have much romantic interest in men. I would frequently ask about any man that she mentioned even casually, but she never really seemed to care. Nor did she seem to care about clothes and makeup. I tried not to get upset, thinking that she didn't have much time to date or worry about her appearance because she was too busy with her classes and her job.

By her second year in college, I had gone from being quietly worried to being truly panicked about Linda. She spoke about men only in platonic ways, and I noticed that an inordinate amount of her conversation focused on one of her female instructors, Laura. Linda brought Laura to dinner, and my suspicions were heightened because Laura appeared more "butch" than feminine. The way the two interacted and the things they talked about made it clear to me that they were spending a lot of time together. My husband and I exchanged looks across the dinner table. After they left, I just had to say it. I turned to my husband and asked, "Did you see it?" He said yes. I said, "Do you think Laura is gay?" He did. Finally we spoke the unspeakable: Could our daughter be a lesbian?

The Confrontation

Linda—Eventually Laura and I became lovers. I was happy, but too afraid to tell a soul what was going on. We went on a trip to San Francisco together, which was exciting and freeing to the sheltered 19-year-old that I was. Afterward I called my mother from the airport to tell her that I'd be home for a couple of days and that I had so much to tell her about my trip. "That's fine, honey," she said with a strange catch in her voice. "Your dad and I have something to talk to you about."

Still riding high from my trip, I was completely unprepared for the confrontation that was to follow. Both my parents were in their bedroom, sitting on the edge of the bed and looking very solemn. My mother turned to me and without missing a beat she asked, "Are you a lesbian?"

Laura had coached me about what to do in the event that my parents asked me anything about being gay. "Lie at all costs. You aren't ready to deal with this yet, and neither are they," she had warned me. But when they confronted me, I was too stunned. "Yes, I think so," I stuttered.

My mother just looked sick and my father's eyes filled with tears. This news really broke him, destroying the perfect image that he had of me. He was afraid that I didn't like men and that I didn't love him. My mother, an adolescent therapist at the time, took a more practical tack: She thought I could be fixed. She told me that I *would* go to therapy. During the whole ordeal, I had been crying and feeling guilty, apologetic, confused and upset, but at that point something snapped. "I don't need to go to therapy. I'm really happy now," I told my parents.

I'm not really a crier, but this confrontation was just so hard. I felt that I'd let my parents down and that doing so was the worst thing. I was always so good, I took pride in that. We all stared at one another without speaking, letting the silence absorb the very strong emotions we each felt. The scene was over, at least for the moment. Finally my mother told me to tell my sister. I went downstairs, crying. My sister was lying on the couch watching TV and I blurted out, "I'm gay." She asked, "Am I?" I said no. Then, like the typical 16-year-old she was, she asked me if I wanted to go shopping.

Clara—The day we confronted Linda was so painful for me that I have blanked it out of my mind; I can't remember anything about it. I couldn't accept the fact that my daughter was a lesbian—I just couldn't believe it. I assumed it was a phase she was going through and that it would go away like an unpleasant dream. This was the seventies, when homosexuals were thought of as sick. I was a child therapist, and I'd been dealing with parents who took the blame for their kids' problems. I figured it would go away faster if she would just get help and if I could get her away from that horrible woman.

I placed all the blame on Laura. I couldn't even bear to hear her name. It was projection, pure and simple. It was easier to focus on this other person whom I didn't really know than to let myself believe that my daughter, whom I loved so much, could do something I found so disgusting.

With all my anger focused on Laura, I thought of confronting her and telling her to stay away from my child. I considered reporting her to the university, to get her fired and sent out of town. But, I worried, then everyone would know. I really didn't know what to do. I decided just to lie low, to think things over until I could figure out how to approach this situation, how to make everything right in my life. My career was going well, but my marriage had begun to fall apart. In the meantime, I avoided my daughter. When she called me, I would contain my anger and disappointment, and we would never bring up *that* subject.

Trying to Come Out of Hiding

Linda—It was a relief to have told my parents the truth and to have stopped hiding from them. My mother wasn't taking it well, but I thought I'd give her time. Clearly she was disappointed and upset, but I knew eventually she'd come to understand. At that point my bigger worry was learning to accept myself.

After I realized I was gay, I had to reinvent myself and the image of my life. I had to let go of everything I thought I was supposed to have, such as a beautiful wedding. I had to figure out who I was apart from the straight world I no longer felt I belonged in. This was a very difficult and lonely period because I couldn't tell anyone. Finally, after two years, I told my best friend.

I didn't know any other gay women besides my lover and a few of her friends. And like everybody else I had been brought up on a steady diet of antigay stereotypes. I felt like one of society's outcasts. I no longer fit into heterosexual society, and I didn't want to fit into the gay community—whatever and wherever it was. I assumed there were only a handful of other lesbians in the world, all short, fat, unattractive women with bad haircuts. All they did was play softball and go to feminist group meetings and try to hide who they were from their coworkers, friends and family. It went without saying that they all hated men. There was a reason these girls didn't have a man. Because I wasn't like this, I wasn't too sure who I was.

So unsure of myself, I was deathly afraid of rejection. I just kept my mouth shut about my sexuality and quietly locked myself away in the closet. I tried to straddle both worlds, happy with my lover and pretending to be accepting of my new life, but secretly scared and insecure. Like one of those tragic mulattos of the past, I was passing but always petrified that someone would uncover my secret. I didn't stop hanging with my friends, I simply stopped talking about myself and steered clear of any personal questions. I listened to dyke and fag jokes and sometimes even laughed along. I went to weddings and would cry, always attributing it to happiness, not loss.

Feeling the Pain

Clara—Despite my hopes, the nightmare was not ending. And the more Linda began to try to explore herself and identify as a lesbian, the angrier I got, and now not at Laura anymore, but at her. How could my daughter do this to me? I was so embarrassed. I was paranoid, thinking that everyone in my community knew and that they were laughing at me, at my failure as a parent. It was doubly humiliating for me—trained as an adolescent therapist—to have raised a daughter who had "gone wrong."

I was devastated and blamed myself. I searched through the past to determine what I had done to make this happen to her. At this point I was in the middle of a divorce. I was also searching for my purpose in life, but I wasn't finding it. People had said I have an aggressive personality, and I wondered if Linda was a lesbian because of my behavior. Maybe I gave her the impression that I hated men. I felt my whole world collapsing.

Resolution and Acceptance

Linda—After college, I moved to New York. As the years went by I began to develop a circle of lesbian friends, women a lot like me who were happy and well adjusted and fun. I started to accept myself and my life and stop worrying that being gay was some kind of punishment or a horrible mistake I could change. Or that it was a phase, a political choice, a form of rebellion or something to be ashamed of.

It has been important for me, too, to realize that being gay is not a curse; in fact, it's been an awakening. I've become more introspective and tolerant of people who are different. Before I "came out," I had always tried to do everything right, everything according to plan—society's plan and my parents' plan—but not my own plan because I didn't really have one. And that behavior—be a good girl, go to college, get married, have a child—was valued by society. So when I turned out to be different, I assumed something was wrong with me. I had no reason to question the world I was brought up in, much less to try to understand anyone who wasn't thinking and behaving exactly the way I was. When I realized I wasn't going to live in the suburbs, I was free to forge my own path and not get stuck in a Black society thing—wearing nice shoes and going to club meetings.

But having felt like an outcast, separate from everyone Black and white, has made me empathize with others who have felt the same way for whatever reason.

Most important, I've also stopped being so afraid of being rejected by people who find out I'm gay. The closet is dark and lonely and not somewhere I plan to hide away. The most important people in my life already know, and they still accept me. No matter how disappointed and angry my mother felt, she never stopped loving me. She and the rest of my family made it okay for me to be me.

Resolution

Clara—After Linda moved to New York, the distance and time gave me the opportunity to be more reflective and less emotional. I asked myself, *Who is my daughter?*

She is still pretty and funny and bright and well regarded. She is kind and cares about other people. She remembers Mother's Day, sends me birthday presents and listens when I need to talk to her. I am proud of her and I love her.

The only difference is her sexual preference. But then I thought, *So what?* She's not on drugs, or harming anyone, or in jail or involved in any of the other terrible scenarios I could imagine. So eventually I was able to let go of my disappointment. I also stopped trying to figure out why she is gay and I stopped blaming myself. Scientists don't know why some people are heterosexual and some homosexual. Psychiatrists don't know, I don't know and no one knows.

Now Linda and I have a close relationship; what we've been through has brought us closer as mother and daughter and as friends. She's a writer and now I own a bookstore, so we have much in common. Sometimes she calls to ask my advice. I remember once she wanted to talk about a problem with her lover. As she started to tell me the situation, I could feel myself say, "Oh, no, I don't want to hear about this." But then I forced myself to listen and I began to relax. What she was going through was no different from things heterosexual couples have to deal with—honesty, communication and patience. I helped her work through her problem and felt happy that she trusted me and could confide in me.

Even though having a lesbian daughter is not what I would have chosen, I've learned to accept Linda for who she is, not what I wanted her to be. Now I can look at my daughter with a sense of pride and a sense of peace.

Questions

1. What are Linda and Clara trying to accomplish in this essay? Is their style of expression effective for accomplishing their goals? What is significant about Linda's choice of *Essence* as a vehicle for sharing her experiences?
2. What issues are involved in the coming out process, both from Linda's perspective and from Clara's? What feelings do the authors express? What issues did they each struggle with individually?
3. What were Linda's motivations in telling her mother? How did they resolve the issue? What stereotypes does this essay contradict?

The Beauty Myth (1991)

Naomi Wolf

Feminist writer and theorist Naomi Wolf, whose 1991 book The Beauty Myth *is excerpted below, was born in San Francisco in 1962. A graduate of Yale University and a Rhodes Scholar, Wolf has lectured extensively on women's issues and authored several books including* Fire with Fire *(1993) and* Promiscuities *(1996). In this selection, Wolf explores Western beauty ideology by examining both its historical roots and its contemporary effects. She argues that modern beauty ideology is based on a mythical perception of "beauty"—a socially constructed set of ideas about how female bodies should appear and behave—that has become more rigid and restrictive even as women have gained political and economic ground.*

At last, after a long silence, women took to the streets. In the two decades of radical action that followed the rebirth of feminism in the early 1970s, Western women gained legal and reproductive rights, pursued higher education, entered the trades and the professions, and overturned ancient and revered beliefs about their social role. A generation on, do women feel free?

The affluent, educated, liberated women of the First World, who can enjoy freedoms unavailable to any women ever before, do not feel as free as they want to. And they can no longer restrict to the subconscious their sense that this lack of freedom has something to do with—with apparently frivolous issues, things that really should not matter. Many are ashamed to admit that such trivial concerns—to do with physical appearance, bodies, faces, hair, clothes—matter so much. But in spite of shame, guilt, and denial, more and more women are wondering if it isn't that they are entirely neurotic and alone but rather that something important is indeed at stake that has to do with the relationship between female liberation and female beauty.

The more legal and material hindrances women have broken through, the more strictly and heavily and cruelly images of female beauty have come to weigh upon us. Many women sense that women's collective progress has stalled; compared with the heady momentum of earlier days, there is a dispiriting climate of confusion, division, cynicism, and above all, exhaustion. After years of much struggle and little recognition, many older women feel burned out; after years of taking its light for granted, many younger women show little interest in touching new fire to the torch.

During the past decade, women breached the power structure; meanwhile, eating disorders rose exponentially and cosmetic surgery became the fastest-growing medical specialty. During the past five years, consumer spending doubled, pornography became the main media category, ahead of legitimate films and records combined, and thirty-three thousand American women told researchers that they would rather lose ten to fifteen pounds than achieve any other goal. More women have more money and power and scope and legal recognition than we have ever had before; but in terms of how we feel about ourselves *physically*, we may actually be worse off than our unliberated grandmothers. Recent research consistently shows that inside the majority of the West's controlled, attractive, successful working women, there is a secret "underlife" poisoning our freedom; infused with notions of beauty, it is a dark vein of self-hatred, physical obsessions, terror of aging, and dread of lost control.

It is no accident that so many potentially powerful women feel this way. We are in the midst of a violent backlash against feminism that uses images of female beauty as a political weapon against women's advancement: the beauty myth. It is the modern version of a social reflex that has been in force since the Industrial Revolution. As women released themselves from the feminine mystique of domesticity, the beauty myth took over its lost ground, expanding as it waned to carry on its work of social control.

The contemporary backlash is so violent because the ideology of beauty is the last one remaining of the old feminine ideologies that still has the power to control those women whom second wave feminism would have otherwise made relatively uncontrollable: It has grown stronger to take over the work of social coercion that myths about motherhood, domesticity, chastity, and passivity no longer can manage. It is seeking right now to undo psychologically and covertly all the good things that feminism did for women materially and overtly.

This counterforce is operating to checkmate the inheritance of feminism on every level in the lives of Western women. Feminism gave us laws against job discrimination based on gender; immediately case law evolved in Britain and the United States that institutionalized job discrimination based on women's appearances. Patriarchal religion declined; new religious dogma, using some of the mind-altering techniques of older cults and sects, arose around age and weight to functionally supplant traditional ritual. Feminists, inspired by Friedan, broke the strangle hold on the women's popular press of advertisers for household products, who were promoting the feminine mystique; at once, the diet and skin care industries became the new cultural censors of women's intellectual space, and because of their pressure, the gaunt, youthful model supplanted the happy housewife as the arbiter of successful womanhood. The sexual revolution promoted the discovery of female sexuality; "beauty pornography"—which for the first time in women's history artificially links a commodified "beauty" directly and explicitly to sexuality—invaded the mainstream to undermine women's new and vulnerable sense of sexual self-worth. Reproductive rights gave Western women control over our own bodies; the weight of fashion models plummeted to 23 percent below that of ordinary women, eating disorders rose exponentially, and a mass neurosis was promoted that used food and weight to strip women of that sense of control. Women insisted on politicizing health; new technologies of invasive, potentially deadly "cosmetic" surgeries developed apace to re-exert old forms of medical control of women.

Every generation since about 1830 has had to fight its version of the beauty myth. "It is very little to me," said the suffragist Lucy Stone in 1855, "to have the right to vote, to own property, etcetera, if I may not keep my body, and its uses, in my absolute right." Eighty years later, after women had won the vote, and the first wave of the organized women's movement had subsided, Virginia Woolf wrote that it would still be decades before women could tell the truth about their bodies. In 1962, Betty Friedan quoted a young woman trapped in the Feminine Mystique: "Lately, I look in the mirror, and I'm so afraid I'm going to look like my mother." Eight years after that, heralding the cataclysmic second wave of feminism, Germaine Greer described "the Stereotype": "To her belongs all that is beautiful, even the very word beauty itself . . . she is a doll . . . I'm sick of the masquerade." In spite of the great revolution of the second wave, we are not exempt. Now we can look out over ruined barricades: A revolution has come upon us and changed everything in its path, enough time has passed since then for babies to have grown into women, but there still remains a final right not fully claimed.

The beauty myth tells a story: The quality called "beauty" objectively and universally exists. Women must want to embody it and men must want to possess women who embody it. This embodiment is an imperative for women and not for men, which situation is necessary and natural because it is biological, sexual, and evolutionary: Strong men battle for beautiful women, and beautiful women are more reproductively successful. Women's beauty must correlate to their fertility, and since this system is based on sexual selection, it is inevitable and changeless.

None of this is true. "Beauty" is a currency system like the gold standard. Like any economy, it is determined by politics, and in the modern age in the West it is the last, best belief system that keeps male dominance intact. In assigning value to women in a vertical hierarchy according to a culturally imposed physical standard, it is an expression of power relations in which women must unnaturally compete for resources that men have appropriated for themselves.

"Beauty" is not universal or changeless, though the West pretends that all ideals of female beauty stem from one Platonic

Ideal Woman; the Maori admire a fat vulva, and the Padung, droopy breasts. Nor is "beauty" a function of evolution: Its ideals change at a pace far more rapid than that of the evolution of species, and Charles Darwin was himself unconvinced by his own explanation that "beauty" resulted from a "sexual selection" that deviated from the rule of natural selection; for women to compete with women through "beauty" is a reversal of the way in which natural selection affects all other mammals. Anthropology has overturned the notion that females must be "beautiful" to be selected to mate: Evelyn Reed, Elaine Morgan, and others have dismissed sociobiological assertions of innate male polygamy and female monogamy. Female higher primates are the sexual initiators: not only do they seek out and enjoy sex with many partners, but "every nonpregnant female takes her turn at being the most desirable of all her troop. And that cycle keeps turning as long as she lives." The inflamed pink sexual organs of primates are often cited by male sociobiologists as analogous to human arrangements relating to female "beauty," when in fact that is a universal, nonhierarchical female primate characteristic.

Nor has the beauty myth always been this way. Though the pairing of the older rich men with young, "beautiful" women is taken to be somehow inevitable, in the matriarchal Goddess religions that dominated the Mediterranean from about 25,000 B.C.E. to about 700 B.C.E., the situation was reversed: "In every culture, the Goddess has many lovers. . . . The clear pattern is of an older woman with a beautiful but expendable youth—Ishtar and Tammuz, Venus and Adonis, Cybele and Attis, Isis and Osiris . . . their only function the service of the divine 'womb.'" Nor is it something only women do and only men watch: Among the Nigerian Wodaabes, the women hold economic power and the tribe is obsessed with male beauty; Wodaabe men spend hours together in elaborate makeup sessions, and compete—provocatively painted and dressed, with swaying hips and seductive expressions—in beauty contests judged by women. There is no legitimate historical or biological justification for the beauty myth; what it is doing to women today is a result of nothing more exalted than the need of today's power structure, economy, and culture to mount a counteroffensive against women.

If the beauty myth is not based on evolution, sex, gender, aesthetics, or God, on what is it based? It claims to be about intimacy and sex and life, a celebration of women. It is actually composed of emotional distance, politics, finance, and sexual repression. The beauty myth is not about women at all. It is about men's institutions and institutional power.

The qualities that a given period calls beautiful in women are merely symbols of the female behavior that that period considers desirable: *The beauty myth is always actually prescribing behavior and not appearance.* Competition between women has been made part of the myth so that women will be divided from one another. Youth and (until recently) virginity have been "beautiful" in women since they stand for experiential and sexual ignorance. Aging in women is "unbeautiful" since women grow more powerful with time, and since the links between generations of women must always be newly broken: Older women fear young ones, young women fear old, and the beauty myth truncates for all the female life span. Most urgently, women's identity must be premised upon our "beauty" so that we will remain vulnerable to outside approval, carrying the vital sensitive organ of self-esteem exposed to the air.

Though there has, of course, been a beauty myth in some form for as long as there has been patriarchy, the beauty myth in its modern form is a fairly recent invention. The myth flourishes when material constraints on women are dangerously loosened. Before the Industrial Revolution, the average woman could not have had the same feelings about "beauty" that modern women do who experience the myth as continual comparison to a mass-disseminated physical ideal. Before the development of technologies of mass production—daguerreotypes, photographs, etc.—an ordinary woman was exposed to few such images outside the Church. Since the family was a productive unit and women's work complemented men's, the value of women who were not aristocrats or prostitutes lay in their work skills, economic shrewdness, physical strength, and fertility. Physical attraction, obviously, played its part; but "beauty" as we understand it was not, for ordinary women, a serious issue in the marriage marketplace. The beauty myth in its modern form gained ground after the upheavals of industrialization, as the work unit of the family was destroyed, and urbanization and the emerging factory system demanded what social engineers of the time termed the "separate sphere" of domesticity, which supported the new labor category of the "breadwinner" who left home for the workplace during the day. The middle class expanded, the standards of living and of literacy rose, the size of families shrank; a new class of literate, idle women developed, on whose submission to enforced domesticity the evolving system of industrial capitalism depended. Most of our assumptions about the way women have always thought about "beauty" date from no earlier than the 1830s, when the cult of domesticity was first consolidated and the beauty index invented.

For the first time new technologies could reproduce—in fashion plates, daguerreotypes, tintypes, and rotogravures—images of how women should look. In the 1840s the first nude photographs of prostitutes were taken; advertisements using images of "beautiful" women first appeared in mid-century. Copies of classical artworks, postcards of society beauties and royal mistresses, Currier and Ives prints, and porcelain figurines flooded the separate sphere to which middle-class women were confined.

Since the Industrial Revolution, middle-class Western women have been controlled by ideals and stereotypes as much as by material constraints. This situation, unique to this group, means that analyses that trace "cultural conspiracies" are uniquely plausible in relation to them. The rise of the beauty myth was just one of several emerging social fictions that masqueraded as natural components of the feminine sphere, the better to enclose those women inside it. Other such fictions arose contemporaneously: a version of childhood that required continual maternal supervision; a concept of female biology that required middle-class women to act out the roles of hysterics and hypochondriacs; a conviction that respectable women were sexually anesthetic; and a definition of women's work that occupied them with repetitive, time-consuming, and painstaking tasks such as needlepoint and lacemaking. All such Victorian inventions as these served a double function—that is, though they were encouraged as a means to expend female energy and intelligence in harmless ways, women often used them to express genuine creativity and passion.

But in spite of middle-class women's creativity with fashion and embroidery and child rearing, and, a century later, with the role of the suburban housewife that devolved from these social fictions, the fictions' main purpose was served: During a century and a half of unprecedented feminist agitation, they effectively counteracted middle-class women's dangerous new leisure, literacy, and relative freedom from material constraints.

Though these time- and mind-consuming fictions about women's natural role adapted themselves to resurface in the postwar Feminine Mystique, when the second wave of the women's movement took apart what women's magazines had portrayed as the "romance," "science," and "adventure" of homemaking and suburban family life, they temporarily failed. The cloying domestic fiction of "togetherness" lost its meaning and middle-class women walked out of their front doors in masses.

So the fictions simply transformed themselves once more: Since the women's movement had successfully taken apart most other necessary fictions of femininity, all the work of social control once spread out over the whole network of these fictions had to be reassigned to the only strand left intact, which action consequently strengthened it a hundredfold. This reimposed onto liberated women's faces and bodies all the limitations, taboos, and punishments of the repressive laws, religious injunctions and reproductive enslavement that no longer carried sufficient force. Inexhaustible but ephemeral beauty work took over from inexhaustible but ephemeral housework. As the economy, law, religion, sexual mores, education, and culture were forcibly opened up to include women more fairly, a private reality colonized female consciousness. By using ideas about "beauty," it reconstructed an alternative female world with its own laws, economy, religion, sexuality, education, and culture, each element as repressive as any that had gone before.

Since middle-class Western women can best be weakened psychologically now that we are stronger materially, the beauty myth, as it has resurfaced in the last generation, has had to draw on more technological sophistication and reactionary fervor than ever before. The modern arsenal of the myth is a dissemination of millions of images of the current ideal; although this barrage is generally seen as a collective sexual fantasy, there is in fact little that is sexual about it. It is summoned out of political fear on the part of male-dominated institutions threatened by women's freedom, and it exploits female guilt and apprehension about our own liberation—latent fears that we might be going too far. This frantic aggregation of imagery is a collective reactionary hallucination willed into being by both men and women stunned and disoriented by the rapidity with which gender relations have been transformed: a bulwark of reassurance against the flood of change. The mass depiction of the modern woman as a "beauty" is a contradiction: Where modern women are growing, moving, and expressing their individuality, as the myth has it, "beauty" is by definition inert, timeless, and generic. That this hallucination is necessary and deliberate is evident in the way "beauty" so directly contradicts women's real situation.

And the unconscious hallucination grows ever more influential and pervasive because of what is now conscious market manipulation: powerful industries—the $33-billion-a-year diet industry, the $20-billion cosmetics industry, the $300-million cosmetic surgery industry, and the $7-billion pornography industry—have arisen from the capital made out of unconscious anxieties, and are in turn able, through their influence on mass culture, to use, stimulate, and reinforce the hallucination in a rising economic spiral.

This is not a conspiracy theory; it doesn't have to be. Societies tell themselves necessary fictions in the same way that individuals and families do. Henrik Ibsen called them "vital lies," and psychologist Daniel Goleman describes them working the same way on the social level that they do within families: "The collusion is maintained by directing attention away from the fearsome fact, or by repackaging its meaning in an acceptable format." The costs of these social blind spots, he writes, are destructive communal illusions. Possibilities for women have become so open-ended that they threaten to destabilize the institutions on which a male-dominated culture has depended, and a collective panic reaction on the part of both sexes has forced a demand for counterimages.

The resulting hallucination materializes, for women, as something all too real. No longer just an idea, it becomes three-dimensional, incorporating within itself how women live and how they do not live: It becomes the Iron Maiden. The original Iron Maiden was a medieval German instrument of torture, a body-shaped casket painted with the limbs and features of a lovely, smiling young woman. The unlucky victim was slowly enclosed inside her; the lid fell shut to immobilize the victim, who died either of starvation or, less cruelly, of the metal spikes embedded in her interior. The modern hallucination in which women are trapped or trap themselves is similarly rigid, cruel, and euphemistically painted. Contemporary culture directs attention to imagery of the Iron Maiden, while censoring real women's faces and bodies.

Why does the social order feel the need to defend itself by evading the fact of real women, our faces and voices and bodies, and reducing the meaning of women to these formulaic and endlessly reproduced "beautiful" images? Though unconscious personal anxieties can be a powerful force in the creation of a vital lie, economic necessity practically guarantees it. An economy that depends on slavery needs to promote images of slaves that "justify" the institution of slavery. Western economies are absolutely dependent now on the continued underpayment of women. An ideology that makes women feel "worth less" was urgently needed to counteract the way feminism had begun to make us feel worth more. This does not require a conspiracy; merely an atmosphere. The contemporary economy depends right now on the representation of women within the beauty myth. Economist John Kenneth Galbraith offers an economic explanation for "the persistence of the view of homemaking as a 'higher calling'": the concept of women as naturally trapped within the Feminine Mystique, he feels, "has been forced on us by popular sociology, by magazines, and by fiction to disguise the fact that woman in her role of consumer has been essential to the development of our industrial society. . . . Behavior that is essential for economic reasons is transformed into a social virtue." As soon as a woman's primary social value could no longer be defined as the attainment of virtuous domesticity, the beauty myth redefined it as the attainment of virtuous beauty. It did so to substitute both a new consumer imperative and a new justification for economic unfairness in the workplace where the old ones had lost their hold over newly liberated women.

Another hallucination arose to accompany that of the Iron Maiden: The caricature of the Ugly Feminist was resurrected to dog the steps of the women's movement. The caricature is unoriginal; it was coined to ridicule the feminists of the nineteenth century. Lucy Stone herself, whom supporters saw as "a prototype of womanly grace . . . fresh and fair as the morning," was derided by detractors with "the usual report" about Victorian feminists: "a big masculine woman, wearing boots, smoking a cigar, swearing like a trooper." As Betty Friedan put it presciently in 1960, even before the savage revamping of that old caricature: "The unpleasant image of feminists today resembles less the feminists themselves than the image fostered by the interests who so bitterly opposed the vote for women in state after state." Thirty years on, her conclusion is more true than ever: That resurrected caricature, which sought to punish women for their public acts by going after their private sense of self, became the paradigm for new limits placed on aspiring women everywhere. After the success of the women's movement's second wave, the beauty myth was perfected to checkmate power at every level in individual women's lives. The modern neuroses of life in the female body spread to woman after woman at epidemic rates. The myth is undermining—slowly, imperceptibly, without our being aware of the real forces or erosion—the ground women have gained through long, hard, honorable struggle.

The beauty myth of the present is more insidious than any mystique of femininity yet: A century ago, Nora slammed the door of the doll's house; a generation ago, women turned their backs on the consumer heaven of the isolated multiapplianced home; but where women are trapped today, there is no door to slam. The contemporary ravages of the beauty backlash are destroying women physically and depleting us psychologically. If we are to free ourselves from the dead weight that has once again been made out of femaleness, it is not ballots or lobbyists or placards that women will need first; it is a new way to see.

NOTES

Cosmetic surgery: *Standard and Poor's Industry Surveys* (New York: Standard and Poor's Corp., 1988).

Pornography main media category: See "Crackdown on Pornography: A No-Win Battle," *U.S. News & World Report*, June 4, 1984. The Association of Fashion and Image Consultants tripled its membership between 1984 and 1989 alone (Annetta Miller and Dody Tsiantar, *Newsweek*, May 22, 1989). During the five or six years prior to 1986, consumer spending rose from $300 billion to $600 billion.

Thirty-three thousand American women, University of Cincinnati College of Medicine, 1984: Wooley, S. C., and O. W. Wooley, "Obesity and Women: A Closer Look at the Facts," *Women's Studies International Quarterly*, vol. 2 (1979), pp. 69–79. Data reprinted in "33,000 Women Tell How They Really Feel About Their Bodies," *Glamour*, February 1984.

Recent research shows: See Dr. Thomas Cash, Diane Cash, and Jonathan Butters, "Mirror-Mirror on the Wall: Contrast Effects and Self-Evaluation of Physical Attractiveness," *Personality and Social Psychology Bulletin*, September 1983, vol. 9, no. 3. Dr. Cash's research shows very little connection between "how attractive women are" and "how attractive they feel themselves to be." All the women he treated were, in his terms, "extremely attractive," but his patients compare themselves only to models, not to other women.

Very little to me: Lucy Stone, 1855, quoted in Andrea Dworkin, *Pornography: Men Possessing Women* (New York: Putnam, 1981), p. 11.

A doll: Germaine Greer, *The Female Eunuch* (London: Paladin Grafton Books, 1970), pp. 55, 60.

Myth: See also Roland Barthes's definition: "It [myth] transforms history into nature. . . . Myth has the task of giving an historical intention a natural justification, and making contingency appear eternal." Roland Barthes, "Myth Today," *Mythologies* (New York: Hill and Wang, 1972), p. 129.

Anthropologist Bronislaw Malinowski's definition of "a myth of origin" is relevant to the beauty myth: A myth of origin, writes Ann Oakley, "tends to be worked hardest in times of social strain, when the state of affairs portrayed in the myth are called into question." Ann Oakley, *Housewife: High Value/Low Cost* (London: Penguin Books, 1987), p. 163.

Platonic: See Plato's discussion of Beauty in *Symposium*. For varying standards of beauty, see Ted Polhemus, *BodyStyles* (Luton, England: Lennard Publishing, 1988).

Sexual selection; Darwin . . . was unconvinced: See Cynthia Eagle Russett, "Hairy Men and Beautiful Women," *Sexual Science: The Victorian Construction of Womanhood* (Cambridge, Mass.: Harvard University Press, 1989), pp. 78–103.

On page 84 Russett quotes Darwin: "Man is more powerful in body and mind than woman, and in the savage state he keeps her in a much more abject state of bondage, than does the male of any other animal; therefore it is not surprising that he should have gained the power of selection. . . . As women have long been selected for beauty, it is not surprising that some of their successive variations should have been transmitted exclusively to the same sex; consequently that they should have transmitted beauty in a somewhat higher degree to their female than to their male offspring, and thus have become more beautiful, according to general opinion, than men." Darwin himself noticed the evolutionary inconsistency of this idea that, as Russett puts it, "a funny thing happened on the way up the ladder: among humans, the female no longer chose but was chosen." This theory "implied an awkward break in evolutionary continuity," she observes: "In Darwin's own terms it marked a rather startling reversal in the trend of evolution."

See also Natalie Angier, "Hard-to-Please Females May Be Neglected Evolutionary Force," *The New York Times*, May 8, 1990, and Natalie Angier, "Mating for Life? It's Not for the Birds or the Bees," *The New York Times*, August 21, 1990.

Evolution: See Evelyn Reed, *Woman's Evolution: From Matriarchal Clan to Patriarchal Family* (New York: Pathfinder Press, 1986); and Elaine Morgan, *The Descent of Woman* (New York: Bantam Books, 1979). See especially "the upper primate," p. 91.

Goddess: Rosalind Miles, *The Women's History of the World* (London: Paladin Grafton Books, 1988), p. 43. See also Merlin Stone, *When God Was a Woman* (San Diego: Harvest Books, 1976).

Wodaabe tribe: Leslie Woodhead, "Desert Dandies," *The Guardian*, July 1988.

In the West African Fulani tribe young women choose their husbands on the basis of their beauty: "The contestants . . . take part in the yaake, a line-up in which they sing and dance, stand on tip-toe and make faces, rolling and crossing their eyes and grimacing to show off their teeth to the judges. They keep this up for hours, aided by the consumption of stimulating drugs beforehand. Throughout all this, old ladies in the crowd hurl criticisms at those who do not live up to the Fulani idea of beauty." [Polhemus, op. cit., p. 21]

See also Carol Beckwith and Marion van Offelen, *Nomads of Niger* (London: William Collins Sons & Co. Ltd., 1984), cited in Carol Beckwith, "Niger's Wodaabe: People of the Taboo," *National Geographic*, vol. 164, no. 4, October 1983, pp. 483–509.

Paleolithic excavations suggest that it has been human males rather than females to whom adornment was assigned in prehistoric societies; in modern tribal communities men generally adorn at least as much as women, and often hold "a virtual monopoly" over adornment. The Sudanese Nuba, the Australian Waligigi, and the Mount Hagen men of New Guinea also spend hours painting themselves and perfecting their hairstyles to attract the women, whose toilette takes only minutes. See Polhemus, op. cit., pp. 54–55.

Technologies: See, for example, Beaumont Newhall, *The History of Photography from 1839 to the Present* (London: Secker & Warburg, 1986), p. 31. Photograph *Academie*, c. 1845, photographer unknown.

Powerful industries: Diet items are a $74-billion-a-year industry in the United States, totaling one-third the nation's annual food bill. See David Brand, "A Nation of Healthy Worrywarts?," *Time*, July 25, 1988.

$33-billion-a-year diet industry: Molly O'Neill, "Congress Looking into the Diet Business," *The New York Times*, March 28, 1990.

$300-million-a-year cosmetic surgery industry: *Standard and Poor's Industry Surveys*, op. cit. 1988.

$7 billion pornography industry, "Crackdown on Pornography," op. cit.

Vital lies: Daniel Goleman, *Vital Lies, Simple Truths: The Psychology of Self-Deception* (New York: Simon and Schuster, 1983), pp. 16–17, quoting Henrik Ibsen's phrase: "The vital lie continues unrevealed, sheltered by the family's silence, alibis, stark denial."

A higher calling: John Kenneth Galbraith, quoted in Michael H. Minton with Jean Libman Block, *What Is a Wife Worth?* (New York: McGraw-Hill, 1984), pp. 134–135.

Ugly Feminist: Marcia Cohen, *The Sisterhood: The Inside Story of the Women's Movement and the Leaders Who Made It Happen* (New York: Ballantine Books, 1988), pp. 205, 206, 287, 290, 322, 332.

Swearing like a trooper: Betty Friedan, *The Feminine Mystique* (London: Penguin Books, 1982), p. 79, quoting Elinor Rice Hays, *Morning Star: A Biography of Lucy Stone* (New York: Harcourt, 1961), p. 83.

Unpleasant image: Friedan, op. cit., p. 87.

QUESTIONS

1. Why does Wolf contend that understanding the beauty myth is critical to an understanding of women's status in contemporary society?
2. What is the "beauty myth"? What are the myth's interrelated components? Why does Wolf call it a "myth"? How does the myth affect women's lives today? Why doesn't it affect men's lives in the same way?
3. How is the beauty myth an ideology? To what does the term *beauty ideology* refer? What are its historical origins? What is a social fiction? How does Wolf employ the images of the Ugly Feminist and the Iron Maiden?
4. What does Wolf mean when she refers to "the colonization of female consciousness"? How is this "colonization" part of a dangerous "private reality" women face? Why does Wolf assert that the beauty myth actually prescribes *behavior* rather than *appearance*?

When I Was Growing Up (1981)

Nellie Wong

Nellie Wong is a poet, writer, socialist and Chinese-American feminist. She is the author of Dreams in Harrison Railroad Park *(1977) and most recently* Stolen Moments. *This poem first appeared in* This Bridge Called My Back: Writings by Radical Women of Color *(1981), a foundational anthology in Women's Studies conceived of and produced entirely by women of color. Wong's poem has been reprinted many times because it speaks powerfully to issues of difference and the effects that glorifying white femininity can have on Asian-American females and other women of color.*

I know now that once I longed to be white.
How? you ask.
Let me tell you the ways.

"When I Was Growing Up" by Nellie Wong. Reprinted from *This Bridge Called My Back: Writings by Radical Women of Color*. Eds. Cherrie Moraga and Gloria Anzaldua. New York: Kitchen Table: Women of Color Press, 1983. pp. 7–8.

when I was growing up, people told me
I was dark and I believed my own darkness
in the mirror, in my soul, my own narrow vision

when I was growing up, my sisters
with fair skin got praised
for their beauty, and in the dark
I fell further, crushed between high walls

when I was growing up, I read magazines
and saw movies, blonde movie stars, white skin,
sensuous lips and to be elevated, to become
a woman, a desirable woman, I began to wear
imaginary pale skin

when I was growing up, I was proud
of my English, my grammar, my spelling
fitting into the group of smart children
smart Chinese children, fitting in,
belonging, getting in line

when I was growing up and went to high school,
I discovered the rich white girls, a few yellow girls,
their imported cotton dresses, their cashmere sweaters,
their curly hair and I thought that I too should have
what these lucky girls had

when I was growing up, I hungered
for American good, American styles,
coded: white and even to me, a child
born of Chinese parents, being Chinese
was feeling foreign, was limiting,
was unAmerican

when I gowing up and a white man wanted
to take me out, I thought I was special,
an exotic gardenia, anxious to fit
the sterotype of an oriental chick

when I was growing up, I felt ashamed
of some yellow men, their small bones,

their frail bodies, their spitting
on the streets, their coughing,
their lying in sunless rooms,
shooting themselves in the arms

when I was growing up, people would ask
if I were Filipino, Polynesian, Portuguese.
They named all colors except white, the shell
of my soul, but not my dark, rough skin

when I was growing up, I felt
dirty. I thought that god
made white people clean
and no matter how much I bathed,
I could not change, I could not shed
my skin in the gray water

when I was growing up, I swore
I would run away to purple mountains,
houses by the sea with nothing over
my head, with space to breathe,
uncongested with yellow people in an area
called Chinatown, in an area I later learned
was a ghetto, one of many hearts
of Asian America

I know now that once I longed to be white.
How many more ways? you ask.
Haven't I told you enough?

Questions

1. Who is the speaker in this poem and to whom is the poem addressed? What words would you use to describe the tone of the poem?
2. Why does Wong repeat the phrase "when I was growing up" throughout the poem?

3. What does the speaker mean when she says white is the "shell of [her] soul"?
4. What makes her feel the way she does? What did she yearn for at that time? Does she feel the same way as an adult as she felt as a child? How do you know?
5. What stereotypes are challenged in this poem? What does this poem say about "difference"?

Men Changing Men (1994)

Robert L. Allen and Paul Kivel

Crimes like battery, sexual assault and rape are often thought to be "women's issues." Media coverage of these topics frequently focuses on increasing women's awareness and encouraging the development of self-defense techniques. The following 1994 essay taken from Ms. Magazine *shifts our attention to the ways men are organizing to prevent violence against women and analyzing the cultural definition of masculinity. Robert Allan and Paul Kivel describe their efforts to help men better understand how their own gender socialization promotes aggressive behavior.*

Batterers need to be penalized for their actions, but the future safety of women and children depends on stopping the violence before it starts. With prevention in mind, "Ms." asked Robert Allan and Paul Kivel to discuss the work they do with boys and men in the Oakland Men's Project (OMP). Formed in 1979, this California-based group is a nonprofit, multiracial organization of men and women, devoted to community education and eradicating male

"Men Changing Men," by Robert L. Allen and Paul Kivel, reprinted from *Ms.*, September/October 1994.

> violence, racism, and homophobia. The group has worked with thousands of boys and men. Its workshops are designed to encourage participants to examine gender roles, violence and discrimination, and alternatives to violence.

Why do men batter women? We have to discard the easy answers. Portraying batterers as ogres only serves to separate "them" from "us." But men who batter and men who don't are not all that different. Male violence is normal in our society and vast numbers of men participate. Men batter because we have been trained to; because there are few social sanctions against it; because we live in a society where the exploitation of people with less social and personal power is acceptable. In a patriarchal society, boys are taught to accept violence as a manly response to real or imagined threats, but they get little training in negotiating intimate relationships. And all too many men believe that they have the right to control or expect certain behavior from "their" women and children; many view difficulties in family relationships as a threat to their manhood, and they respond with violence.

Young people's definitions of femininity and masculinity often reflect rigid expectations of what they must live up to in order to be a "real" woman or a "real" man. Time and again we hear boys say that they are supposed to be tough, aggressive, in control, that they are not to express any feelings except anger, not to cry, and never to ask for help. And many boys expect girls to acquiesce to men and be dependent on them.

How do boys get these ideas about male identity and manhood? Often from parents, but our whole society contributes to the process. As many as one of every six boys are sexually assaulted, and many, many more are hit, yelled at, teased, and goaded into fighting to prove they're tough. At the project, we believe that many boys become convinced that they will be violated until they learn to use force to protect themselves. Then they move to take their pain and anger out on others the way older males have done to them.

In our work we often use role play as a way of getting at some of these issues. One particularly effective exercise involves a ten-year-old and his father; the father arrives home from work and demands that the boy turn off the TV, then berates him for the messiness of his room. The boy tries to explain; the father tells him to shut up, to stop making excuses. Fueling the father's anger is the fact that he's disappointed by the boy's school report card. The father shoves the report card in his son's face and demands to know why he has gotten a "D" in math. The boy says he did his best. The father tells him that he is stupid. The boy protests and begins to stand up. The father shoves him down, saying, "Don't you dare get up in my face!" The boy is visibly upset, and begins to cry. The father explodes: "Now what? You little mama's boy! You sissy! You make me sick. When are you going to grow up and start acting like a man?"

When we do this exercise in schools, it gets the boys' undivided attention because most have experienced being humiliated by an older male. Indeed, the power of this exercise is that it is so familiar. When asked what they learned from such encounters, the boys often say things like: A man is tough. A man is in control. A man doesn't cry. A man doesn't take crap.

We write the boys' comments on a blackboard, draw a box around them, and label it the "Act Like a Man" box. We talk about how males in this culture are socialized to stay in the box. Eventually we ask: What happens if you step out of it, if you stop acting tough enough or man enough? Invariably we hear that you get called names like "fag," "queer," "mama's boy," "punk," "girl." Asked why, the boys say it's a challenge, that they're expected to fight to prove themselves. Homophobia and fear of being identified with women are powerful messages boys get from an early age, and they are expected to fight to prove that they're tough and not gay—that they're in the box.

Using exercises, like the father/son interchange, helps us examine how the male sex role often sets men up to be dominating, controlling, and abusive. We ask: How safe is it to stay in the "Act Like a Man" box? Usually, most admit that it isn't safe, because boys and men continually challenge each other to prove that they're in the box. When a boy or man is challenged, he can prove he's a man either by fighting the challenger or by finding someone "weaker"—a female or a more vulnerable male—to dominate. Hurting girls relieves any anxiety that we may not be tough enough and establishes our heterosexual credentials. It's both a sign of our interest (we're paying attention to them) and a symbol of our difference (we're in control).

Because we are taught that women are primarily sexual objects, this behavior seems perfectly natural. And many men come to believe that a woman is just another material possession. We initiate dates, pay for our time together, protect them on the streets, and often marry them. We are trained to think that in return, girls should show their appreciation by taking care of us emotionally, putting their own concerns and interests aside, and putting out sexually.

This unspoken contract is one that many heterosexual men operate by, and it often leads to the assumption that women are our dumping grounds. If we've had a hard day at work, were embarrassed or humiliated by a boss—challenged in the box—the contract leads us to believe that we can take those feelings out on "our" women, and thus regain our power. If we end up hitting her, then we have to blame her in order to deny our aggression and keep our self-esteem intact. So we say things like: She asked for it. She pushed my buttons. She deserved it.

Invariable it comes as a surprise to us that women don't meekly accept our violence. So we respond by minimizing and justifying our actions: I didn't mean it. You're too sensitive. That's the way guys are. It was just the heat of the moment.

In order to get men to take responsibility for their own actions, we have to get them to talk about what they did, and what they said, and what they felt. Making the connection between how they have been trained and hurt and how they have learned to pass that pain on by hurting women or young people is essential.

To get men to reflect on their experiences and behaviors, we use exercises we call "stand ups." We ask everyone to be silent, and then slowly pose a series of questions or statements, and ask men to stand every time one applies to them. For example, we may ask, Have you ever:

- worried you were not tough enough?
- been called a wimp, queer, or fag?
- been told to "act like a man"?
- been hit by an older man?
- been forced to fight?
- been physically injured and hid the pain?
- been sexually abused, or touched in a way you didn't like?
- used alcohol or drugs to hide your pain?
- felt like blowing yourself away?

Later in the workshop we ask, Have you ever:

- interrupted a woman by talking louder?
- made a comment in public about a woman's body?

- discussed a woman's body with another man?
- been told by a woman that she wanted more affection and less sex from you?
- used your voice or body to intimidate a woman?
- hit, slapped, shoved, or pushed a woman?
- had sex with a woman when you knew she didn't want to?

Each participant is asked to look around and see other men standing, which helps break down their sense of isolation and feelings of shame. Since we are not a therapy group, no one is questioned or confronted about his own experiences. All of our work involves challenging the notion that males are naturally abusive and that females are natural targets of male abuse. We give boys and men a way of analyzing social roles by drawing insights from their own experiences, and help them to recognize that social interactions involve making choices, that we can break free of old roles by supporting each other in choosing alternatives to violence.

An important part of our work is getting men and boys to look at how power, inequality, and the ability to do violence to others are structured into social relationships in this country. We discuss how these inequalities are maintained and how violence against one targeted group encourages violence against others. This is not to excuse men's behavior; it is done in the belief that in order to make better choices, men must understand the framework of power and violence that constantly pressures us to be in control and on top.

There are growing numbers of men who are critical of sexism. All too often they are isolated and fearful of raising their concerns with other men because they worry about being targeted for violence. We try to help them break through the fear and reach out to other men. But we also work to get men to understand how they are damaged by sexism and how male violence against women keeps us from the collective action needed to confront racial, gender-based, and economic injustice.

For us personally this is powerful, life-changing work. We were each drawn to it because of troubling issues in our own lives: issues around our relationships with our fathers (one emotionally abusive, the other emotionally distant); relationships with women partners where we found ourselves repeating controlling, sexist behaviors that made us feel guilty, ashamed, defensive; and the fear that we might do to our children what had been done to us as children. Through the work we have discovered that many men share these concerns, but they are hesitant to talk about this with other men. Sadly, we have all learned that "real" men don't admit vulnerability. But despite their initial hesitation, many men are eager to talk about their lives, and to change the controlling and abusive behavior they've been trained to pass on. Doing this work is healing for us and for those we work with.

Men are responsible for battery and for stopping male violence. If we are to counter the myth that men's abuse of women is natural, men must challenge each other to stop the violence. We must defy notions of manhood that lead us to injure or kill those we say we love. We must confront male friends when we see them heading down the destructive path of domestic violence and urge them to get help. While it is critical that domestic violence cases be taken more seriously by the police and criminal justice system, it is equally important to examine and to change underlying social attitudes and practices that promote and excuse domestic violence. This is truly men's work.

QUESTIONS

1. What are the effects of shifting our attention from violence as a "women's issue" to men's responsibility for preventing crimes against women? How is violence against women also a crime against men?
2. In our culture, how do men have to behave to stay in the "Act Like a Man" box? How are little boys and men hurt by these messages that they receive from childhood? According to Allen and Kivel, how is violence promoted by these social constructions of masculinity? How do they perpetuate homophobia?
3. How can individual men make a difference even though they may not have the opportunity to participate in such a group?

Recovery From Violence (1991)

Margaret Anderson

Recognizing and breaking free from a battering relationship consumed Margaret Anderson for more than four years. Reflecting on details she recorded in her journal, Anderson recounts the social and individual circumstances that introduced violence into her life. Exemplifying the survival process of many women whose relationship is scarred by a battering companion, Anderson's brief autobiographical study highlights the utility of a feminist political analysis for developing personal power.

I have difficulty telling this story, not because my history is too painful, but because I simply can't remember much of what happened. I've found it very hard to accept that, as a recovering alcoholic, there are large chunks of time that I don't remember or can't remember clearly. I drank constantly during the four-year duration of my battering relationship. The alcohol has wiped out many of my memories.

To write this story, then, I had to research myself like a term paper. I returned to my old journals—those that I rarely reread—that dealt with my relationship with Mike. Reading the words of a seventeen-, eighteen-, nineteen- and twenty-year-old me that I hardly remember, I discovered that over the years I have filled in the memory gaps with nostalgia and with imagination. I forced myself to scrub away the whitewashing that I've done to compensate for such a sad, confused history so that I can speak honestly. This is the story of my struggle to love myself.

I am sure now that if I had stopped drinking while I was seeing Mike, our relationship would have ended. Alcohol was one of the strongest bonds between us; and it was the substance which allowed me time and again to ignore my survival instincts and to return to the same problems, the same arguments and the same cycle of violence.

The Beginning

I received straight A's my senior year of high school and had just been accepted to college. I began to venture outside the narrow parameters of total dedication to achievement that I had constructed for myself during high school. I had just started to drink, years after most of my classmates. I had only experimented half-heartedly with dating.

Mike was dark and brooding. He rode a motorcycle and played the guitar. He possessed an intoxicating sense of the romantic, and he flirted masterfully. He was just what I wanted—the complete opposite of my world of good behavior.

During the first months of our relationship, Mike and I shared lots of whimsy and a passion for words. I had spent most of my life devouring books, and he would stay up for hours tinkering with the rhyme of a song lyric. We found common ground in our love of mythology. We took walks in the rain, we flew kites, we went swimming at midnight. Although my journal logs this phase as a short one, followed by violence, I feel lucky to have preserved these initial happy memories.

Sex between us intoxicated me. I had just begun to discover and to explore my sexual self, and Mike and I were both caught up in ourselves as sexual beings. I almost always had sex after I had been drinking. I didn't experience sober sexual intimacy until three years after Mike was out of my life. We used sex as a last resort. Near the end of our relationship, we could barely carry on a civil conversation about the simplest things. Sex became our only way to communicate with each other. Mike was my first, and for many years, my only source of intimate information about myself. I could not associate the person who hit me and called me names with the person who made love to me. I used sex to convince myself that the relationship worked and that I could feel good about being with Mike.

Nine months into our relationship, Mike started being violent. I initially thought that I had pushed him too hard, started an argument at the wrong time, that his rages were something about him that I could change with enough patience and attention. Like most violent relationships, ours followed a pattern. One small disagreement would lead to another; our communications would misfire. Resentment would build to a crescendo, which always ended with us drunk, screaming at each other, and Mike's violence. Then the storm would clear, and we would make up passionately and be blissfully happy for days or weeks until the next storm started to build.

In some ways, this was familiar. I grew up in a landscape of verbal and physical violence. I never doubted that my parents loved me fiercely, and I often felt their support, yet simple stresses exploded into uncontrollable anger in my family. In anger, my father became irrational, violent and dangerous. Anger grabbed my mother like a seizure, and my brother and I learned to wait quietly for her rages to pass.

When I was three years old, my father hit my mother for the last time. I remember him clearly, standing over her shouting. Just as clearly, I remember how long she was gone as she walked, in midwinter, to the police station. She filed charges against my father because she refused to bring her children up in a home with a battered mother. This is my earliest memory, and while our family did not escape other forms of my father's violence, my mother made sure that my brother and I never perceived physical violence as a "normal" or acceptable atmosphere for a family. We saw it rather as something unique to our family and completely uncontrollable.

The Violence

Mike's anger controlled him, and if he mixed anger with alcohol, he almost always resorted to violence. I spent the evening of my grandmother's funeral pleading with him not to destroy our lawn furniture; an argument over what he wore to the funeral had set him off. After another argument, Mike smashed his hands through our front screen door, shaving off most of the skin on his hands. My mother made him repair the door and told him that he was no longer welcome in our house.

One week later, Mike and I each went out with friends and ended up at the same bar. He was so drunk that he barely recognized me, but he remembered that he was angry that we hadn't gone out together that night. He kissed my friend; I dumped a beer over his head and went home. At two o'clock in the morning he appeared in my bedroom, ripped a poster off my wall and hit me five times. As I tried to get him out of the house with my brother's help, he hit my brother. I was shutting the front door on him when he put both hands through the plate glass panel in the door and shattered it. A six-inch piece of glass cut my neck, but by the time we realized how much I was bleeding, Mike had wandered into the street and was trying to avoid being hit by a car.

I took my mother's car and drove Mike to his house. When I crossed the threshold, covered with blood, his mother said to me, "What did you expect? You stood him up tonight." What she meant was not so much that I deserved to be battered, but that Mike could not control his behavior and therefore could not be held responsible for it. It was up to me to shoulder the responsibility, since it had to be shouldered by someone.

In my journal the next day, I wrote:

> I almost don't feel like really writing now, but I think I need a record of this to keep around—to check up on and to keep me scared.... I only moved to defend myself when he went for Steve [my brother]. Even though the glass could have hit me in the eye or his blows could have been harder and landed in a more dangerous place . . . I never really believed that he could hit me.... What am I supposed to think of myself? . . . I keep asking myself why people who claim they care about me would treat me like this.... He told me that all I ever meant to him was a good lay. . . . I feel cheap and I feel dirty.... I'm not angry, I just have this

feeling of betrayal and disgust with both of us. . . . It's because I loved him so much that I gave up myself. . . .

Mike and I were still together two and a half years later. I didn't look back on that journal entry very often because it told the truth. Later, I fielded Mike's drunken, abusive phone calls to my dormitory. I pulled him out of drunken fights with his fraternity brothers. He hit me or called me names more frequently, so that I finally *did* get angry and started hitting back in a rage.

As our relationship grew older and more dangerous, we fought more frequently. We screamed at each other regularly, and Mike was not afraid to call me names in front of other people. After the fights, he would cry, buy me flowers, be twice as attentive, turn into a gentle lover. Then the cycle would start all over again.

Identifying the Abuse

Several violent episodes passed before I began to see violence as a pattern in our relationship, before I began to understand what was happening to me. Before I saw the pattern, I usually blamed myself for the disastrous outcomes of our fights and was often convinced that Mike was the victim instead of me. (After the broken-glass episode, Mike and his mother both asked repeatedly that my mother drop the charges against him for destruction of property, but neither would speak of the violence that led to those charges.)

I am convinced now that keeping a journal played a pivotal role in helping me to identify our relationship as abusive. My journal was the only place that I recorded my own voice without first editing it to fit others' expectations. My journal tracks my uneasiness with our relationship beginning a few months after Mike and I started dating. There, I repeated my own voice until, months later, I began to hear and remember what I was saying. Ashamed to talk about the violence with my friends and afraid to talk about it with my parents, I used my journal as a place to process my feelings. In my journal, I repeated "I don't deserve this," until one day I believed it.

Extracting Myself

I spent a long time weaning myself from Mike. I depended upon him; I had leaned on him during the hard transition from adolescence to adulthood. For a long time, I chose to remember the good times that we had shared and the honeymoon periods after the violence. I created a mythology for myself that attributed Mike's rages to his troubled family history. I convinced myself that I could help Mike change, that we had strong bonds between us, that his violence was so sporadic that it posed no real danger to me.

I kept taking chances with Mike, chances that he would never seriously injure me, chances that he would put aside his rages. I lied to friends and parents about the frequency of our contact because I was ashamed that I couldn't manage without him. I used Mike like a drug: I kept seeing him, hoping that the time spent with him would make me feel good again. Like any other drug, though, the good that Mike did became less frequent, and the bad days began to stack up.

I took tiny steps away from him. I started studying feminist literature in college. I collected friends who didn't see Mike as a prince, but as a jerk who telephoned drunk at four o'clock in the morning to mutter abusive gibberish at me. Every day that I made my own decisions, every time that I could get through a week or a month without a call or letter from him, I put a little more distance between us.

During this time, my journal acted as my only real outlet for anger. I only allowed myself to get mad when I wrote in my journal; fear of my own emotions and a desire to appear "normal" kept me from sharing most of my anger with my friends and family. I feared anger; when I was growing up, getting mad was the special territory of adults. Children who got angry were better off quiet. Adults who got angry raged around us until their feelings dissipated. I had no models for a healthy way of dealing with anger.

My journal allowed me space to catalog the brutality of our relationship, making it impossible for me to dismiss the violent episodes as isolated incidents. Without the journal, I would have kept on taking a drink every time I had the urge to get out of the relationship.

Distance helped, too. Nine months of the year, I attended a women's college one thousand miles away from Mike. We kept up frequent phone and letter contact, but the heady physical effects of our sex life could not touch me during the school year. Had we seen more of each other during semesters, my risk of serious injury would have increased greatly.

Away from our abusive fights, I was able to build my self-reliance in small ways. I learned to have fun without Mike, to make decisions that affected only me and to structure a life that did not necessitate seeing him every day. Slowly, depending upon myself built my self-confidence. Armed with stronger self-confidence, I could define myself on my own terms, rather than seeing myself as Mike's girlfriend.

Feminists or not, most of the women I encountered in college had clear ideas about what they wanted in life and were forging plans to meet their goals on their own. Feminist studies became part of the atmosphere on campus, and I began to develop a sense of the political. Feminism gave me the tools that I needed to analyze my relationship with Mike and the strength to leave the relationship behind. When I read feminist literature, I no longer felt so isolated and I found models for freeing myself. Feminism also taught me that survival means getting angry, means placing the blame on the person who does the violence, means saying no.

Finally, Mike's own behavior helped me to break away from him. Although he started dating someone else toward the end of our relationship, I still found it difficult to stay away from him. We slept together for a long time into his new relationship, and this sexual dimension did not end until I finally could tell him that I'd had enough.

At some point, I had to lie one too many times to cover up Mike's behavior. He became more and more volatile. He smashed his fist through his new girlfriend's wall. I had believed until that point that I was the only woman who could really "drive" him to violence.

Two years ago I stopped drinking and began a recovery program for alcoholism. Recovery helped me to put the final pieces in place, to explain how I had stayed in such an abusive relationship. Recovery also helped me to recognize abusive patterns in my own behavior and how to deal with anger before it swept me away.

I can look back on my relationship not with shame but with pride. I am proud of my own courage, which enabled me to grow strong. I am proud that I had the strength to say no to an abusive relationship. I can look back at my younger self and see in her the beginnings of a fighter, someone who would insist that she deserved something better than violence. That woman became someone who loves herself enough to settle for nothing less than happiness and self-respect.

QUESTIONS

1. Why does Margaret Anderson tell her story? Why is it a difficult story to tell?
2. How does Anderson describe "the beginning" of the violence in her relationship with Mike? How does she initially respond to Mike's violence? Why does she respond this way? How did Anderson rationalize Mike's actions in order to remain in the relationship?
3. How did Anderson's journal writing facilitate her recognition that Mike's violence was a pattern? How did recognizing that the violence was a pattern facilitate Anderson's emotional release from the relationship?

The Scope of the Problem (1993)

Carol Bohmer and Andrea Parrot

This article addresses the problem of rape in the context of college campus. It illustrates the variety of behaviors which can be defined as rape, showing that most rapes are not committed by strangers leaping out of dark alleys, but by people the students know. Although terms like date rape and acquaintance rape are commonly heard, the article clarifies that these terms are not legal categories; the law requires the same proof whether the victim and defendant knew one another or not, though proof of lack of consent is often more difficult in trials involving acquaintances. In fact, many cases of campus sexual assault are not handled by the courts at all but rather by the college. How colleges respond to the complaints, as this selection discusses, varies tremendously. Andrea Parrot is a social scientist and Carol Bohmer is a lawyer and sociologist; both authors have years of

"The Scope of the Problem" by Carol Bohmer and Andrea Parrot. Reprinted from *Sexual Assault on Campus: the Problem and the Solution*, New York: Lexington Books, 1993.

experience in rape education and analysis and as survivor advocates.

Most people, including those who have experienced it, have trouble understanding sexual assault. This is especially true if the victim and assailant are acquainted, are friends, or are dating. Many of the common questions about sexual assault on a college campus will be addressed in this chapter.

WHO ARE THE VICTIMS OF CAMPUS SEXUAL ASSAULT?

The case that follows includes many of the elements common to cases of sexual assault on campus. In this case the victim did report the sexual assault to the campus authorities, but she was manipulated into not pursuing legal or judicial authorities.

> Ellen, a first-year student, went to several parties the first Saturday of the fall semester. She had a lot to drink over the course of the evening. She was then taken by one of the men she had met at one of the parties to his residence hall, where there was a toga party under way. They both dressed in sheets and drank more alcohol at the residence hall party. Ellen passed out and when she gained consciousness, she discovered his penis in her mouth.

Ellen was a typical victim of campus sexual assault in that she was female, a freshman in college, and had been drinking alcohol. Victims of rape may be men or women of any age; however, they are usually females between the ages of 15 and 24. Most of them are of college age, an age when they are dating most frequently (Koss et al., 1987). Most sexual assaults occur between acquaintances, frequently on dates. The sexual assault victims we will be discussing in this paper are most often college women between 17 and 21. It is possible for men to be raped by male assailants—or, more rarely, by female assailants—but because the vast majority of acquaintance rapes involve male assailants and female victims, this paper will primarily focus on this type of sexual assault.

The two most important determining factors regarding whether a date rape will occur are the number of men a woman dates (Burkhart and Stanton, 1985), and the degree of intoxication of those men (Polonko et al., 1986). The first factor is based on probability of exposure, in part because it is impossible to tell a date rapist by the way he looks, and in part because women are socialized to ignore cues that may indicate that some men are a threat. For example, if a man calls a woman a derogatory name (such as "bitch") or continues to tease her when she asks him to stop, he is harassing her and is likely to exploit her. If he harasses, exploits, and/or objectifies her in a non-sexual situation, he is likely to do so in a sexual situation as well. Most women are socialized to put up with harassment, however, because saying something assertive is considered contrary to proper feminine behavior. The more times a woman experiences harassing kinds of behavior, the more they become part of her social environment, and the more she learns to "grin and bear it."

Some sexual assault victims have such low self-esteem that they feel that they are worthless without a relationship, and that it is better to be associated with any man than no man at all. This attitude is also enforced in American culture. The victim may say, "As soon as he gets to know the real me, he will fall in love with me, and will stop doing that. He will change for me." Or she may say, "I know he did something to me that I didn't like, but that is all I deserve." The victim may have watched her father harass or assault her mother, making her believe that this is the way adult sexual relationships are supposed to be. She may even have been sexually assaulted as a child; forced sexual experiences may be the only kind of sexual relationships she knows. Some victims may not want to believe that someone they love could do anything as terrible as rape them, so these victims may define the sexual assault as their own fault rather than believe that their boyfriends are rapists. For example, a victim may say, "I got him so excited that he couldn't stop himself."

With regard to the second factor, the more intoxicated a man is, the greater the likelihood that he will ignore a woman's protests or be unable to interpret her words and actions as she intended them. This is especially true if she does not want to have sex but he does, which is a common pattern in acquaintance sexual assaults.

> While visiting from another institution, John got drunk at a fraternity party and raped a woman at the party. His friends, who were fraternity brothers, helped to get her drunk and then encouraged the assault by cheering him on. After the party the woman filed a complaint with the college administration, but

because the alleged rapist was not a student at the college, the administration was not able to do anything to him.

Studies have not consistently indicated any female personality traits that make a woman more likely to become a date or acquaintance rape victim. Our research indicates that the typical scenario of sexual assault on college campus includes the woman's drinking at a party (especially a fraternity party) and playing drinking games, a situation where she has been given a drink in which the alcohol has been disguised as punch. First-year college students are most likely to become the victims of sexual assault while in college (Koss et al., 1987). Sexual assault, however, can and does also happen in other circumstances.

Sexual assault victims sometimes have sex again with their assailant. In many cases in which the victim has sex with the assailant again, the latter was the boyfriend of the victim. The victim may believe that, although he did force her to have sex, he will treat her better and not rape her once he really gets to know what a wonderful person she is (and, presumably, falls in love with her). Only after repeated sexual assaults over time does she realize that he will not change, and so she ends the relationship.

Neil Gilbert, a professor of social work at Stanford University, believes that if a woman does not know that what has happened to her is rape, then it is not rape (Collison, 1992). This type of attitude is probably pervasive among the administrations of some colleges. Gilbert cites FBI statistics, which consist disproportionately of reports of stranger rape, to prove that the 20–25 percent estimate of sexual assaults on female college students is inflated. The FBI estimates that fewer than one in ten stranger rapes are actually reported to them, however, and data from national studies suggest that fewer than one in a hundred acquaintance rapes are reported to the police (Burkhart, 1983; Parrot, 1992). Because most rapes and sexual assaults that occur in college are between acquaintances, they are not likely to be reported to the police or even the college administration. This is especially true if administrators have made it clear to victims that they don't believe sexual assault happens on their campus.

Who are the assailants?

Approximately 5–8 percent of college men know that raping acquaintances is wrong, but choose to do it because they know the odds of their being caught and convicted are very low (Koss et al., 1987; Koss, 1992; Hannan and Burkhart, 1994). There is a larger group of men who rape acquaintances but do not believe it is rape. They often believe they are acting in the way men are "supposed to act"—that "no" really means "maybe," and "maybe" really means "yes." Once a case becomes public, several other women often come forth who are willing to testify that the assailant sexually assaulted them as well, even though the other women had not pressed charges themselves. This was the case in the William Kennedy Smith trial, although the three women who also claimed to have been raped by him were nor permitted to testify.

Some studies have compared the incidence of sexual assault among various groups of men. One study indicated that 35 percent of fraternity men reported having forced someone to have sexual intercourse. This figure was significantly higher than for members of student government (9 percent) or men not affiliated with organizations (11 percent) (Garrett-Gooding and Senter, 1987). Based on an FBI survey, basketball and football players from NCAA colleges were reported to the police for committing sexual assault 38 percent more often than the average for males on college campuses (Hoffman, 1986).

The men who are most likely to rape in college are fraternity pledges (Bird, 1991; Koss, 1991). It is unclear whether this is because either forced sexual intercourse or sexual intercourse under any circumstances is a condition of pledging, or because the pledges are trying to act in a way that they believe the brothers will admire. The process of pledging a fraternity often desensitizes men to behaviors that objectify women, and it also creates a "groupthink" mentality (Sanday, 1990). As a result, once men become pledges, or fraternity members, some of them may commit a sexual assault to be "one of the brothers." All of these factors, plus the heavy alcohol consumption that occurs in fraternities, contribute to the likelihood that a sexual assault will occur on campus. Not all fraternity pledges who abuse alcohol, however, actually commit sexual assault. Conversely, women should not automatically feel safe with a man who is not in a fraternity and who is a teetotaler.

> Tom sexually assaulted Carol, the girlfriend of one of his fraternity brothers. Carol passed out from drinking too much at a fraternity party, and Tom had sex with her while she was unconscious in her boyfriend's bedroom. When she started moaning her boyfriend's name during the rape, Tom panicked and went to get the boyfriend, encouraging him to have sex with her so that if she regained consciousness, she would see him instead of Tom. Friends of Carol saw Tom leave the room and then reappear with her boyfriend, who he pushed into the room. Tom, however, had inadvertently left his tie in the bed, which was seen as evidence that he had been there with Carol. Tom was subsequently convicted of sexual assault by the campus judicial board.

The likelihood to commit a sexual assault also increases if men choose to live in all-male living units when co-educational units are also available. In fact, men who elect to live in all-male residences often do so in order to be able to behave in a violent or antisocial way, such as punching walls or getting drunk and vomiting in the hallways. There is significantly more damage done in all-male living units than on male floors of co-educational residences for this reason (Walters et al., 1981).

Another group at risk for committing rape in college are athletes competing in such aggressive team sports as football, lacrosse, and hockey. Athletes are most likely to sexually assault after a game, when they are out either celebrating a win or drowning their sorrows after a loss. Drinking parties are frequently part of the post-game ritual, with female fans helping the athletes celebrate or commiserating with them. The likelihood of a sexual assault is greatest at this point if a female "groupie" appears to be "throwing herself" at an athlete with the intent of being seen with him or because she wants to be his friend. The athlete may be unable to distinguish between her desire for friendship and his perception that she is throwing herself at him because she wants sex. Further, he may believe that this is what he deserves as a result of his "star" status. There have been many celebrated cases of high school, college, and professional athletes who were successfully charged with rape or sexual assault by college and civil authorities.

Assailants are not limited to fraternity members and athletes, however, and the vast majority of fraternity men and athletes do not rape. The rate is higher among these two groups because of their position of privilege on campus, and because of their involvement with alcohol. The characteristics that are most important in determining if a man will become an acquaintance rapist are macho attitudes, antisocial behavior, and abuse of alcohol (either on a regular basis, or through binge experiences) (Malamuth and Dean, 1991; Rapaport and Posey, 1991). Athletes and fraternity men may exhibit some or all of these traits.

> Bill, a fraternity pledge, was a virgin at the time he was pledging. He was told by the brothers that they did not accept virgins into their house, and so he would have to do something about his virginity status. When he protested that he did not have a girlfriend, he was told that he should bring a girl to their fraternity formal, and the brothers would do the rest. He invited a very naïve first-year student, Lori, to the party. Once there, she was given punch spiked with grain alcohol. When Lori blacked out, Bill took her to the bedroom of one of the brothers, put a condom on, and forced her to have sex over her feeble protests. She was also a virgin at the time, and she became pregnant because the condom broke during the rape.

DIFFERENT TYPES OF CAMPUS SEXUAL ASSAULT AND RAPE

Each different type of sexual assault has specific characteristics and problems associated with it. Campus sexual assaults vary by the status of the victim (student, faculty, staff, visitor, and so on), the status of the assailant, the number of assailants involved, and the degree of acquaintanceship between those involved. Rape or sexual assault on college campuses may be committed by an acquaintance or a stranger; most typically, the assailant is someone the victim knows. For the purposes of this article we have defined *campus sexual assault* as assault cases in which at least one of the people involved is associated with the institution.

Sexual assault of a member of the college community by a stranger from outside the campus community

We probably hear about this type of sexual assault more often than any other. Women are much more likely to report a sexual assault in which they are seen as having little or no culpability. Therefore, victims are more likely to report a sexual assault to the police or campus authorities if they do not know the assailant, do not share the same friends, and consequently do not receive any pressure from friends or acquaintances to keep quiet so the assailant's life will not be "ruined." Stranger rape usually occurs more in urban than rural areas because of higher crime rates in urban areas.

> On the night of January 2, 1989, a female employee of the University of Southern California was attacked near the school's credit union building by an unknown man who dragged her into some bushes, where she was beaten, stabbed, robbed, and raped. The attack lasted 40 minutes, during which time no one came to the woman's aid. She was rescued by two passersby, who scared off the assailant and then helped her to walk to the security office about a block away. It turned out that only one security officer was in the field at the time of the attack. Six months before the attack, there was a report that identified the building as a security risk, but no one had ever followed up on the report's recommendations, which included increasing the lighting and cutting back the bushes.

> A young woman at Clarkson University was assaulted while walking home through an isolated area behind the field house. A fire watchman who was inside the field house reported it to another fire watchman who was on patrol on another part of campus. The watchman in the car came to the building to investigate. He came upon two people having what he believed to be consensual sex. He called the other fire watchman and they were unsure of how to respond. When they went to check the scene again, they found the woman alone, bloody, and unconscious. They then called the village police, who responded and apprehended the man after he had raped and beaten the woman. She later died in the hospital. Clarkson College was sued and settled out of court. The college has subsequently hired a director of campus safety with a law enforcement background and has dramatically upgraded the training for its campus safety personnel (Cooper, 1992).

Sexual assault by a stranger (other than a student) from within the campus community is more likely in large campus communities than on smaller campuses, where most people tend to know each other. These rapes may be between students and faculty, administrators, or college staff members or visitors to the campus community.

Rape by a student unknown to the victim

This type of sexual assault is also more common in larger schools, and may happen in circumstances such as after the assailant notices the victim in a bar or at a large party. It may also occur if a woman has a "bad" reputation, passes out at a party after drinking alcohol, and is used sexually by male students who are strangers to the victim. In some instances, the victim is in a presumably safe place but is attacked by a stranger who has gained access based on false pretenses (for example, posing as a student or pizza delivery person). It is typical in gang rape that at least some of the assailants are strangers to the victim.

> In 1986, Lehigh freshman Jeannie Clery was raped, sodomized, and murdered while sleeping in her bed at 6:00 a.m. That night another student, who had been drinking and who did not know her, entered her residence hall through three automatically locking doors that were propped open, entered her room, and sexually assaulted and strangled her. Her parents sued the university for failing to provide a safe environment for their daughter and for violation of "foreseeable action." They settled for an undisclosed sum, and in addition, they committed Lehigh to extensive improvements in dormitory security.

Acquaintance rape and sexual assault

"Acquaintance rape" and "date rape" are not legal categories; the term *rape* usually applies to any forced intercourse, regardless of the degree of acquaintance. We are using the terms *acquaintance rape* and *date rape* for clarity of understanding in a sociological rather than a legal sense.

> Amy, a senior in high school, was visiting her sister, Jill (a first-year student), for the weekend at a small liberal arts college. They went to a lacrosse game, and Jill had a party in her room afterward. One of the lacrosse players, Adam, attended the party after the game, and Amy spent over an hour with him there. Amy and Adam both got drunk and went into an adjoining room during the party for about an hour. When they emerged, he went home, and Amy told Jill that Adam had raped her. Amy and Jill reported the event to the authorities, and Adam was suspended. Adam

> sued the college on the grounds that the campus policy explicitly stated that the college community would protect its students, but it said nothing about protecting visitors. (Parrot and Bechhofer, 1991)

Acquaintance sexual assaults are by far the most common type of rape both on and off the campus; however, they are rarely reported to authorities. Date rape (the most common type on college campuses) and acquaintance rape are estimated to happen to one-fifth of college women, whereas one-quarter of college women will experience either attempted or completed forced sex (Koss et al., 1987). These sexual assaults happen most often during the woman's first year, although a victim may also experience further episodes later on. Sexual assaults often happen to victims in the first week of college, before they know the social "rules." At colleges where first-year students live on campus and then must move off campus during their sophomore year, however, the incidence increases when students no longer have the protection of the structured college living environment (Parrot and Lynk, 1983; Parrot, 1985).

Gang rape and sexual assault

Although gang rape occurs on college campuses, it is not unique to them. It usually occurs in all-male living units where alcohol and peer pressure are abundant. Fraternity gang rape is especially difficult to prove because an accused's fraternity brothers are usually unwilling to provide evidence to the local or campus police. In fact, of the documented cases of alleged gang rape by college students from 1980 to 1990, 55 percent were committed by fraternity members, 40 percent were committed by members of team sports (football, basketball, and lacrosse), and only 5 percent were committed by men who were not affiliated with formal organizations (O'Sullivan, 1991). Other studies also show that a majority of gang rapes committed on college campuses occur in fraternity houses (Tierney, 1984).

Many of the people who are involved in gang rape are "followers" rather than initiators (Groth and Birnbaum, 1979). One of five Kentucky State University defendants charged with sodomizing a fellow student told police that at first he left the woman alone when he found her partially undressed in his room, because she was unwilling to have sex with him. When he later returned and found his friends assaulting her, he joined them (O'Sullivan, 1991).

> Tanja was raped in her dormitory in September of her first year of college at the University of California at Berkeley. An unsupervised party had been held in the dorm during which alcohol was consumed, despite the agreement between students and the university that there would be no drinking in the dorms. After this party, Tanja went to the room of an acquaintance, Donald, to borrow a cassette tape. There she met Donald's twin brother Ronald, who forced her down the interior stairs of the building to a dark landing where a light bulb had been shattered. He forced Tanja to have intercourse and oral sex with him. Ronald then took Tanja to a room occupied by John and Christian, where Donald soon joined them. Donald suggested that they all go to his room, where he encouraged the other three men to have oral sex with Tanja against her wishes. When she protested forcefully, Donald told the others to leave, but told her that if she didn't stop yelling, he would beat her. Donald then forced Tanja to have intercourse with him, while the other three friends watched, laughing. Tanja was finally permitted to leave. All four men were members of the university football team.

Like other acquaintance rape victims, the victim in a gang rape may be drunk or passed out at the time and therefore may have no memory of the rape; if she does remember it, her memory may be incomplete. She may have voluntarily gone to the location of the rape and may have consented to have sex with one of the men, but not with all of them. If she has a reputation for sleeping around, she may fear that she will not be believed if she reports the event to the police or the campus authorities. In fact, regardless of her reputation, when a woman is being gang raped, the last men are likely to feel more justified in forcing her because they feel that she deserves it for being so "loose." Gang rape may occur when women who are believed to be "easy" are imported from off campus for this purpose (Sanday, 1990).

In the event of a fraternity gang rape, powerful alumni and current brothers may put pressure on the institution to squelch the case. Information is often covered up in these cases to protect the assailant or to prevent the charter of the fraternity from being revoked. Members of the group that raped the victim, as well as the rapists themselves, may also harass her or put pressure on her not to report the assault, or to drop the charges. For all of these reasons, charges are rarely filed in gang rape cases, whether they occur on or off campus. If they are filed and the case goes to trial, the result is often an acquittal. In such cases, it is usually the word of the victim against that of the assailants, and the assailants' stories usually agree with each other. In addition, the assailants are often "nice boys" from "good families," in contrast with the victim's frequently "bad" reputation. In such cases it is difficult to convince the entire jury beyond a reasonable doubt that she was not a willing participant.

Peggy Sanday (1990) suggests that gang rape is often the means by which homophobic men who want to share a sexual experience with other men are able to do so through a woman. Sanday believes that these men want to have sex with each other, but will not do so because of the societal taboo against homosexual behavior. Therefore they select a woman whom they do not know and have sex with her in the presence of their male friends as a means of sharing a sexual experience in a "socially acceptable" heterosexual way. This process is unspoken, and perhaps unconscious, because these men would never admit wanting to have sex with another man. They are also misogynistic if they are able to abuse a woman in this manner to fulfill their own desires.

Judge Lois Forer (1991) believes that gang rape is becoming less acceptable off campus, but is viewed much less negatively on campus. In gang rape, as in acquaintance rape, if we hear of only a small number of cases being reported to the police or campus judicial authorities, it probably means that many more are actually taking place. We very rarely hear, for example, about gang rapes being reported to the authorities in which the victim has a "bad" sexual reputation (as many of them do).

St John's University case study

The rape trial involving members of the St John's University lacrosse team was a highly celebrated case that involved alcohol, athletics, and a groupthink mentality. It will be presented here as a case study because it illustrates the very points we are making about campus sexual assault. The St John's case includes many of the common elements present in the response to a campus sexual assault when the victim reports to the authorities.

> The three men on trial from St John's University (Andrew Draghi, Walter Gabrinowitz, and Matthew Grandinetti) were accused of

> making a woman perform oral sex on them, using force at some moments and at other times taking advantage of her helplessness from liquor that the victim says a fourth student (Michael Calandrillo) pressured her to drink. Not all of the men were tried together, because some of the defendants agreed to provide testimony against the other assailants.
>
> The woman testified that she was told by Michael that he would drive her home from an evening college meeting, but that he needed to stop by at his nearby house for gas money. She agreed to that arrangement. According to the prosecutor, however, when they entered the house she was the victim of sexual advances by Michael and was forced to drink cups of vodka and orange soda, a mixture that caused her to fade in and out of consciousness. When she awoke periodically, she found Michael's housemates (and former teammates) shoving their penises, in turn, into her mouth. The woman asserted that she tried to ward off her attackers verbally but that she was too weak. A Queens, New York, jury in 1991 rejected her allegations, and the three defendants were acquitted. (Parrot, 1993)

The facts in the St John's case illustrate many of the issues that often contribute to not-guilty verdicts. The victim waited many months before she reported the incident, and there was another significant time period between the report and the trial. When she provided accounts of the alleged crime to her minister, detectives, and lawyers, there were subtle differences in her story, such as exactly how much liquor she drank (from one to three cups). As in most acquaintance rape cases, the major legal issue here was not whether the event in fact took place, but whether the woman consented. The victim said she did not consent; the jury did not believe her.

It is important to understand that a verdict of not guilty does not necessarily mean that the assailant is innocent. It simply means that there was not sufficient evidence to convince all the jurors, beyond a reasonable doubt, that he committed the crime of which he was accused. Although this is, of course, true for all crimes, the acquittal rate in rape trials is higher than for other serious felonies. Jurors often do not believe that the defendant committed the crime because he was a credible witness, or because the victim was a poor witness; because there was not enough corroborating evidence; or because they could not understand why such a nice, upstanding (often married) pillar of the community would have to resort to raping a woman of questionable character in order to have sex.

This last line of reasoning assumes that men rape for sex. Although sexual organs are used in rape, that does not make it sex. As Linda Sanford, author of *Women and Self Esteem,* says, "If I hit you over the head with a rolling pin, you wouldn't call it cooking, would you?" In the same way, if a penis is used to commit violence, it does not make the act sex.

Stranger rapists often plan rape, whereas acquaintance or date rapists often plan sex. In acquaintance rape it is only when the assailant's plan for a perfect evening (ending with sex) goes wrong that he resorts to violence to get what he wants and may think he is owed. But even though the motivation may be different in stranger and acquaintance rape, the consequence is the same for the victim.

In many cases of acquaintance rape, the man may truly *not* believe that what he did was rape, or even that he did anything wrong. He may believe that a woman does not really mean no when she says it, and that all she needed was a little push, and she will be happy about the outcome. This scenario is played out in the media time after time, from *Gone with the Wind* to the soap opera *General Hospital,* the television series *Moonlighting,* and the movie *Baby Boom.* Just because an alleged assailant believes he is innocent, however, does not mean that he is within the law. The law does not define the crime of rape in terms of what the defendant thought, but rather uses a more objective standard.

Newspaper accounts of the trial of the members of the St John's lacrosse team suggested that this trial represented a miscarriage of justice, and that the legal system of the old South had returned because the victim was black, the defendants were white, and the defendants were found not guilty. Many feminists agreed that the verdict will have a chilling effect on the willingness of sexual assault victims to press charges.

Although the defendants were acquitted, St John's University nevertheless expelled the three men. The university waited until after the trial, however, to pass judgment on the men through the campus judicial process. The university's president found that each of the students was guilty of "conduct adversely affecting his suitability as a member of the academic community of St John's," noting that the court verdict acquitting the three of sodomy and criminal charges involved "different standards" from those related to the code of behavior that governs students' actions toward one another and toward teachers.

Many St John's University students felt that this was a harsh verdict for a Catholic university and that better punishment would have been some type of forgiveness and rehabilitation, such as psychotherapy. Catholic colleges seem to respond more harshly, in general, than most other colleges in the judicial handling of sexual assault cases on their campuses. Sexual assault is considered immoral and is not usually tolerated there, even if other segments of society do tolerate or even condone those behaviors.

Although the St John's case was typical in many ways, it differs from the norm because it actually went to trial. The victims of sexual assault rarely report either to the police or to the campus judicial system. Approximately 90 percent of sexual assault cases involving people who know each other are never reported to the police. Some victims prefer to report the rape to the campus judicial authorities; however, the majority of victims of acquaintance sexual assault do not tell anyone about it (Biden, 1991)...

WHAT HAPPENS WHEN VICTIMS REPORT TO CAMPUS OR CRIMINAL AUTHORITIES

Even when victims do report to the police, they are frequently disbelieved or blamed. This phenomenon was seen in the William Kennedy Smith case, in which the victim did report being raped. Although this case was not a campus sexual assault, the issues are similar. Because it was so highly publicized, we will use it as an example for purposes of illustration. Patricia Bowman's character was called into question; she was criticized for being in a bar drinking, for going to his home voluntarily, and for using poor judgment. The same things happen when campus sexual assault victims report to the campus authorities. But in the campus system, because rules of evidence are more flexible than in the criminal courts, victims are also often asked inappropriate questions about their sexual behavior (for example, "Do you have oral sex with all the men you date? Do you like it?).

In most acquaintance sexual assault cases, the victim is usually blamed by her peers and her support system. Martha Burt (1991) found that a majority of Americans think that at least half of all rape reports are false and that they are invented by women to retaliate against men who have wronged them. Many people believe that the charge of acquaintance rape or gang rape occurs because a woman feels guilty after a sexual encounter with a man and cries "rape" in order to ease her conscience. The fact is that only 2 percent of rape reports prove to be intentionally reported falsely to the police (Brownmiller, 1975).

Many victims find it cathartic and healing to tell their stories in court and to play a role in their assailant's punishment. But a plea bargain is often negotiated for a lesser charge, and the victim feels cheated when the assailant pleads guilty to a much less serious crime than that which he committed against her.

> Mary, a graduate student, was raped by another student in her apartment and reported the assault to the police. (Because the rape was not on college property, it was not within the jurisdiction of that particular college.) The district attorney accepted the case and was preparing it for trial. In order to obtain information from the alleged assailant about another crime, however, the district attorney offered the assailant a plea bargain, and the latter received a light sentence. Mary was very angry and disappointed at having been denied the right to "have her day in court" or to see the man sentenced to what she considered an appropriate penalty. At least in her case, however, the assailant was sentenced for some offense and as a result will have a criminal record.

The low reporting and conviction rates are generally characteristic of what are called *simple rapes*: those with no violence, a single attacker, and no other crime committed at the time (Estrich, 1987). Acquaintance rapes are usually simple rapes. The report and criminal conviction rates are much higher in the case of aggravated rapes, but those are far less likely than simple rapes to take place, especially on a college campus. Therefore, more assailants may be punished if acquaintance rape cases are heard by the college judicial board or officer, because the campus system can operate under different rules of evidence. Campus judicial processes are able to find more defendants guilty of sexual assault violations, all other things being equal, than the criminal courts, provided that the system is well designed and administered. The most serious penalty that may be administered in the campus system, however, is expulsion from the institution, which is not comparable to the loss of liberty that may follow a guilty verdict in the criminal justice system.

In many cases of sexual assault reported to the criminal justice system, the case is not accepted by the district attorney or indicted by the grand jury, which may make the victim feel powerless or very angry, especially if she wants to see her assailant behind bars. Victims who report their assaults to the campus criminal judicial system often also experience anger, frustration, and disappointment. For example, victims may be told that their case is not eligible for action by the campus judicial system because it occurred outside of the jurisdiction of the system. Other cases may fail because the victim is not taken seriously by law enforcement officials or campus officials, or because of long delays, among other reasons.

If the case is handled within a campus system, the result may be an acquittal. Although on some campuses, the cases of campus sexual assault that are brought to the judicial body for hearing almost always result in a guilty verdict, this is not universally the case. The outcome depends, in large part, on the thoroughness of the investigation and the mind-set of the administrator(s) hearing the case. The way the campus code is written may also make a guilty verdict very difficult. Alternatively, there may not be enough evidence to convict the defendant, even when the rules of evidence are more flexible.

Even if the defendant is found guilty, he may receive an extremely light sentence (for example, 30 hours of community service). Additionally, the victim often has to face harassment by other students on campus who believe that she was not really raped, that it was her fault, that she is ruining the assailant's life, or that it was not "that big a deal." She may also be harassed by the assailant or his friends, especially if the former is a member of a fraternity that stands to be sanctioned if he is found guilty. Fear of this kind of harassment is more likely if the victim is on a small campus, where students tend to know almost everyone and everything that occurs on campus. All of these factors may contribute to reluctance on the part of women to report campus sexual assault....

PUBLIC ATTITUDES ABOUT ACQUAINTANCE RAPE

The role of public opinion in general, and the influence of highly publicized cases of sexual assault in particular, help to shape the way campus sexual assault is viewed. This article is about the problem of campus sexual assault in general, and those cases resulting in civil suits are but one small segment of the cases that occur. Case studies that did not occur on a college campus, involving the campus judicial process, or result in civil litigation are also included here if they are celebrated and have played a major role in developing societal attitudes about acquaintance rape. Examples of such cases include the William Kennedy Smith and Mike Tyson rape trials and the confirmation hearings for Clarence Thomas's appointment to the Supreme Court. Each of these events took place within a 12-month period early in the 1990s and were instrumental in shaping public opinion about "real rape" and attitudes blaming the victim.

We have learned a great deal about how the American public views rape, sexual assault, and sexual harassment involving acquaintances from cases that have received wide publicity. The victim is held to a higher standard than is the assailant; her testimony must be perfectly consistent and impeccable. She is blamed for her behavior if she has been drinking, and for not being able to stop him. His drinking behavior, on the other hand, excuses his sexual needs. ("He couldn't stop himself"; "He got carried away.")

Most people in our culture are socialized to believe rape myths. Rape myths allow us to believe that a "real rape" is one in which a victim is raped by a stranger who jumps out of the bushes with a weapon, and in which she fought back, was beaten and bruised, reported the event to the police, and had medical evidence collected immediately. In a "real rape," the victim has never had sex with the assailant before, is preferably a virgin, was not intoxicated, was not wearing seductive clothing, and has a good reputation. If a rape occurred under these circumstances, most people would agree that the woman was indeed raped. Unfortunately, acquaintance sexual assaults contain few, if any, of these elements. In many acquaintance rape situations the victim had been drinking, did voluntarily go with the man to his apartment or room, was not threatened with a weapon, did not fight back, did not report the event to the police immediately, did not have medical evidence collected, and may have even had sex with the assailant voluntarily before.

In many of the highly publicized cases of 1990 and 1991, the verdict was simply based on the man's word against the woman's.

It is a matter of whom we believe and why. Societal messages have suggested that men must always be ready and willing to have sex, that a woman who says "no" never means it, and that sex is a man's right if he spent money on the date (Muehlenhard et al., 1985). Some men also feel that a woman is asking for sex if she gets drunk, goes to a man's apartment, or asks him over to hers. These ideas are in stark contrast to the legal definitions of rape and sexual assault in the United States. Most states have laws that define rape as a situation in which sexual intercourse is forced on one person by another against the victim's will and without the victim's consent, or if the victim submits out of fear for his or her safety or life. In theory, the victim does not have to say "no" more than once, and does not have to explain why he or she wants the offender to stop. Many people, however, do not believe that an event was rape if the woman is not bruised and hysterical, and if the offender was not a stranger (Burt, 1980, Johnson, 1985). Legally, these factors do not have to be present for a sexual assault to have occurred.

In some cases, members of society believe that the victim should have known better, such as in the Mike Tyson case. Even though Tyson was convicted of rape and sexual assault, the behavior of his victim, Desiree Washington, was still questioned, and victim-blaming statements were abundant. Many of the following comments were made by people who disbelieved the victim. Why did she go up to his hotel room unescorted? She must have known of his reputation. He was reported as having sexually harassed beauty pageant contestants earlier that day, and she surely must have seen that. In reality, most women have a hard time believing that men they know would hurt them if they have never hurt them before. If attacked, women often have a difficult time defending themselves against most men. In the case of the former heavyweight boxing champion of the world, she could never have fought her way out if he behaved inappropriately.

Tyson's reputation as a man who had previously been involved in sexual violence was very different from that of William Kennedy Smith, who was a physician and a member of a very influential family. Desiree Washington's background (as a pillar of the community, an upstanding member of her church, and a member of the National Honor Society) was very different from that of Smith's accuser, Patti Bowman. Bowman had obviously had sex before (because she was a mother) and was drinking in a bar where she met Smith. Undoubtedly, racial factors were also a likely contributor to Tyson's conviction, in contrast to the acquittal in the William Kennedy Smith trial.

The public often assumes that victims will make false accusations for some kind of personal gain. Anita Hill was accused of making up charges against Clarence Thomas because she was either a woman scorned, emotionally imbalanced, looking for a movie or book contract and a way to become famous, or a pathological liar. Patricia Bowman, the woman who accused William Kennedy Smith of rape, was portrayed as a "wild girl" with a "taste for glitz" by the media. Sexual assault and rape victims are often charged by public opinion with trying to ruin a man's life; when a public figure is charged, the victim is viewed as being out for fame and fortune as well.

College students are aware of news events of this nature, and one can assume that they are influenced by them. Potential rapists may believe that they can rape with impunity as long as they choose the right kind of victim.

Victims are likely to have learned the lesson that there are many factors, unrelated to the sexual assault, that will have bearing on whether their cases will be treated seriously. If victims do decide to report the assault, they must know that their chances of a conviction are not good, and that their chances of being further harassed and blamed are high. Current and highly publicized cases will undoubtedly have an important impact on the number of sexual assaults committed and the number of cases reported to authorities, both on and off the campus.

REFERENCES

Biden, J. (1991) *Violence against Women: The Increase in Rape in 1990* (Washington, DC: Committee on the Judiciary, United States Senate).

Bird, L. (1991) "Psycho-social and environmental predictors of sexually assaultive attitudes and behaviors among American college men," PhD dissertation at the University of Arizona.

Brownmiller, S. (1975) *Against Our Will: Men, Women and Rape* (New York: Simon and Schuster).

Burkhart, B. (1983) "Acquaintance rape statistics and prevention," paper presented at the Acquaintance Rape and Prevention on Campus Conference in Louisville, KY.

Burkhart, B. R. and Stanton, A. L. (1985) "Sexual aggression in acquaintance relationships," in G. Russel (ed.), *Violence in Intimate Relationships* (New York: Spectrum Press).

Burt, M. (1980) "Cultural myths and supports for rape," *Journal of Personality and Social Psychology*, 38: 217–30.

Burt, M. (1991) "Rape myths and acquaintance rape," in A. Parrot and L. Bechhofer (eds), *Acquaintance Rape: The Hidden Crime*, pp. 26–40 (New York: John Wiley and Sons).

Collison, M. (1992) "A Berkeley scholar clashes with feminists over validity of their research on date rape," *Chronicle of Higher Education*, February 26.

Cooper, Dean (1992) Personal communication from the dean of students, Clarkson College, October 15.

Estrich, S. (1987) *Real Rape: How the Legal System Victimizes Women who Say No* (Cambridge, MA: Harvard University Press).

Forer, Lois (1991) Personal communication, March 18.

Garrett-Gooding, J. and Senter, R. (1987) "Attitudes and acts of sexual aggression on a university campus," *Sociological Inquiry*, 59: 348–71.

Groth, N. and Birnbaum, H. J. (1979) *Men who Rape* (New York: Plenum Press).

Hannan, K. E. and Burkhart, B. (1994) "The typography of violence in college men: frequency, and comorbidity of sexual and physical aggression," *Journal of College Student Psychotherapy*.

Hoffman, R. (1986) "Rape and the college athlete: part one," *Philadelphia Daily News*, March 17, p. 104.

Johnson, K. M. (1985) *If You are Raped* (Holmes Beach, FL: Learning Publications).

Koss, M. (1991) Keynote address presented at the First International Conference on Sexual Assault on Campus, Orlando, FL.

Koss, M. (1992) "Alcohol, athletics, and the fraternity rape connection," paper presented at the Second International Conference on Sexual Assault on Campus, Orlando, FL.

Koss, M. P., Gidicz, C. A., and Wisniewski, N. (1987) "The scope of rape: incidence and prevalence of sexual aggression and victimization in a national sample of higher education students," *Journal of Consulting and Clinical Psychology*, 55(2): 162–70.

Malamuth, N. and Dean, C. (1991) "Attraction to sexual aggression," in A. Parrot and L. Bechhofer (eds), *Acquaintance Rape: The Hidden Crime* (New York: John Wiley & Sons).

Muehlenhard, C. L., Friedman, D. E., and Thomas, C. M. (1985) "Is date rape justifiable? The effects of dating activity, who initiated, who paid, and man's attitudes toward women," *Psychology of Women Quarterly*, 9(3): 297–310.

O'Sullivan, C. (1991) "Acquaintance gang rape on campus," in A. Parrot and L. Bechhofer (eds), *Acquaintance Rape: The Hidden Crime*, pp. 140–56 (New York: John Wiley and Sons).

Parrot, A. (1985) "Comparison of acquaintance rape patterns among college students in a large co-ed university and a small women's college," paper presented at the Annual Meeting of the Society for the Scientific Study of Sex, San Diego, CA.

Parrot, A. (1992) "A comparison of male and female sexual assault victimization experiences involving alcohol," paper presented at the Annual Meeting of the Society for the Scientific Study of Sex, San Diego, CA.

Parrot, A. (1993) *Coping with Date Rape and Acquaintance Rape*, 2nd edn. (New York: Rosen).

Parrot, A. and Bechhofer, L. (eds) (1991) *Acquaintance Rape: The Hidden Crime* (New York: John Wiley & Sons).

Parrot, A. and Lynk, R. (1983) "Acquaintance rape in a college population," paper presented at the Eastern Regional Meeting of the Society for the Scientific Study of Sex, Philadelphia, PA.

Polonko, K., Parcell, S., and Teachman, J. (1986) "A methodological note on sexual aggression," paper presented at the National Convention of the Society for the Scientific Study of Sex, St Louis, MO.

Rapaport, R. R. and Posey, D. (1991) "Sexually coercive college males," in A. Parrot and L. Bechhofer (eds), *Acquaintance Rape: The Hidden Crime* (New York: John Wiley & Sons).

Sanday, P. (1990) *Fraternity Gang Rape* (New York: New York University Press).

Tierney, B. (1984) "Gang rape on college campuses," *Response to Violence in the Family and Sexual Assault*, 7(2): 1–2.

Walters, J., McKellar, A., Lyston, M., and Karme, L. (1981) "What are the pros and cons of coed dorms?" *Medical Aspects of Human Sexuality,* 15(8): 48–56.

QUESTIONS

1. Who are most frequently the victims and assailants in cases of campus sexual assault? What factors, according to the authors, are most commonly associated with incidents of campus rape and assault?
2. How can you tell if someone consents to sex? Must consent be verbal? Why or why not? Do you think men and women have different perceptions of what consent means? Why or why not?
3. What myths surround campus sexual assault? How has this article expanded your thinking about this issue?
4. How should a college respond to complaints of campus sexual assault? Should colleges have legal responsibility and jurisdiction over crimes on their property? Why or why not?

ADDICTIVE LOVE AND ABUSE (1991)

Ginny NiCarthy

Love is a deeply entrenched cultural ideal in American society—television, cinema and literature abound with tales of couples falling in love or tormented by love that has been lost. But what, specifically, is love? And is it always a positive, healthy experience? In an attempt to clarify these questions, the following article, taken from Dating Violence: Young Women in Danger, *presents the differences between nurturing love and love that is destructive.*

Nurturing, Romantic and Addictive Love

Love has been described in many ways, but for purposes of this discussion, it is useful to distinguish among nurturing, romantic and addictive love relationships. Conceptions about these types of love informed our work and added to our discussions during the course, although they were not presented formally to the students.

Nurturing Love

Nurturing love incorporates a wish that the loved person will grow and flourish, developing her or his fullest potential. This implies that each partner encourages the other's pleasure in additional close friendships as well as satisfactions in independent activities. A partner is even capable of accepting the other's wishes if he or she wants to reduce the degree of intimacy between them. If the relationship ends before one partner is ready, he or she will experience grief, but not self-destructive devastation.

Romantic Love

In romantic love, everything about the relationship or the loved one is filtered through a screen that makes it seem perfect. Songs, stories, films and advertising insist that there is one person in the universe who is just right for each of us and that we'll know this person is *the one* the instant we set eyes on him or her. When we think we have found that person, unattractive or threatening traits are simply not recognized. Others are redefined or reevaluated so that they seem like positive characteristics. "Selfish," "stubborn," or "thoughtless" become "independent," "determined" or "poetically absent-minded." "Possessive" becomes "devoted."

This process is enhanced by the lovers' determination to put only the best foot forward. It is exacerbated when immediate sexual involvement confounds sex with love and, even more, when resistance to even brief separations is interpreted as proof of true love. Sooner or later disillusionment is sure to follow.

In most cases, the desire for extreme "togetherness" and suspension of critical faculties gradually diminish on the part of one or both partners. The type of relationship that develops over time may depend upon how the couple handles the period that follows this "honeymoon" state. At this point, the relationship can evolve into a nurturing or an addictive one. At best it develops into deeper, more complex, mutual appreciation—perhaps with romantic interludes. It includes recognition and acceptance of each other's limitations.

Addictive Love

Addictive love is a learned habit, not a disease. It is a habit handed down from one generation to another. Women, even more than men, have been socialized in Western societies to believe they cannot have a full life without one special partner. (Until very recent times, that partner has been assumed to be a person of the opposite sex.) Economic and domestic roles are designed to make women financially dependent on men. Women have been defined as the emotional sex, the ones who nurture intimacy and "need" romantic partners. Men are assumed to manage quite well without the love of an intimate partner. Thus women get the idea they are lucky to have a man who will *let* them love him. They believe men do not really need them. As women grow older, some realize how little these beliefs resemble reality. But teens are especially susceptible to dichotomous views of male and female roles. Even among many adult women, dependency on men is seen as both natural and practical, and economic and emotional dependency have become confounded.

Numerous societal forces come together to encourage women in a dependent love (addiction) long before they are of an age to commit to a man. Much has changed in the past thirty years, but assumptions about "true love" die hard. In this society it is still "normal," even admirable, for a woman to give up many things for the sake of her man (or her children and other family members). In fact, a woman who places her career or other interests ahead of her intimate relationships is considered selfish or overly ambitious. (Although small changes have begun, men are admired for sacrificing everything to their work in order to support their families—to be "responsible breadwinners.")

A couple is in for serious trouble if one or both believe they cannot survive without the other, whether because they fear loss of love or of security. The desire to be together every minute develops into a need or demand for the partner to be continually available. Addiction implies an urge far beyond desire. The refrain in the addicted person's mind becomes a variation on "I'll die if he doesn't call me," "I can't live without her," "She's everything to me." The words of popular songs provide numerous examples of those sentiments, although in everyday conversation they may be expressed in less histrionic language, especially by people in midlife and by men.

When men become addicted, they are often adept at hiding it from their partners—and even from themselves. Because dependence does not fit with a "manly" image, addicted men are less likely than women to admit to being "hooked." A man may claim he does not need his woman, yet insist she has no right to "neglect" him; he may say she is uncaring, unfeminine and selfish; he may frequently threaten to leave her. His demands are expressed in terms of control and criticism rather than admission of his need.

Signs of Addictive Love Include the Following:

- A conviction that the loved person is needed for survival.
- Diminishing numbers of happy, stimulating, interesting or satisfying experiences with the partner, compared with the time spent in recrimination, apologies, promises, anger, guilt and fear of displeasing.
- A reduction in feelings of self-worth and self-control on the part of the addicted person.
- An increasingly contingent way of life; that is, all plans hinge on the partner's availability.
- A reduced capacity to enjoy the time away from the partner; a sense of marking time until he or she is available.
- Frequently breaking promises to limit dependency on the partner: "I won't call him," "I won't insist she account for her time since I last saw her," "I won't wait for the phone to ring."
- A feeling of never being able to get enough of the loved one.
- Increasing efforts to control the partner.

Addiction and Abuse

It is not the addiction that differentiates women who are abused from others. Dependency does not *cause* abuse, and many women addicted to their partners are not abused. Likewise, many abused women are not addicted. (They are afraid to leave for a variety of reasons, not the least of which is terror that the men will follow through on threats to injure or kill them.) But women who *are* addicted to violent partners are especially vulnerable, and doubly at risk because their emotional dependency is an added barrier to escape.

An abusive man takes advantage of an addicted woman's perceived need for him and uses force to control her. The woman's addiction tempts her to ignore or excuse his abusiveness. She fears that any objection she makes will result in abandonment. She equates abandonment with being totally alone in the world, a situation she will do almost anything to avoid. Her failure to resist or leave is perceived by her partner as permission to continue and even escalate his abusive control. Then, whenever he feels an urge to release tension or wants to blame someone else for his inadequacies or the conditions of his life, he uses the addicted woman as a handy target without fear of reprisals.

Paradoxically, the more the man abuses her, the more the woman is likely to think she deserves it. The more she "deserves" it, the less likely it seems that anyone else could care for her. If this man who insists he *loves* her treats her this way, surely, no one else would want her. All these psychological roads lead back to terror of being left and being totally alone.

If the man is also addicted, he may be willing to do anything he can think of to stave off the threat of losing his loved one. He may use techniques that keep women cowed and afraid to assert their own needs. Many men rely on these techniques to gain women's loyalty, and they confuse compliance with loyalty or devotion.

Addiction is not the cause of the abuse. However, as can be seen even from the brief description above, male and female socialization to traditional roles increases tendencies for addicted men to abuse women and for addicted women to be abused by male lovers. Men's presumed independence and dominance and women's supposed passivity and submissiveness play into individual vulnerability to both addiction and abuse.

QUESTIONS

1. What are the characteristics that distinguish healthy love from addictive love? What are some of the signs of addictive love? How can abuse develop from addictive love?
2. Why does our culture concentrate so much on ideal love? Why might this be dangerous to young women? What other social forces make women particularly vulnerable to addictive love?
3. What effects do cultural constructions of love have on men? How can it distort their own experiences in relationships?

INTRODUCTION TO *BODY AND SOUL: THE BLACK WOMEN'S GUIDE TO PHYSICAL HEALTH AND EMOTIONAL WELL-BEING* (1994)

Linda Villarosa

Linda Villarosa recognized the need for a comprehensive health care resource for black women during a conference she attended in the 1980s. Stunned by the traumatic health experiences participants disclosed, Villarosa felt compelled to battle the "conspiracy of silence" affecting black women by offering a publication designed to empower. The underrepresentation of black female doctors, inadequate levels of health insurance, and fewer studies on people of color in medical research contribute to black women's marginalization as patients in the health care system. In this introduction to Body and Soul: The Black Women's Guide to Physical and Emotional Health and Well-Being *(1994), Villarosa insists that good health is about power, intuition and communication. Villarosa is the editor of* Essence *magazine and the co-author of* Finding Our Way: The Teen Girls' Survival Guide *(1995).*

I remember the day I became acquainted with the National Black Women's Health Project. Several years ago I attended a one-day conference sponsored by the New York City chapter called "Empowerment, Health, Reproductive Rights: An Agenda for Women of All Colors." More than two hundred participants showed up early that Saturday morning, people of all ethnicities, men and women, gay and straight, all jammed into the auditorium at John Jay High School in Brooklyn. I settled deep into my seat, notepad in hand, ready to be talked at.

Instead the organizer informed us that we were to divide into race/gender groups, go into separate rooms, and talk about times in our lives when we had felt empowered and healthy and had enjoyed reproductive freedom and times when we had felt the opposite. This seemed like a highly unusual move. This was a conference; I had expected some experts with lots of letters after their names to sit up on the stage and tell me what to think. What did my life and what I felt have to do with an agenda for reproductive rights?

There were about fifty of us in my group, which was one of two groups of Black women. Before anyone spoke, we sat together in a circle, quietly getting to know one another. I looked around at the beautiful, calm, intelligent faces and hoped I would make some new friends.

But I was unprepared for what was about to happen. One sister jumped in with the first of many tales of disempowerment. She had had to be rushed to the emergency room because blood was gushing from her vagina. She begged the doctors to remove the IUD that was imbedded in her tissue, but they refused. Hysterical, she yanked the IUD out herself, causing pain more excruciating than she had ever felt. "I am now sterile," she said quietly.

"Introduction," by Linda Villarosa, reprinted from *Body and Soul: The Black Women's Guide to Physical Health and Emotional Well-Being.*

Another woman was told that she might have cancer, and that she needed to come into the clinic for tests. With her legs spread on a table and with no anesthetics, a young white doctor cut out a cone-shaped piece of her cervix. When she screamed out in pain and terror, he looked at her and said, "What's that all about? You have no nerve endings there." Retelling the story, she began to sob so hard that two sisters got up to hold her.

Another woman had been raped repeatedly by an angry boyfriend, another had been sexually abused, another had watched her uncle beat her aunt to death, and still another had been sterilized without her consent.

I was stunned by the pain that lay behind the faces of these serene, intelligent women. I volunteered to be the historian for the group, needing a task to distance myself from the grief that was being deposited in the room. When it was my turn to speak, I felt subdued and constrained, overwhelmed by what I had heard from the other sisters. Haltingly, I talked about my mother, how I felt blessed to have learned about my body, sex, sexuality, and reproduction from her at an early age. At ten, I was unbearably embarrassed to have to listen to her, but she forced me to sit still and made sure I understood. After I told the story, I began to cry, no longer able to hold back the sorrow I felt for the other women. The sister next to me held my hand until it stopped shaking.

Yet when I left that room, rather than feeling sad, I felt empowered, proud to be in the company of survivors. I will never forget that day; the emotions I experienced as I listened to the sisters share will stay with me for the rest of my life. But it made me think about what NBWHP founder Byllye Avery calls our conspiracy of silence. Most of the women in the room had never felt safe enough to share those experiences with anyone, and maybe they never have again.

I think of how the conspiracy existed among the women in my life. Because we never talked about our "personal business." At age thirty-six, my mother went into the hospital to get her tubes tied. But during the operation, the surgeon punctured one of her ureters and severed the other. She ended up having a hysterectomy, needed another operation, and had to be hospitalized for three months. For three more months she had to wear a bag strapped to each thigh to collect urine that couldn't be collected into the bladder. It took me years to ask my mother why she needed a hysterectomy in the first place or how she felt. Why hadn't I ever asked her if she was angry about the two large scars that stretch across her belly? When we finally talked about her ordeal, she said that she had been terrified she would die and wouldn't be able to raise my sister and me.

When I was a teenager, my grandmother used to ask me to massage the pain out of her hip, but it wasn't until she died that I found out she had suffered through months of excruciating bone cancer. She had put off going to the hospital because she didn't want to die before she could attend my high school graduation. She never shared her sadness or her fear of dying. Eventually I talked to my mother about it, and she told me that my grandmother had also had breast cancer and had had to have a breast removed. She also had an illegal abortion in the 1940s. I had never known.

Last year I read an essay my best friend wrote and learned that as a little girl, she had endured seven years of sexual abuse. I felt sad and ashamed to realize that I hadn't known of the anguish and anger she felt over having her childhood stolen from her.

The first large gathering of Black women dealing with health issues was inspired by the need to break this conspiracy of silence. Two simple sentences buried somewhere in a health atlas motivated Byllye Avery to organize the 1983 National Conference on Black Women's Health Issues: "A survey reported that more than half of Black women 18 to 35 years old rated themselves in psychological distress. That distress was rated higher than that of diagnosed mental patients."

That startling finding illustrated the kind of emotional pain so many of us carry with us as we move through our lives and pointed to a conspiracy of silence so many Black women have when it comes to our personal and health problems. The conference was organized to give sisters permission to talk about how we felt—physically, emotionally, and spiritually—and to understand that there is no shame in being afraid, no shame in reaching out to grasp another woman's hand for support. It was also created so that we could develop our own approaches to healing ourselves, rather than having some great white father somewhere deciding what is best for us.

From the energy and ideas generated by that conference the National Black Women's Health Project (NBWHP) was born. It began in 1983 as a few scattered self-help support groups in Atlanta, Philadelphia, and New York, arranging for three or more

Black women to meet monthly to "take the stress off." There are now nearly 150 such groups around the country and throughout the world. With the women trained by the Project to guide themselves, the discussions range from rapes and abuse the women have quietly suffered to how to do a breast self-examination and where to get a Pap smear.

But even as hundreds of thousands of us have torn down that invisible wall of silence, many problems remain.

- Black women live fewer years than white women.
- Our breast cancer is caught later, and we are more likely to die from it.
- The majority of women and children infected with HIV disease are Black.
- Our children are more likely to be born small, and they die more frequently before reaching one year of age.
- We have heart disease at younger ages, a heart attack is more likely to prove fatal, and we have twice as many cases of high blood pressure as whites.
- Nearly 50 percent of us are overweight.
- We are more likely to smoke, and we are less likely to quit than white women.
- We have higher rates of sexually transmitted infection and pelvic inflammatory disease.
- Over half of us have been beaten, been raped, or survived incest.

As I looked at these statistics, I thought about how little had changed since that first Black women's health conference in 1983. With this thought in mind, I drove up to Pennsylvania to talk to Byllye Avery. I needed to ask her what we can do—as individual Black women and collectively—to change this.

As we sat in Byllye's home surrounded by her beautiful African artifacts in a room painted her favorite color—purple—I realized the first thing we can do: Find our spiritual homes. Make the places where we live reflect ourselves, so that whatever healing needs to be done can begin. Fill it with people who affirm who we are and respect what we need to do with our lives.

Byllye and I spent the next few hours talking about ourselves and our sisters. Too many Black women are like empty wells that never get replenished. We give and give, but get little back. Many of us are dying inside. Unless we are able to go inside, to touch ourselves, to breathe fire and life into ourselves, we can never be healthy or even know what good health feels like.

Good health starts with self-esteem. In order to be healed, we must all believe that we are worthy of it. We must love and trust ourselves and know that feeling good is something we deserve and we can have.

Good health is about power. We have the power to understand how our bodies work and how they feel, and we are empowered to heal our bodies and our souls. Too often we don't know the power we have within ourselves. Instead we give up that power to other people. We need to stop letting doctors get away with piling up all this money, buying all these machines. All this foolishness is putting money back into their pockets on the treatment end instead of the prevention end. This can stop only when we take care of ourselves and avoid the illnesses that keep the medical system in business.

Good health is about intuition. That means being in tune with everything and everyone around us. In this scientific world we don't give credence to the idea that our intuition can lead us to the right place. When faced with health challenges, we must collect all the information, talk to all the doctors, and then go inside ourselves and take direction from our inner voices. We have to believe in ourselves and believe in our ability to make the decision that will lead to healing.

Finally, good health is about talking. We can no longer afford to participate in silence. We have to talk to our children about their bodies and their sexuality. We have to talk to our men to let them know that when they hurt us, they hurt themselves. And we have to talk to each other, to be willing to share our stories, rather than pretend that we haven't had to struggle or face challenges. With talking goes listening, sitting quietly, and understanding and learning from the experience of other women.

I still struggle when I have to talk about myself and how I feel. When I can't make the words come out of my mouth, I put them on paper. That's what this book has been about for me and for all of the women who worked on it. It is written by Black women, for Black women as a way for all of us to grow and learn as we work to improve our personal and collective health.

Reading this book may be your first step toward good health or one of many steps in a long journey. Take this information and use it. This book is no more than you're willing to put into it. Take it with you to the doctor. Share it with a friend or neighbor. Discuss it with your daughter or your mother. Talk about it in your support group.

We couldn't cover every subject about Black women's health in depth here, but where we fall short we've provided the titles of books you can read and the names of organizations with phone numbers and addresses for you to contact.

As you read this book, look for yourself on each page and in the experiences of other women. Examine your reactions, attitudes, and feelings to the things you read. What are you willing to do to make changes in your life, in order to be a different, more healthy person physically, emotionally, and spiritually? Are you willing to clean your mind and your body of whatever is holding you back?

This book should be part of your growth. There is no such thing as being grown up, because we are in a continual process of growth. You will be in a different place after you read this book. Make that a place where your healing can begin. Imagine that place bathed in your favorite colors and covered in bright African fabric. It is yours, and you deserve it.

—LINDA VILLAROSA
Brooklyn, New York

QUESTIONS

1. What common experiences emerged among conference participants? Why might some Black women feel so uncomfortable talking about their health problems? How has the "conspiracy of silence" affected Black women's health care and their feelings about health?

2. Why might Black women need a separate resource manual specific to their needs, or a separate space to discuss health care issues? What might be the difference between health care "access" and "equity"?

3. How do the elements of good health that Villarosa presents expand your thinking about health? How can Black women work to empower themselves in the health care system?

Social and Cultural Reasons for Abuse (1985)

Myrna Zambrano

A variety of myths persist concerning why women are victims of domestic battery. In the following brief selection, Myrna Zambrano, a graduate of Yale University and a counselor for battered women, presents ten of these myths, describes their flaws, and offers a more accurate portrait of the circumstances surrounding domestic abuse.

Is It True What They Say About Battered Women?

People say many things about why women are beaten by their husbands or boyfriends. You may have heard that it's because the family is poor, or the woman has a job and isn't home, or because she is not very smart. But women of *all* cultures and races, of all income levels, and of all personalities can be and are physically and emotionally abused by the men they are involved with. Most of what is said about battered women is meant to excuse behavior that is violent, irrational, and illegal. Most of what is said is cleverly designed to get around the basic fact that one person beating another is wrong and cannot be excused. Most of it also blames the person being beaten instead of the person doing the beating. But why should the men be protected and the women blamed? When people, or the men themselves, try to make excuses for the violence or blame women as the cause, they are denying and ignoring a very serious, complex problem. Perhaps worse, they perpetuate "myths" about domestic violence—false ideas and false reasons why men abuse women (and why women should accept it as natural) that circulate throughout society in movies, magazines, bars and beauty salons until they are so widespread that no one questions them and everyone believes they are true. The most terrible and untruthful thing is that these myths make abused women believe that it is all their fault and that they can control the violence if they really want to.

Don't believe these myths—they are false. They don't change or help the situation, they allow it to get worse. They let men get away with cruelty and brutality, and make women fearful and submissive. Instead of believing what people say, you can learn some of the facts about domestic violence that can help to change your anger and frustration into action and fulfillment.

Myths and Realities

Myth #1 Battered women like it or else they would leave.

False. No one likes being threatened, slapped, shoved, thrown around, choked, hit or kicked. But it is difficult to leave a man who is your only support, or who has sworn to kill you if you leave. It is difficult to leave if you don't know where to go and have children to think about and provide for. A woman doesn't stay in a violent relationship because she likes it, she stays because many times pressure from her family, church and community leaves her feeling she has few, if any, alternatives.

Myth #2 If the battered woman sticks it out long enough, the relationship will change for the better.

False. If the woman doesn't leave, get legal help or counseling, the beatings and mental torture are likely to get worse, not better. Many women stay hoping the abuse will eventually stop. Some finally leave when the violence is so bad they want to kill the abuser or know that the next time he will kill them. It's dangerous to wait until this point of desperation; almost half of all women killed in the United States are killed by their boyfriends or husbands.[1]

Myth #3 If he didn't drink he wouldn't beat his wife or partner.

False. Although in many relationships alcohol appears to provoke or encourage violent behavior, women are physically abused by men who are sober and by men who don't drink. Alcohol is just a part of the reason he hits. At times the alcohol gives men a false sense of power. It cannot be said that it is the only cause, or that if he stops drinking the beating will stop.

Myth #4 Women deserve to be beaten because of the way they behave.

False. No one deserves to be beaten no matter what she does. Women who are beaten know only too well that it happens most of the time for no reason at all. If the dinner is served late she gets beaten, if she serves dinner on time she gets beaten. He is never pleased or satisfied with anything she does. His anger and his desire to have total control are the causes of his outbursts, not her actions.

Myth #5 If he works, is a good provider, and good with the children, a woman shouldn't ask for more. She should tolerate some of his character defects.

False. A husband who is good with the kids and brings home a paycheck shouldn't be excused from violent behavior. *Violence in the home shouldn't be tolerated under any circumstances.* The wife deserves to be well-treated, just like any member of the family. No one would approve of staying with a man because he only beat the children!

Myth #6 Battering doesn't affect the children. They are just kids and don't notice these things.

False. Battering most definitely affects children. In fact, a high percentage of men who are batterers saw their own mothers beaten.[2] Battering can be learned. It is very possible that if your children witness beatings, they too will grow up to be batterers or the victims of abuse. Also, living in the midst of an explosive situation frequently contributes to learning and personality problems in children. Although kids may not talk about the violence, they know it exists, and it has a deep impression on them.

Myth #7 This is God's will and no one should interfere.

False. God may plan for much of what happens in our lives, but he would never plan for a woman to be regularly beaten by her partner. We may not be able to avoid something like a fatal disease or the death of a child, but what control we do have over our lives can be used to help stop the violence. It is far more likely that it is God's will that we live in peace and harmony than in the middle of violence.

Myth #8 Yes, women shouldn't be beaten, but what goes on in a home is no one else's business.

False. Domestic violence is everyone's problem. Women are maimed and killed every day. Physical assault is wrong and it is illegal. We are all responsible for its end. Your husband has no more right to harm you than a stranger, who would be convicted and sent to jail if he beat you or tried to rape you in your home.

Myth #9 If women would fight back, men wouldn't keep on beating them.

False. Even if women do fight back they are beaten, sometimes even more severely. Most women are physically smaller than most men and no match when it comes to a fist fight.

Myth #10 Battering is a problem of the poor and uneducated.

False. Battering is a crime against women that affects *all* communities. Abused women can be rich or poor; they can be white, Black, or Latina; they can have a high school education or a college degree. Although you may know only of poor women who are beaten, wealthy women are also victims of domestic violence. These women usually have more resources to keep their bruises from public view. They can see private doctors instead of emergency rooms, they can consult lawyers instead of legal aid, they may live in less crowded areas where people don't hear what's going on. They are less likely to ask for help from public agencies and are better able to keep their problems private. Admitting you are being battered does not show you are poor or uneducated. It says that you are being taken advantage of physically and mentally and that your partner needs immediate help. The violence in your home should not be a shameful secret that keeps you from getting help. [1985]

REFERENCE

1. R. E. Dobash, R. Dobash, *Violence Against Wives: A Case Against the Patriarchy,* The Free Press, 1979, page 17.
2. M. Straus, R. Gellis, S. Steinmetz, *Behind Closed Doors: Violence in the American Family,* Anchor Press, 1980, p. 100.

QUESTIONS:

1. What are some of the myths Zambrano presents about victims of domestic abuse? What are some of the myths about the causes of abuse? What role does alcohol play? According to Zambrano, what role do class and race play in domestic abuse?
2. What are some of the consequences of these myths for female victims? Given the myths/realities presented here, why might it be difficult for women to seek help?

Study Says Equality Eludes Most Women in Law Firms (1996)

Nina Bernstein

Although women comprise 50% of students in many law schools and the number of female lawyers has increased, widespread gender inequities continue to plague the legal profession. Nina Bernstein, a journalist for the New York Times, *scrutinizes the troubling findings from a recent American Bar Association study undertaken to evaluate women's progress in the legal profession.*

Despite surging numbers of female lawyers, bias against women remains entrenched in the legal profession and results in steep inequities of pay, promotion and opportunity, according to an American Bar Association panel's report, the first of its kind in eight years.

"We expected that our evaluation would yield evidence of steady progress," said Laurel G. Bellows, a Chicago lawyer and chairwoman of the Commission on Women in the Profession, which produced the report. "Our predictions were, unfortunately, too optimistic. Now, we must say that the passage of time and number of women is not going to cure this problem."

Though women now sit on the Supreme Court, head the Justice Department and preside over the bar association itself, the stubborn barriers faced by rank and file female lawyers are reflected in pay disparities at every level of experience and in all types of legal practice, the report found. And in the profession's highest echelons, in law firm partnerships, law school faculties and on the bench, the percentage of women, while increasing, remains inexcusably low, the report says, when measured against huge increases in the numbers of qualified women.

In many respects, commission members noted, the findings fly in the face of a perception among male lawyers that the professional playing field has not merely been leveled, but has tilted in favor of women, who now comprise about 23 percent of all the nation's lawyers and nearly half of all law students.

This perception was voiced repeatedly in a male focus group at the A.B.A.'s midyear meeting in Miami, said the organization's former president William W. Falsgraf, a Cleveland lawyer who was vice chairman of the first A.B.A. Commission on Women in the Profession.

He said of the men: "Particularly the younger ones were saying, 'This has gone far enough,' and, 'We're having a heck of a time finding jobs in the law, and if we even find them they're not very good and it's time to stop giving one group of people special consideration because we're all in trouble.'"

But studies cited by the commission suggest that in fact, women have been disproportionately hurt by the recent shrinking of law firms after a rapid expansion in the 1980s. A 1995 study of eight large New York City firms, for example, found that promotion rates for women, which were already lower than the rates for men, dropped to 5 percent from 15 percent among those who were hired after 1981 and were considered for partnership in the recessionary 1990s. Promotion rates for their male counterparts declined less, to 17 percent, from 21 percent.

Especially troubling to the commission are signs that while job opportunities are shrinking, even the slow and uncertain progress that has been made is being eroded in some areas by a resentful backlash or persistent stereotypes. From law schools come reports of women whose performance has suffered because of a resurgence of overt male hostility that recalls the early 1970's, when only 3 percent of law students were female. Income comparisons, notably a 1993 analysis by local bar associations in Colorado, suggest that though male and female lawyers now start out with equal pay, an earnings gap opens in the first year of practice and widens rapidly.

Among Colorado lawyers with only one to three years of experience, for example, the average annual income was $30,806 for women but $37,500 for men. For those with 10 to 20 years of experience, women averaged 76 percent as much as men, or $68,466 to the men's $90,574. And even as women increasingly replace men as chief legal officers of Fortune 500 companies, national surveys show female corporate counsels earning less than their male counterparts at every level of seniority, with pay gaps that range as high as 35 percent.

"What it suggests is not a glass ceiling at the end, but a process that begins right off the bat, and we're not facing that as a profession yet," said Kathleen Donnell, a veteran Denver lawyer who analyzed the Colorado data.

There are bright spots in the report. To date, a record 31.5 percent of President Clinton's appointments to the Federal bench were women, and over all his nominees received higher ratings for their qualifications than those of previous administrations. The Department of Justice is cited as a leader in cre ating a hospitable workplace for women, offering part-time work, job-sharing, flexible schedules and on-site child care.

"Equal opportunity for women in the law is important to all of society." Hillary Rodham Clinton, who was chairwoman of the A.B.A.'s first commission on women in 1987, said after being given an advance copy of the report on Friday. "Hopefully, the Administration is leading by example."

Jamie S. Gorelick, President Clinton's appointee as Deputy Attorney General, who spent 18 years in private practice, is not surprised that so many women are drawn to government service. Currently, they comprise 35 percent of the executive branch's 25,000 lawyers.

"In Government we don't have any minds and talents to waste, unlike the private sector," she said. "There's an opportunity for women to show their stuff and I think that alone will have an enormous effect on the private marketplace."

But the commission report is less optimistic. In the private sector, it notes, very few lawyers—1 to 4 percent—dare to take advantage of the "family friendly" policies adopted by most law firms in the last decade. Those who do often are tarred as not seriously committed to the law.

Even women who have demonstrated their commitment for a decade or more often face a combination of crude and subtle barriers to advancement, like the partner at a large national law firm whose commercial real estate client celebrated the success of a two-year leasing project she had directed by taking her male colleagues to a topless bar. Exclusion from male networks, reinforces the belief that women are less effective as "rain makers," lawyers who can bring in business—a belief used in turn to skew promotion evaluations against them, the commission found.

The gulf between visible progress and persistent bias is captured in studies of law schools in Chicago and Philadelphia that found classes in which women are effectively silenced by male students who heckle them as "femi-Nazis" and overwhelmingly male faculty who ignore them. One male professor in Chicago told students in a discussion of a Supreme Court opinion written by Justice Sandra Day O'Connor that it was written by a woman and "women always change their minds."

Estelle D. Rodgers, a commission member, said, "The status of women in the profession has changed surprisingly little in very important ways that affect people's real lives."

She recalled the testimony of a woman at the first commission hearings in 1988 who described going into labor at her top flight law firm in the middle of an important meeting with Japanese clients and making her presentation between contractions for fear of losing her credibility. Ms. Rodgers, now a lawyer with the American Civil Liberties Union in Washington, graduated from law school in 1973 and left a large private firm for public interest work after the birth of her first child in 1978.

Today's young female lawyers say that they are less willing to make extreme personal sacrifices to adapt to a work culture defined by and for white men, and that they expect employers to accommodate their life needs, the report says. But many are coming to a rude awakening.

In the commission's hearings last year a lawyer who was recently the first to give birth in a firm of 100 lawyers described how on her return from a brief, hard-won maternity leave she asked for more regular hours and instead was assigned to write all the litigation team's overnight and weekend motions.

"Once she said she needed more regular hours, a kind of baiting went on," recalled Mary Cranston, the commission's liaison representing large law firms, and herself a partner in San

Francisco's Pillsbury, Madison & Sutro, long a leader in hiring and promoting women.

The good news, the report says, is that women are not giving up. Many who left law firms have formed their own, or gone to corporate law departments where they are gaining the authority to choose which outside lawyers will get company business.

"There's an old girls' network that's starting to develop," Miss Cranston said in a comment echoed across the country.

It is only by taking advantage of the power of their numbers in such ways, the report says, that women lawyers can permanently change the structure of the profession.

Questions

1. What progress is evident from the American Bar Association study? What evidence of gender bias was revealed? Why is it significant that inequities between men and women exist in the legal profession?
2. What is the difference between equity and equality? Why do pay gaps persist even in such a high paying profession? Is the gender bias less significant because it exists in a higher paying profession?
3. If increasing the numbers of women law students and lawyers is insufficient in addressing inequalities, what is the answer?

WHY MARRY? (1996)

Frank Browning

In the following selection from the New York Times, *Frank Browning explores the subjects of "family" and "marriage" within the context of homosexual relationships. Browning broadens the traditional scope of the question, "How is family defined?" by presenting how "family" is understood within gay, lesbian, and bisexual partnerships.*

Thursday morning, and it's my turn to move our cars for street cleaning. Gene has already bribed the cats into silence with food. So begins the day here in Windsor Terrace, a quiet Brooklyn neighborhood populated by many kinds of families: a lesbian couple next door—and beyond them an Italian widow who rents out rooms, an Irish-American grandmother who shares her house with her daughter's family, the multigenerational Korean family that owns the corner grocery.

We gay couples, of course, are not considered families under the law, a fact that the bishops and Buchananites insist will never change and that many gay activists have identified as America's next great civil rights struggle. Indeed, a court case in Hawaii may soon lead to that state's recognition of same-sex marriage.

I suppose it's a good thing for gay adults to be offered the basic nuptial rights afforded to others. We call that equal treatment before the law. But I'm not sure the marriage contract is such a good plan for us.

The trouble with gay marriage is not its recognition of our "unnatural unions." The problem is with the shape of marriage itself. What we might be better off seeking is civic and legal support for different kinds of families that can address the emotional, physical and financial obligations of contemporary life. By rushing to embrace the standard marriage contract, we could stifle one of the richest and most creative laboratories of family experience.

We gay folk tend to organize our lives more like extended families than nuclear ones. We may love our mates one at a time, but our "primary families" are often our ex-lovers and our ex-lovers' ex-lovers.

The writer Edmund White noticed this about gay male life 20 years ago; he called it the "banyan tree" phenomenon, after the tree whose branches send off shoots that take root to form new trunks. Nowhere has the banyan-tree family proved stronger than in AIDS care, where often a large group of people—ex-mates and their friends and lovers—tend the sick and maintain the final watch.

Modern marriage, by comparison, tends to isolate couples from their larger families and sometimes from friends—especially if they are ex-lovers. And a nuclear family with working parents has often proved less than ideal in coping with daily stresses or serious illness.

The marriage model could prove especially problematic for rearing children. In a gay family, there are often three parents—a lesbian couple, say, and the biological father. Sometimes, four or five adults are committed to nurturing the children. In such cases, a marriage between two might bring second-class status to the rest of the extended family and diminish their parental roles.

(Those who think that only a father and mother can successfully raise a child should visit Italy, Japan, Greece, Thailand or American family archives, which show that before World War II, grandparents, aunts, uncles and older siblings had vital child-rearing roles.)

Precisely because homosexuals have resided outside the law, they have invented family forms that respond to late 20th-century needs, while formulating social and moral codes that provide love, freedom and fidelity (if not always monogamy).

All I need do is look up and down Windsor Terrace to see that the family includes all sorts of relationships and obligations.

Each of us, hetero or homo, has a stake in nurturing a diverse landscape of families. Only a minority of us have marriages like Donna Reed's or Harriet Nelson's. Even Pat Buchanan knows that.

QUESTIONS

1. What is Browning's perspective on extending the standard marriage contract to gay, lesbian, and bisexual partnerships? What argument does Browning offer for his perspective?
2. Why does the "banyan tree" phenomenon apply to "family" in gay, lesbian, and bisexual contexts? What benefits and liabilities might the phenomenon create, both for adult participants and for children?

THE MOMMY WARS: HOW THE MEDIA TURNED MOTHERHOOD INTO A CATFIGHT (2000)

Susan Douglas and Meredith Michaels

Professors Susan Douglas and Meredith Michaels analyze representations of "celebrity" mothers in the popular press. Sexy, glamorous, contented, images of wealthy, white mothers such as Christie Brinkley and Kirstie Alley pervade popular magazines and assault readers with a vision of motherhood attainable only by lavish consumerism and extraordinary wealth. In contrast, images of "welfare mothers" demonize women who receive state support, portraying them as complaining and undeserving drains on the economy. The authors argue that these contrasting images construct motherhood as a competition between women—a catfight—in which some women triumph and some women fail because of what appear to be personal inadequacies rather than social and economic barriers. These divisive images also feed our rampant consumer culture in which energetic buying seems the only route to ideal motherhood.

Douglas is a Professor of Communication Studies at the University of Michigan and the author of Where the Girls Are, *an in depth analysis of the impact of the mass media on gender identity and development. Meredith Michaels is a Professor of Philosophy at Smith College and the co-author of* Fetal Subjects, Feminist Positions.

It's 5:22 p.m. You're in the grocery check-out line. Your three-year-old is writhing on the floor, screaming, because you have refused to buy her a Teletubby pinwheel. Your six-year-old is whining, repeatedly, in a voice that could saw through cement, "But mommy, puleeze, puleeze," because you have not bought him the latest Lunchables, which features as the four food groups: chips, a candy bar, fake cheese, and artificial coloring.

To distract yourself, and to avoid the glares of other shoppers who have already deemed you the worst mother in America, you leaf through *People* magazine. Inside, Uma Thurman gushes, "Motherhood is sexy." Moving on to *Good Housekeeping*, Vanna White says of her child, "When I hear his cry at 6:30 in the morning, I have a smile on my face, and I'm not an early riser." Brought back to reality by stereophonic wailing, you feel about as sexy and euphoric as Rush Limbaugh in a thong.

Meanwhile, *Newsweek*, also at the check-out line, offers a different view of motherhood. In one of the many stories about welfare mothers that proliferated until "welfare reform" was passed in 1996, you meet Valerie, 27, and "the three children she has by different absentee fathers." She used to live with her mother, "who, at 42, has six grandchildren." But now Valerie resides with other families, all of whom "live side-by-side in open trash-filled apartments." Hey, maybe you're not such a failure after all.

Motherhood has been one of the biggest media fixations of the past two decades. And this is what so many of us have been pulled between when we see accounts of motherhood in the me-

---

"The Mommy Wars: How the Media Turned Motherhood into a Catfight," by Susan Douglas and Meredith Michaels. Reprinted from *Ms.* Magazine, February/March 2000. pp. 62–67.

dia: celebrity moms who are perfect, most of them white, always rich, happy, and in control, the role models we should emulate, versus welfare mothers who are irresponsible, unmarried, usually black or Latina—as if there were no white single mothers on the dole—poor, miserable, and out of control, the bad examples we should scorn.

Beginning in the late 1970s, with the founding of *People* and *Us*, and exploding with a vengeance in the '90s with *InStyle*, the celebrity-mom profile has spread like head lice through popular magazines, especially women's. "For me, happiness is having a baby," gushed Marie Osmond on a 1983 cover of *Good Housekeeping*, and Linda Evans added in *Ladies' Home Journal*, "All I want is a husband and baby." These celeb biographies, increasingly presented as instruction manuals for how the rest of us should live our lives, began to proliferate just as there was a dramatic rise in the number of women who worked outside the home while raising small children. Pulled between established wisdom—if you worked outside the home before your child entered kindergarten you were bound to raise an ax murderer—and the economic and psychic need to work, many of these mothers were searching for guidance. And celebrity mom magazine articles seemed to provide it.

Celebrity moms were perfect for the times. They epitomized two ideals that sat in uneasy but fruitful alliance. On the one hand, they exemplified the unbridled materialism and elitism the Reagan era had spawned. On the other, they represented the feminist dream of women being able to have a family and a job outside the home without being branded traitors to true womanhood. Magazine editors apparently figured they could use stars to sell magazines and to serve as role models.

But now, in the year 2000, things have gotten out of control. Celebrity moms are everywhere, beaming from the comfy serenity and perfection of their lives as they give multiple interviews about their "miracle babies," what an unadulterated joy motherhood is, and all the things they do with their kids to ensure they will be perfectly normal Nobel laureates by the age of 12. These stories are hardly reassuring. They make the rest of us feel that our own lives are, as the great seventeenth century philosopher Thomas Hobbes put it, nasty, brutish, and short. So why should we care about something so banal as the celebrity mom juggernaut? One answer is that it bulldozed through so much of American popular culture just when working mothers, single mothers, and welfare mothers were identified, especially by conservative male pundits, as the cause of everything bad, from the epidemic of drug use to the national debt to rising crime rates. Remember all the hand-wringing by George Will, William Bennett, and Allan Bloom about America's "moral decay"? The biggest culprit, of course, was the single welfare mother. These guys attacked celebrity single mothers now and then, but the mud never stuck—not even, heaven help us, on that fictional celebrity single mother Murphy Brown.

As the push "to end welfare as we know it" gained momentum and reached its climax in the welfare reform of 1996, the canonized celebrity mom and the demonized welfare mother became ever more potent symbols, working in powerful opposition to each other. We rarely saw these very different mothers in the same publication, or even considered them in the same breath. Celebrity moms graced the covers of magazines designed for self-realization and escape; welfare mothers were the object of endless stories in newspapers and newsmagazines and on the nightly news that focused on public policy and its relation to the tenuous state of morality in America.

But what if we put these portrayals side by side and compare what these different mothers were made to stand for? Could it be that the tsunami of celebrity-mom profiles helped, however inadvertently, to justify punitive policies toward welfare mothers and their children? While the "you can have it all" ethos of these pieces made the rest of us feel like failures as mothers, and upped the ante in the eyes of employers and coworkers about how much working mothers can handle, a little side-by-side reading also exposes some rather daunting hypocrisy. Often, one group is glamorized and the other castigated for precisely the same behavior.

Let's take a look at a celebrity mom first. Kirstie Alley, for example. It's 1994. The star of *Cheers* and the *Look Who's Talking* movies graces the cover of *InStyle*, a magazine that pays fawning tribute to the charming indiosyncrasies and lifestyle choices of our nation's most glamourous. Among Kirstie's recent choices is the purchase of her third house. *InStyle* advises us respectfully that "as with all of her houses, Kirstie paid cash." On a tour of her new Bangor, Maine, retreat (the renovation of which was paid for by a quick voice-over job she did for Subaru), we discover that both Kirstie and her house are "at once down-to-earth and whimsical."

Kirstie must be down-to-earth, of course, because now, at long last, she is a mother. Her "playful sense of style" is made evident by the decoupage grapes that grace her son True's high chair. "It was painted and cracked to make it look old," *InStyle* informs us. (Why not simply rely on natural toddler effluvia to give the chair that petroglyph look?) True has just turned one; his whimsical high chair faces an equally whimsical ceramic pig holding a blackboard on which a new word appears each day to encourage his reading.

In our tour through Kirstie's hideaway, we encounter an entourage—decorators, a nanny, a cook, and various personal assistants. Kirstie spends True's two-hour nap time working out with her personal trainer and then being served a healthful, fat-free lunch by the cook. Lounging in her living room (painted to "echo" the surrounding firs and elms), reflecting on the challenges of motherhood, Kirstie gushes, "Being a mother has given me a whole new purpose. Every day when I wake up it's like Christmas morning to me, and seeing life through True's eyes gives me a whole new way of looking at the world." Perfect house. Perfect husband. Perfect child. Perfect career. Perfect life. Kirstie is a perfect mother. *InStyle* invites you to curl up on the sofa with Kirstie, but then implies that you'd probably just spill your tea on it.

Forward to 1997. There's Kirstie again, now the star of the television series *Veronica's Closet*, beaming at us once more from *InStyle*. "A new man, a new show, a brand-new life," proclaims the cover. Since 1994, her island mansion has "become a place to play." Each of the 15 bedrooms is decorated with Kirstie's "eclectic and playful eye." According to *InStyle*, most people would have found decorating this 16,000-square-foot house daunting, but not Kirstie. "I'm very fast," she explains. "I don't shop. I just point: boom, boom, boom." Having outgrown his high chair, True now has his own miniature lobster boat. In addition, he and his new sister, Lillie, can frolic in their personal nursery-rhyme garden, complete with Mother Goose figures especially commissioned by "fun-loving" Kirstie because, as she puts it, "I hope I give my children a spirit of play."

Kirstie swears by the facial treatment she receives every morning on her terrace as the fog burns off Penobscot Bay. It involves "blasting her face with oxygen and enzymes . . . through a plastic hose hooked up to two pressurized tanks." Though her life was perfect in 1994, she has since set aside her husband, Parker Stevenson, in favor of her "soul mate," James Wilder, who "is a cross between Houdini, Errol Flynn, and Marlon Brando." Apparently Kirstie uses the same technique for choosing her lovers as she does for choosing sofa fabrics. With James, "it was like comet to comet. Boom . . ."

Not that we ought to single out Kirstie (although such self-serving bilge makes it irresistible). Celebrity-mom profiles are almost all alike and haven't changed much over the years, except that the houses and toys are more lavish. Celebrity moms are shown embracing motherhood after years of sweating under klieg lights, which apparently brings them in touch with their true, essential, feminine natures. Most important, motherhood is a powerfully transforming experience, akin to seeing God. It always changes these women, and always for the better. "I feel more enriched and compassionate toward others since having my son," says Elle McPherson.

Ladies' Home Journal tells us that Christie Brinkley's third child, daughter Sailor (her father, Brinkley's fourth husband, is a descendant of Captain Cook), "barely tipping the scale at eight pounds . . . has become Brinkley's anchor, a midlife miracle well worth waiting for." Of her second child, Jack (from her third marriage, which lasted only a few months), Christie was equally lyrical: "It's like I went to hell and came back with this angel."

We assume that most (but not all) of these celebrity moms are not trying to gloat, or to rub our noses in our own poor lifestyle choices (which invariably include the failure to choose being thin, white, gorgeous, and rich). And we've all said mushy things about how much our kids mean to us, especially in the immediate aftermath of birth, before the months of sleep deprivation and projectile vomiting produce a slightly more jaundiced view of the joys of motherhood.

But there's little deviation in the celebrity mom profile: it is a sturdily ossified genre, and those who choose to contribute to it must embody and emphasize certain traits. She is everything that you—poor, stupid, imcompetent slob—are not: serene, resourceful, contented, transformed, perky, fun-loving, talented, nurturing, selfless, organized, spontaneous, thin, fit, pore-free, well-rested, well-manicured, on-the-go, sexy and rich. She has absolutely no ambivalence about motherhood, would prefer to spend all her time with her kids if only she could, and finds that when she comes home from a draining day, her children recharge her as if they were Energizers. She is never furious, hysterical, or uncertain. She is never a bitch. She is June Cleaver with cleavage and a successful career. In a 1997 cover story titled "The New Sexy Moms," *People* told us that "postpartum depression isn't an option for such celebrity moms as Whitney Houston, Madonna, and supermodel Miki Taylor." Being subjected to sleep deprivation and raging hormones was a choice for these women, and they just said no.

The celebrity-mom profile is predicated on the interview, in which we hear extensively from the mother herself. This is a media form designed to showcase the mother's subjective processes and inner life and, thus, to celebrate her distinctive individuality. We're meant to hang on her every word, no matter how banal. She hasn't fallen through the cracks, ended up part of some vast, nameless, harried horde like the rest of us. What makes her such a great mother and enviable person is her ability to take action, make smart choices, and impose discipline on herself while being loving and spontaneous with her kids. The myth of the determined individual, fully capable of vaulting over all sorts of economic, political, and social barriers, is beautifully burnished in these profiles. It's all up to you, if only you'll try, try, and try again. There are no such things in this gauzy world as economic inequalities, institutional sexism, racism, or class privilege. Nor are there tired, pissed-off partners or kids who've just yelled, "I hate you! I wish you were dead!"

Celebrity children don't wreak havoc with work, they enhance it and even fortify their mothers' bargaining position with the boss. Says actress Gigi Rice, "Now, if they want you to do a job, you say, 'well, my baby comes with me.' What are they going to say—no?" In addition, *People* tells us, "Contractually mandated star perks typically include first-class airfare for the entire entourage, a separate trailer for the kiddies and a 24-hour limousine on standby to ferry them wherever they want to go, paid hotel accommodations for the nanny, even a nanny allowance." Sounds just like your workplace, *n'est-ce pas?*

Celebrity moms exemplify what motherhood has become in our intensified consumer culture: a competition. They rekindle habits of mind, pitting women against women, that the women's movement sought to end, leaving the notion of sisterhood in the dust. More perniciously, these portraits resurrect so many of the stereotypes about women we hoped to deep-six 30 years ago: that women are, by genetic composition, nurturing and maternal, that they love all children and prefer motherhood to anything, especially work—so they should be the main ones responsible for raising the kids. In the pages of the glossies, motherhood becomes a contest in which the reader is always the loser. Why do Kirstie and Cindy and Whitney love being mothers in some unequivocal way that you do not? Because they're good and you're bad.

Ah, but you could be worse. What about media motherhood on the other side of the tracks? Celebrity mom profiles place us on the outside looking in; stories about welfare mothers invite us to look down from on high. Welfare mothers have not been the subject of honey-hued profiles in glossy magazines. They are not the subjects of their own lives, but objects of journalistic scrutiny. We don't hear about these women's maternal practices—what they do with their kids to nurture them, educate them, soothe them, or keep them happy. It is simply assumed that these women don't have inner lives. Emotions are not ascribed to them; we don't hear them laugh or see their eyes well up with tears. One of the most frequent verbs used to describe them is "complain," as when they complain about losing health care for their kids when they go off welfare. When they are quoted, it is not their feelings about the transformative powers of motherhood to which we are made privy. Rather, we hear their relentless complaints about "the system." In many articles about welfare, we don't hear from the mothers at all, but instead from academic experts who study them, or from politicians whose careers are devoted to bashing them. The iconography of the welfare mother is completely different, too—she's not photographed holding her child up in the air, whizzing her about. In fact, she's rarely, if ever, shown smiling at all. It's as if the photographer yelled "scowl" just before clicking the shutter.

These mothers are shown as sphinx-like, monolithic, part of a pathetic historical pattern known, familiarly, as "the cycle of dependency." In a major article in *Newsweek* in August 1993 titled "The Endangered Family," we learned that "For many African Americans, marriage and childbearing do not go together." Not to mention the 25 percent of white women for whom they don't go together either, or the celebrity single mothers like Jodie Foster, Madonna, and Farah Fawcett.

It isn't just that the conservative right has succeeded in stereotyping welfare mothers as lazy, promiscuous parasites; the media in which these mothers appear provide no point of identification with them. At best, these mothers are pitiable. At worst, they are reprehensible opposites of the other mothers we see so much of, the new standard-bearers of ideal motherhood—the doting, conscientious celebrities for whom motherhood is a gateway to heaven.

During the height of welfare bashing in the Reagan, Bush, and Clinton administrations, the stereotype of the "welfare queen" gained mythological status. But there were other, less obvious, journalistic devices that served equally well to dehumanize poor mothers and their children. Unsavory designations proliferated with a vengeance: "chronic dependents," "the chronically jobless," "welfare mothers in training," "hardcore welfare recipients," "never-married mothers," "welfare careerists," and "welfare recidivists" became characters in a distinctly American political melodrama. Poor women weren't individuals; instead their life stories became case-studies of moral decay, giving substance to the inevitable barrage of statistics peppering the media's presentation of "Life on the Dole." In publications everywhere, we met the poster mother for welfare reform. She only had a first name, she lived in the urban decay of New York, Chicago, or Detroit, she was not married, she had a pile of kids each with a different absent father, and she spent her day painting her nails, smoking cigarettes, and feeding Pepsi to her baby.

As sociologists have pointed out, even though there consistently have been more white people than black on welfare, the news media began, in the mid-1960s, to rely almost exclusively on pictures of African Americans to illustrate stories about welfare, reinforcing the stereotype that most welfare recipients are black. Occasionally readers are introduced to the runner-up in the poster competition: the white welfare mother, whose story varies only in that she lives in a trailer in some godforsaken place we have never heard of and is really, really fat.

For example, in a 1995 edition of CBS's *48 Hours,* titled "The Rage Over Welfare," we met two overweight white women who live on welfare in New Hampshire. The very first shots—just to let us know the kind of lazy, selfish mothers we are in for—are close-ups of hands shuffling a deck of playing cards and, next, a mom lighting a cigarette. The white male journalist badgers one of the women, who says she can't work because she has epilepsy and arthritis in both knees. "People with epilepsy work. People with bad knees work. People do," he scolds. As she answers, "I don't know what kind of a job I could find," the camera again cuts to her hands shuffling the cards, suggesting, perhaps, a bright future in the casino industry if she'd only apply herself.

Or there's Denise B., one of the "True Faces of Welfare," age 29, with five daughters, from ages one to 13. "All, after the first, were conceived on welfare—conceived perhaps deliberately," *Reader's Digest* sniffs, conjuring up the image of Denise doing some quick math calculations, saying to herself, Oh boy, an extra 60 bucks a month, and then running out to find someone to get her pregnant. The other thing we learn about Denise is that she's a leech. Why not get a job, even though she has toddlers? Because she's lazy. "To get a good job, she would first have to go to school, then earn her way up to a high salary," *Reader's Digest* reminds us, and then lets the ingrate, Denise, speak. "'That's going to take time,' she says, 'It's a lot of work and I ain't guaranteed to get nothing.'" What we learn of Denise's inner life is that she's a calculating cynic. Her kids don't make her feel like every day is Christmas; no, we're supposed to think she uses her kids to get something for nothing.

Even the *New York Times*' Jason De Parle, one of the more sympathetic white male journalists to cover welfare, gets blinded by class privilege. Roslyn Hale, he wrote in 1994, who had been trying to get off welfare, had a succession of jobs that "alternatively invite and discourage public sympathy." She had worked as a maid and as a clerk in a convenience store during the overnight shift when drunks came in and threatened her with a knife. Hale "blames economics for her problems," De Parle reports, since these were crappy jobs that paid only minimum wage. "And sometimes she blames herself. 'I have an attitude,' she admitted." Hello? What middle-class woman would not have "an attitude" after having been threatened at knifepoint or being expected to be grateful for such jobs? In the *Boston Globe*'s "Welfare Reform Through a Child's Eyes" we see little Alicia, who now has a room of her own, Barbies, four kittens, and a ferret because her mother got a job. But although this story appears to be through the child's eyes (never the mother's), it's actually through the judgmental eyes of the press. Sure, the mom has quit drinking, quit crack, and is now working at a nursing center. But the apartment is "suffused with the aroma of animal droppings and her mother's cigarette smoke." Presumably everyone but welfare mothers and former welfare mothers knows how to make their litter boxes smell like gardenias.

One of the sentences most commonly used to characterize the welfare mother is "Tanya, who has ____ children by ____ different men . . ." (you fill in the blanks). Their lives are reduced to the number of successful impregnations by multiple partners—like zoo animals, but unlike Christie Brinkley, although she has exactly the same reproductive M.O. And while the celebrity magazines gush that Christie, Kirstie, and Cindy are sexier than ever, a welfare mother's sexuality is depicted as her downfall.

In the last three years, we've seen the dismantling of the nation's welfare system. Meanwhile, the resentment over the ridiculous standards we're supposed to meet is rising. Sure, many of us ridicule these preposterous portraits of celebrity mom-dom, and we gloated when the monumentally self-righteous "I read the Bible to Cody" Kathie Lee Gifford got her various comeuppances. But the problem is bigger than that: the standards set by celebrity motherhood as touted by the media, with their powerful emphasis on individual will, choice, and responsibility, severely undercut sympathy for poor mothers and their children. Both media characterizations have made it easier for middle-class and upper-middle-class women—especially working women facing speed-ups at work and a decline in leisure time—to resent welfare mothers instead of identifying with them and their struggles.

Why does the media offer us this vision? Not surprising, many reporters bought into the myths that began in the Reagan era, with its dogma of trickle-down economics, its attacks on the poor and people of color, and its antifeminist backlash, through which patriarchy got a new name—family values. Becoming rich and famous came to be the ultimate personal achievement. Reagan's message was simple—the outlandish accumulation of wealth by the few is the basis of a strong economy.

In that context, celebrity-mom profiles haven't been just harmless dreck that help sell magazines. They have encouraged self-loathing, rather than reassurance, in those of us financially comfortable enough not to have to worry about where our kids' next meals are coming from. And they play a subtle but important role in encouraging so many of us to think about motherhood as an individual achievement and a test of individual will and self-discipline. That mind-set—the one that promotes individual responsibility over community and societal obligations—justifies letting poor women and their children fend for themselves until mom makes the right lifestyle choices.

These stories suggest that we, too, can make it to the summit if we just get up earlier, laugh more, and buy the right products. These stories are about leaving others behind, down below. Phony images of joyful, ever-nurturing celebrity moms sitting side-by-side in the newsstands next to humorless, scowling welfare mothers naturalize a pecking order in which some kids deserve to eat well, have access to a doctor, or go to Disney World, and others do not. Under the glossy veneer of maternal joy, generosity, and love lurks the worst sort of narcissism that insists it's every woman for herself. Paying lip service to a collagen-injected feminism, celebrity momism trivializes the struggles and hopes of real women, and kisses off sisterhood as hopelessly out of style.

Questions

1. How are "celebrity moms" portrayed in the popular press? How are "welfare moms" portrayed? Give specific examples. Why do Douglas and Michaels think these contrasting images are damaging? What specifically do they damage?

2. List every social support and resource you can think of that women need to fulfill the duties associated with mothering. Be as specific as possible, drawing from your own experience if relevant. What financial and social resources do celebrity moms have access to that women who receive state support do not? How do these resources shape celebrity women's attainment of the idealized perfect mother?

3. Why might it be dangerous to glorify celebrity women as ideal mothers? Why do different standards of mothering exist for different groups of women? For example, why are women on welfare with children forced to work under new

welfare laws while other women are encouraged to stay at home with their children?

4. Brainstorm about what kind of information about the daily lives of "welfare" moms and "celebrity" moms might be left out of popular accounts. For example, what might be an obstacle to working full time for a single mother who receives state support? Also, who is taking care of the children of "celebrity" moms?

5. Why do you think that the popular press focuses so frequently on celebrity moms? Why does the public find these stories appealing? Why, in contrast, might the stories about mothers on welfare be unappealing or cause discomfort?

For Immigrant Maids, Not a Job but Servitude (1996)

Doreen Carvajal

In the following 1996 New York Times *article, journalist Doreen Carvajal reports that for immigrant women, the line between job and servitude is thin. Because working conditions and wages in many fields are hard to regulate, recent arrivals to the U.S. are vulnerable to exploitation, particularly in the field of domestic work. Carvajal describes some of the difficulties domestic workers face, and their efforts to organize for change.*

GLEN COVE, Long Island—The story of Etelbina Flores is the stuff of a television novela, a Spanish soap opera of a timid immigrant maid who toils in a wealthy suburban house for hourly wages too meager to buy a feather duster.

Her own house is like the crowded steerage compartment of a bulky ship, containing five Salvadoran families with lives too tenuous to question authority. Yet something snapped the day her

Great Neck boss accused her of a $400 theft and, she says, she was forced to submit to a strip search to prove her innocence; she dropped her mop and sued.

"I am not a thief," Ms. Flores said defiantly. "I didn't like what they were saying."

The dirty little secrets behind the closed doors of some upper middle class houses in the suburbs from New York to Los Angeles are the immigrant women who work up to 15-hour shifts, six days a week, for wages amounting to $2 an hour.

Some disgruntled domestic workers like Ms. Flores, who can barely write her own name, are trying to bare those secrets with rebellious strategies ranging from court challenges and professional mediation to self-esteem training and a new, untested weapon of last resort—demonstrations outside the employers' houses. They are receiving encouragement and legal advice from organizations that work with immigrants.

"It's really remarkable to us the difference that we see in the women who've been trained in their legal rights," said Jennifer Gordon, a Harvard-trained lawyer who heads one such organization, the Workplace Project in Hempstead, L.I. "As we see more and more women becoming trained, we see them getting stronger and stronger."

Ms. Gordon said employers treat domestics differently from all other workers.

"They don't think they have any obligation to pay minimum wages," she said, "but they say they treat her like family. But if your sister came to live with you, would you pay her $1.90 an hour and make her work 80 hours a week?"

In the hierarchy of domestic workers, laboring in the suburbs and living with an employer is considered the lowest rung of the ladder because women are isolated without transportation and often are compelled to work hours without defined limits. Days start before breakfast and can linger until a baby stops crying in the middle of the night. Some women rarely leave the house.

The popular Spanish term for this job sums up the more cynical view of the occupation—"encerrado," locked up.

Some have paid as much as a week's salary in advance to immigrant agencies or friends who help them find jobs. Typically, it is the new immigrants with shaky legal status and few options who take these positions at wages that start at about $150 a week in the New York area, $100 in California.

To reach them, community organizers have tried a variety of strategies to contact workers before they get their frantic telephone calls complaining about a family quarrel, a financial dispute or a dismissal.

In Jackson Heights, Queens, along a crowded strip of Indian and Bangladeshi shops and restaurants, social workers for a group called Sakhi for South Asian Women circulate leaflets to reach immigrant women who are recruited from India to work in the houses of upper middle class Indian families living in Westchester County and northern New Jersey.

Their message, translated in English, Hindi, Bengali and Urdu, contains basic information for women who rarely leave their employers' homes and are paid monthly in rupees—the equivalent of about $320. These are the women who complain to the agency about living in drafty basements, isolated by language and suburban address, their passports and money held in safekeeping by their employers.

"We try to tell them the right kind of conditions to demand—break-time, holidays and things like that," said Neela Trivedi, who coordinates a domestic workers' project for Sakhi, which means "woman friend" in Urdu.

The Workplace Project on Long Island sends its organizers to the cafeterias of Roman Catholic churches with large Spanish-speaking congregations to find domestics who need help.

On a Sunday morning at St. Peter of Alcantara Church in Port Washington, after Mass and the coffee hour had ended, dozens of Salvadoran women and men lingered to listen to Dina Aguirre deliver a testimonial about her own bittersweet experiences as a domestic in Garden City.

She was dressed for church instead of work, a woman of 20 in a long green dress and black high heels, who had moved here seven months ago from Guatemala where she had been studying to be a school teacher. She speaks little English and lacks immigration documents, a résumé that gave her few choices.

"I worked for three weeks without getting paid," she said. "I worked from 7 in the morning until 7 at night and sometimes till 11. I asked the woman to pay me and she said, 'I don't owe you anything because you ruined my blouse.' She said, 'Give me your address, and I will send you a bill for all that you owe me.'"

Her Garden City employer, Ana Marie Lobos, declined to discuss Ms. Aguirre's brief employment, but insisted that she had been paid. Ms. Aguirre agrees that she finally did get a paycheck, but only after suing in small claims court and receiving an award of $600.

Her tactic is increasingly being used by other domestic workers in the suburbs of Long Island who have discovered how difficult it is to make a claim for back wages. In some cases, the women had already turned unsuccessfully to their local police department for help or the State Department of Labor, where claims can take as long as 18 months to investigate.

But those who win court claims don't necessarily feel victorious; they still have to collect the money.

The calendar belonging to Yanira Juarez, 25, is filled with entries marking the paydays that passed without payment from her employer in Bellport, L.I., where she worked as a housekeeper. Ultimately, she won her claim in court for back wages of more than $2,000, but the award remains unpaid.

"I returned and I returned again with a friend who spoke English to tell her that I needed the money," Ms. Juarez said. "She took my address and said, 'I will send it.' I'm still waiting."

Such complaints are so common that various social agencies have created special units to offer advice and counseling to domestic workers. The Coalition for Humane Immigrant Rights of Los Angeles circulates a comic book called "Super Domestica," a caped maid who offers negotiating tips in Spanish.

"Use the relationship that you have with your patrona to negotiate an agreement," declared Super Domestica as she hurtled through the clouds in knee-high boots. To reach "encerradas" isolated in their employers' homes, the group also regularly sends its organizers to three Beverly Hills parks where the women gather with their charges. The group offers seminars for domestics in tax planning and self-esteem, which they contend is critical training for women who don't have the skills to assert themselves.

The Workplace Project on Long Island is also circulating an advice comic book about scornful bosses and overworked maids, but their proposed solutions are far more aggressive. They are organizing workers to form "justice committees" of domestic workers who will appear at an employer's doorstep to show their court orders and demand back wages.

"I find that a lot of employers feel that they're doing employees a favor by giving them a job," said Ms. Gordon, the founder of the project. "And they're shocked when they complain."

Often employers raise the threat of reporting undocumented immigrants to the authorities, but in turn they could face sanctions because it is illegal to hire someone who lacks work authorization documents or a residency permit, the so-called green card.

The employers themselves offer starkly different versions of disputes involving their domestic workers.

David Brush, a Point Lookout, L.I., resident, was flabbergasted when his former nurse's aide, Aurora Chavarria, a Colombian immigrant, sued him in small claims court for $2,600 for three months of back wages. The case is pending.

"There should be agencies that are regulated by the government that are going to check that these women are not illegal," he said. "I paid her $100 a day. You tell me why she's complaining. What she did is sit on her tail, watching the Latin channel on TV. All these people, they seem to know exactly what to do. They learn just how hard they can push. It's like it's organized. It's too well organized."

Mr. Brush noted that while he employed Ms. Chavarria to nurse his wife, at least $7,000 worth of suits disappeared along with $2,000 in pants and shoes. "I'm not blaming her," he said. "But when she came here these things were still here."

Accusations of theft or damaged property are often intertwined with a worker's claim for back wages. It's a constant anxiety for workers who fear being falsely accused, said Marta Lopez-Garza, an associate professor in sociology at Occidental College in Los Angeles who studied the Mexican, Salvadoran and Guatemalan women who dominate domestic work in the West.

Those tensions are compounded for workers who are undocumented and fear that their employers could report them to federal authorities.

That was the case of Ms. Flores, 24, the undocumented immigrant from El Salvador, who speaks only Spanish and relies on her husband, Martires Villatoro, to read for her. She found a $125-a-week job last summer working as a live-in domestic for a Great Neck family, who used a Spanish-speaking friend to communicate instructions to Ms. Flores.

Her employment ended four weeks later in an explosive quarrel: the employer accused her of stealing $400 stuffed in the husband's coat pocket. She said she was forced to strip in front of the husband and wife to prove she didn't have the cash.

"She's a big liar," insisted her former employer, Flora Charkhy. As they demanded information about the missing money, she said, Ms. Flores insisted on disrobing. "She suddenly started taking off her clothes. I said, 'Don't do that, please!'"

Ms. Flores sued in small claims court and their dispute ended in professional mediation. The result: $150 in back wages for Ms. Flores, who is now hoping to find work in a beauty salon.

"I was very sad because it was very difficult for me," Ms. Flores said. "But God knows what happened."

QUESTIONS

1. What are working conditions like for immigrant maids? Why are domestic workers treated differently than other workers? What does the Spanish word "encerrado" mean and why is it an appropriate word to describe the labor conditions of domestic workers?
2. How are women workers and their advocates fighting back? What obstacles do they face?
3. Why is domestic work an important feminist issue? How can women work across the lines of social class to address this issue? Does some women's progress in the workforce come at the expense of other women?

WE ARE FAMILY (1996)

National Council for Research on Women

The Family and Medical Leave Act, signed into law in 1993, is a step toward increasing job security for those individuals—usually women—who must take time off from work to care for ill children. Yet, according to this brief article, FMLA does not go far enough.

What do you do? Your one-year-old daughter has meningitis; day care can't watch her in this condition; and family and friends are either working or too far away to help out. Someone has to stay home with the baby, and that someone is you.

You hesitate. In the last two years, you've been on maternity leave, missed work for a week to care for an elderly parent, and suffered a bout of the flu last winter. Will missing a few more days of work have repercussions? Will your job be waiting for you when your daughter is healthy enough to go back to the childcare center?

Under the Family Medical Leave Act (FMLA), signed into law by President Clinton in 1993, if you work for a company that employs 50 or more workers, you are entitled to up to 12 weeks of *unpaid, job-protected* leave to care for a newborn, a newly adopted child, or a seriously ill child, spouse, or parent. FMLA also allows you to care for yourself if you are unable to work due to illness or temporary disability, including childbirth.[1]

On the face of it, FMLA is a good law for women. It allows them to care for their families and not only stay on the job but keep themselves moving on the fast track. According to the Washington, DC-based independent, nonprofit research center, the Institute for Women's Policy Research, "In the late 1980s about one-quarter of women who left jobs did so because of pregnancy or other family reasons."[2] Given that nationwide, working women give birth to more than 2 million babies each year and that the proposed cuts to Medicare threaten to greatly reduce the level of professional homecare available to a growing population of elderly Americans, the task of tending to the nation's families—its newest and oldest members—takes on Goliath proportions, especially for working women.[3] If it weren't for the FMLA, many families would be operating without a safety net.

That said, FMLA is not the be all and end all of family-leave policy. A year after FMLA became law, researchers at the University of California at Berkeley found that four in ten companies affected by FMLA were not adhering to its provisions.[4] Likewise, in an October 1994 telephone survey of nearly 700 workers, the Bureau of National Affairs found that 52 percent of those called knew little or nothing about the act.[5] Once briefed, most said they would hesitate to take advantage of FMLA because they could not afford to go on unpaid leave, even job-protected leave. Almost half of the employees with annual incomes between $15,000 and $20,000 expressed this concern, as did 40 percent of those with children under age 18.

Two studies conducted for the Commission on Family and Medical Leave at the US Department of Labor and released in October 1995 looked at the impact of FMLA on workers and their employers. Researchers found that most FMLA-covered companies report having incurred little or no costs due to the law and that only two to four percent of FMLA-covered employees have made use of the law since January 1994.[6] Like earlier studies, the employee survey also found that the majority of respondents who needed to take leave during this time period but didn't, said they couldn't afford to forgo their paychecks.[7]

Recognizing that unpaid leave means no leave for many workers, the Institute for Women's Policy Research (IWPR) would like to see FMLA expanded to include a paid-leave program modeled after the Temporary Disability Insurance (TDI) benefits currently available to workers in California, Hawaii, New Jersey, New York, Rhode Island, and Puerto Rico. If a worker must go on leave for a nonwork-related condition—including pregnancy, childbirth, automobile accidents, heart disease, or cancer—TDI partially replaces missed wages.

IWPR reports emphasize that "TDI is a pay-as-you-go system rather than a new entitlement paid out of general tax revenues."[8] Employers and employees pay for the benefit, not the general public. The distinction could make a world of difference in this era of federal-budget cutting and social-policy backpedaling. IWPR estimates the cost per worker for paid leave for both health- and family-care absences would range from $151 to $213 annually, well below the costs of government-run social security programs like Supplemental Security Income and Aid to Families with Dependent Children, and on par with the costs of Unemployment Insurance.[9]

IWPR projects that paid-family-medical leave would help women stay on the job longer, which is good news for women at the bottom and top of the income ladder. Research shows that women with paid maternity leaves are more likely to return to work and low-income women are more likely to stay off welfare. Given these outcomes, paid leave promises to yield high returns in the private and public sectors. Paid-family-medical leave is in the best interest of the government, business, and America's families: an opportunity whose time has come.

Notes

1. In addition, to be eligible, employees must have worked for the employer for at least 12 months and for 1250 hours during the year preceding the leave. FMLA requires employers to maintain an employee's health benefits during the leave, and they may not require employees to forfeit any previously accrued seniority or benefits as a result of the leave. However, employers are not required to count the leave time as time accrued for purposes of seniority or other benefits.
2. Young-Hee Yoon, Heidi Hartmann, and Jill Braunstein, "Using Temporary Disability Insurance to Provide Paid Family Leave: A Com-

parison with the Family Medical Leave Act," (Washington, DC: Institute for Women's Policy Research, 1995). Pamphlet, 1.

3. Mike Meyers, "Taking Pregnancy Leaves," *Star Tribune* (February 6, 1995).
4. Julianne O'Gara, *Making Workplaces Work: Quality Work Policies for Small Business* (Washington, DC: Business and Professional Women's Foundation, 1995), 22.
5. Jeffrey Goldfarb, "Employment: Majority of US Workers Are Unaware of FMLA Provisions, BNA Survey Finds," *Analysis and Reports* (Washington, DC: Bureau of National Affairs, 1994), C1.
6. Commission on Family and Medical Leave, "New Studies Measure Impact of Family & Medical Leave Law" (Washington, DC: US Department of Labor, 1995). Photocopy.
7. Katherine A. McGonagle et al., "Commission on Leave Survey of Employees on the Impact of the Family and Medical Leave Act." (Ann Arbor, MI: Institute for Social Research, 1995): Photocopy, 23. See also, David Cantor et al., "The Impact of the Family and Medical Leave Act: A Survey of Employers" (Rockville, MD: Westat, 1995), Photocopy.
8. Yoon, Hartmann, and Braunstein, 4.
9. Ibid., Table 2.

Questions

1. What advantages does FMLA offer, particularly for women? Why is this Act under-utilized by employees?
2. Why would a plan modeled after Temporary Disability Insurance (TDI) be advantageous? What resistance might meet such a plan?
3. Are we interested in a more family-friendly workforce? Whose responsibility is it to provide a more family-friendly climate for workers? What economic and emotional benefits would be reaped from a more secure workforce? Would you be willing to pay the amount estimated to ensure a benefit like TDI to working parents? Why/Why not?

For Better or Worse? (1996)

Jonathan Rauch

Heterosexual marriage is recognized by the U.S. Supreme Court as a fundamental right. Granting homosexuals the right to marry is not a "special right," but extending a fundamental right to all citizens. Making the case for gay (and straight) marriage, the author argues "to bar any class of people from marrying as they choose is an extraordinary deprivation." This article, which appeared in The New Republic, *casts gay and lesbian couples in the role of enriching the institution of marriage, rather than undermining or "destroying" it.*

Whatever else marriage may or may not be, it is certainly falling apart. Half of today's marriages end in divorce, and, far more costly, many never begin—leaving mothers poor, children fatherless and neighborhoods chaotic. With timing worthy of Neville Chamberlain, homosexuals have chosen this moment to press for the right to marry. What's more, Hawaii's courts are moving toward letting them do so. I'll believe in gay marriage in American when I see it, but if Hawaii legalizes it, even temporarily, the uproar over this final insult to a besieged institution will be deafening.

Whether gay marriage makes sense—and whether straight marriage makes sense—depends on what marriage is actually for. Current secular thinking on this question is shockingly sketchy. Gay activists say: marriage is for love, and we love each other, therefore we should be able to marry. Traditionalists say: marriage is for children, and homosexuals do not (or should not) have children, therefore, you should not be able to marry. That, unfortunately, pretty well covers the spectrum. I say "unfortunately" because both views are wrong. They misunderstand and impoverish the social meaning of marriage.

So what is marriage for? Modern marriage is, of course, based upon traditions that religion helped to codify and enforce. But religious doctrine has no special standing in the world of secular law and policy (the "Christian nation" crowd notwithstanding). If we want to know what and whom marriage is for in modern America, we need a sensible secular doctrine.

At one point, marriage in secular society was largely a matter of business: cementing family ties, providing social status for men and economic support for women, conferring dowries, and so on. Marriages were typically arranged, and "love" in the modern sense was no prerequisite. In Japan, remnants of this system remain, and it works surprisingly well. Couples stay together because they view their marriage as a partnership: an investment in social stability for themselves and their children. Because Japanese couples don't expect as much emotional fulfillment as we do, they are less inclined to break up. They also take a somewhat more relaxed attitude toward adultery. What's a little extracurricular love provided that each partner is fulfilling his or her many other marital duties?

In the West, of course, love is a defining element. The notion of lifelong love is charming, if ambitious, and certainly love is a desirable element of marriage. In society's eyes, however, it cannot be the defining element. You may or may not love your husband, but the two of you are just as married either way. You may love your mistress, but that certainly doesn't make her your spouse. Love helps make sense of marriage emotionally, but it is not terribly important in making sense of marriage from the point of view of social policy.

If love does not define the purpose of secular marriage, what does? Neither the law nor secular thinking provides a clear answer. Today marriage is almost entirely a voluntary arrangement whose contents are up to the people making the deal. There are few if any behaviors that automatically end a marriage. If a man beats his wife, which is about the worst thing he can do to her, he may be convicted of assault, but his marriage is not automatically dissolved. Couples can be adulterous ("open") yet remain married. They can be celibate, too; consummation is not required. All in all, it is an impressive and also rather astonishing victory for modern individualism that so important an institution should be so bereft of formal social instruction as to what should go on inside of it.

Secular society tells us only a few things about marriage. First, marriage depends on the consent of the parties. Second, the parties are not children. Third, the number of parties is two. Fourth, one is a man and the other a woman. Within those rules a marriage is whatever anyone says it is.

Perhaps it is enough simply to say that marriage is as it is and should not be tampered with. This sounds like a crudely reactionary position. In fact, however, of all the arguments against reforming marriage, it is probably the most powerful.

Call it a Hayekian argument, after the great libertarian economist F. A. Hayek, who developed this line of thinking in his book *The Fatal Conceit*. In a market system, the prices generated by impersonal forces may not make sense from any one person's point of view, but they encode far more information than even the cleverest person could ever gather. In a similar fashion, human societies evolve rich and complicated webs of nonlegal rules in the form of customs, traditions and institutions. Like prices, they may seem irrational or arbitrary. But the very fact that they are the customs that have evolved implies that they embody a practical logic that may not be apparent to even a sophisticated analyst. And the web of custom cannot be torn apart and reordered at will because once its internal logic is violated it falls apart. Intellectuals, such as Marxists or feminists, who seek to deconstruct and rationally rebuild social traditions, will produce not better order but chaos.

So the Hayekian view argues strongly against gay marriage. It says that the current rules may not be best and may even be unfair. But they are all we have, and, once you say that marriage need not be male-female, soon marriage will stop being anything at all. You can't mess with the formula without causing unforeseen consequences, possibly including the implosion of the institution of marriage itself.

However, there are problems with the Hayekian position. It is untenable in its extreme form and unhelpful in its milder version. In its extreme form, it implies that no social reforms should ever be undertaken. Indeed, no laws should be passed, because they interfere with the natural evolution of social mores. How could Hayekians abolish slavery? They would probably note that slavery violates fundamental moral principles. But in so doing they would establish a moral platform from which to judge social rules, and thus acknowledge that abstracting social debate from moral concerns is not possible.

If the ban on gay marriage were only mildly unfair, and if the costs of changing it were certain to be enormous, then the ban could stand on Hayekian grounds. But, if there is any social policy today that has a fair claim to be scaldingly inhumane, it is the ban on gay marriage. As conservatives tirelessly and rightly point out, marriage is society's most fundamental institution. To bar any class of people from marrying as they choose is an extraordinary deprivation. When not so long ago it was illegal in parts of America for blacks to marry whites, no one could claim that this was a trivial disenfranchisement. Granted, gay marriage raises issues that interracial marriage does not; but no one can argue that the deprivation is a minor one.

To outweigh such a serious claim it is not enough to say that gay marriage might lead to bad things. Bad things happened as a result of legalizing contraception, but that did not make it the wrong thing to do. Besides, it seems doubtful that extending marriage to, say, another 3 or 5 percent of the population would have anything like the effects that no-fault divorce has had, to say nothing of contraception. By now, the "traditional" understanding of marriage has been sullied in all kinds of ways. It is hard to think of a bigger affront to tradition, for instance, than allowing married women to own property independently of their husbands or allowing them to charge their husbands with rape. Surely it is unfair to say that marriage may be reformed for the sake of anyone and everyone except homosexuals, who must respect the dictates of tradition.

Faced with these problems, the milder version of the Hayekian argument says not that social traditions shouldn't be tampered with at all, but that they shouldn't be tampered with lightly. Fine. In this case, no one is talking about casual messing around; both sides have marshaled their arguments with deadly seriousness. Hayekians surely have to recognize that appeals to blind tradition and to the risks inherent in social change do not, a priori, settle anything in this instance. They merely warn against frivolous change.

So we turn to what has become the standard view of marriage's purpose. Its proponents would probably like to call it a child-centered view, but it is actually an anti-gay view, as will become clear. Whatever you call it, it is the view of marriage that is heard most often, and in the context of the debate over gay marriage it is heard almost exclusively. In its most straightforward form it goes as follows (I quote from James Q. Wilson's fine book *The Moral Sense*):

> A family is not an association of independent people; it is a human commitment designed to make possible the rearing of moral and healthy children. Governments care—or ought to care—about families for this reason, and scarcely for any other.

Wilson speaks about "family" rather than "marriage" as such, but one may, I think, read him as speaking of marriage without doing any injustice to his meaning. The resulting proposition—government ought to care about marriage almost entirely because of children—seems reasonable. But there are problems. The first, obviously, is that gay couples may have children, whether through adoption, prior marriage or (for lesbians) artificial insemination. Leaving aside the thorny issue of gay adoption, the point is that if the mere presence of children is the test, then homosexual relationships can certainly pass it.

You might note, correctly, that heterosexual marriages are more likely to produce children than homosexual ones. When granting marriage licenses to heterosexuals, however, we do not ask how likely the couple is to have children. We assume that they are entitled to get married whether or not they end up with children. Understanding this, conservatives often make an interesting move. In seeking to justify the state's interest in marriage, they shift from the actual presence of children to the anatomical possibility of making them. Hadley Arkes, a political science professor and prominent opponent of homosexual marriage, makes the case this way:

> The traditional understanding of marriage is grounded in the "natural teleology of the body"—in the inescapable fact that only a man and a woman, and only two people, not three, can generate a child. Once marriage is detached from that natural teleology of the body, what ground of principle would thereafter confine marriage to two people rather than some larger grouping? That is, on what ground of principle would the law reject the claim of a gay couple that their love is not confined to a coupling of two, but that they are woven into a larger ensemble with yet another person or two?

What he seems to be saying is that, where the possibility of natural children is nil, the meaning of marriage is nil. If marriage is allowed between members of the same sex, then the concept of marriage has been emptied of content except to ask whether the parties love each other. Then anything goes, including polygamy. This reasoning presumably is what those opposed to gay marriage have in mind when they claim that, once gay marriage is legal, marriage to pets will follow close behind.

But Arkes and his sympathizers make two mistakes. To see them, break down the claim into two components: (1) Two-person marriage derives its special status from the anatomical possibility that the partners can create natural children; and (2) Apart from (1), two-person marriage has no purpose sufficiently strong to justify its special status. That is, absent justification (1), anything goes.

The first proposition is wholly at odds with the way society actually views marriage. Leave aside the insistence that natural, as opposed to adopted, children define the importance of marriage. The deeper problem, apparent right away, is the issue of sterile heterosexual couples. Here the "anatomical possibility" crowd has a problem, for a homosexual union is, anatomically speaking, nothing but one variety of sterile union and no different even in principle: a woman without a uterus has no more potential for giving birth than a man without a vagina.

It may sound like carping to stress the case of barren heterosexual marriage: the vast majority of newlywed heterosexual couples, after all, can have children and probably will. But the point here is fundamental. There are far more sterile heterosexual unions in America than homosexual ones. The "anatomical possibility" crowd cannot have it both ways. If the possibility of children is what gives meaning to marriage, then a postmenopausal woman who applies for a marriage license should be turned away at the courthouse door. What's more, she should be hooted at and condemned for stretching the meaning of marriage beyond its natural basis and so reducing the institution to frivolity. People at the Family Research Council or Concerned Women for America should point at her and say, "If she can marry, why not polygamy?"

Obviously, the "anatomical" conservatives do not say this, because they are sane. They instead flail around, saying that sterile men and women were at least born with the right-shaped parts for making children, and so on. Their position is really a nonposition. It says that the "natural children" rationale defines marriage when homosexuals are involved but not when heterosexuals are involved. When the parties to union are sterile heterosexuals, the justification for marriage must be something else. But what?

Now arises the oddest part of the "anatomical" argument. Look at proposition (2) above. It says that, absent the anatomical justification for marriage, anything goes. In other words, it dismisses the idea that there might be other good reasons for society to sanctify marriage above other kinds of relationships. Why would anybody make this move? I'll hazard a guess: to exclude homosexuals. Any rationale that justifies sterile heterosexual marriages can also apply to homosexual ones. For instance, marriage makes women more financially secure. Very nice, say the conservatives. But that rationale could be applied to lesbians, so it's definitely out.

The end result of this stratagem is perverse to the point of being funny. The attempt to ground marriage in children (or the anatomical possibility thereof) falls flat. But, having lost that reason for marriage, the anti-gay people can offer no other. In their fixation on excluding homosexuals, they leave themselves no consistent justification for the privileged status of *heterosexual* marriage. They thus tear away any coherent foundation that secular marriage might have, which is precisely the opposite of what they claim they want to do. If they have to undercut marriage to save it from homosexuals, so be it!

For the record, I would be the last to deny that children are one central reason for the privileged status of marriage. When men and women get together, children are a likely outcome; and, as we are learning in ever more unpleasant ways, when children grow up without two parents, trouble ensues. Children are not a trivial reason for marriage; they just cannot be the only reason.

What are the others? It seems to me that the two strongest candidates are these: domesticating men and providing reliable caregivers. Both purposes are critical to the functioning of a humane and stable society, and both are much better served by marriage—that is, by one-to-one lifelong commitment—than by any other institution.

Civilizing young males is one of any society's biggest problems. Wherever unattached males gather in packs, you see no end of trouble: wildings in Central Park, gangs in Los Angeles, soccer hooligans in Britain, skinheads in Germany, fraternity hazes in universities, grope-lines in the military and, in a different but ultimately no less tragic way, the bathhouses and wanton sex of gay San Francisco or New York in the 1970s.

For taming men, marriage is unmatched. "Of all the institutions through which men may pass—schools, factories, the military—marriage has the largest effect," Wilson writes in *The Moral Sense*. (A token of the casualness of current thinking about marriage is that the man who wrote those words could, later in the very same book, say that government should care about fostering families for "scarcely any other" reason than children.) If marriage—that is, the binding of men into couples—did nothing else, its power to settle men, to keep them at home and out of trouble, would be ample justification for its special status.

Of course, women and older men don't generally travel in marauding or orgiastic packs. But in their case the second rationale comes into play. A second enormous problem for society is what to do when someone is beset by some sort of burdensome contingency. It could be cancer, a broken back, unemployment or depression; it could be exhaustion from work or stress under pressure. If marriage has any meaning at all, it is that, when you collapse from a stroke, there will be at least one other person whose "job" is to drop everything and come to your aid; or that when you come home after being fired by the postal service there will be someone to persuade you not to kill the supervisor.

Obviously, both rationales—the need to settle males and the need to have people looked after—apply to sterile people as well as fertile ones, and apply to childless couples as well as to ones with children. The first explains why everybody feels relieved when the town delinquent gets married, and the second explains why everybody feels happy when an aging widow takes a second husband. From a social point of view, it seems to me, both rationales are far more compelling as justifications of marriage's special status than, say, love. And both of them apply to homosexuals as well as to heterosexuals.

Take the matter of settling men. It is probably true that women and children, more than just the fact of marriage, help civilize men. But that hardly means that the settling effect of marriage on homosexual men is negligible. To the contrary, being tied to a committed relationship plainly helps stabilize gay men. Even without marriage, coupled gay men have steady sex partners and relationships that they value and therefore tend to be less wanton. Add marriage, and you bring a further array of stabilizing influences. One of the main benefits of publicly recognized marriage is that it binds couples together not only in their own eyes but also in the eyes of society at large. Around the partners is woven a web of expectations that they will spend nights together, go to parties together, take out mortgages together, buy furniture at Ikea together, and so on—all of which helps tie them together and keep them off the streets and at home. Surely that is a very good thing, especially as compared to the closet-gay culture of furtive sex with innumerable partners in parks and bathhouses.

The other benefit of marriage—caretaking—clearly applies to homosexuals. One of the first things many people worry about when coming to terms with their homosexuality is: Who will take care of me when I'm ailing or old? Society needs to care about this, too, as the AIDS crisis has made horribly clear. If that crisis has shown anything, it is that homosexuals can and will take care of each other, sometimes with breathtaking devotion—and that no institution can begin to match the care of a devoted partner. Legally speaking, marriage creates kin. Surely society's interest in kin-creation is strongest of all for people who are unlikely to be supported by children in old age and who may well be rejected by their own parents in youth.

Gay marriage, then, is far from being a mere exercise in political point-making or rights-mongering. On the contrary, it serves two of the three social purposes that make marriage so indispensable and irreplaceable for heterosexuals. Two out of three may not be the whole ball of wax, but it is more than enough to give society a compelling interest in marrying off homosexuals.

There is no substitute. Marriage is the *only* institution that adequately serves these purposes. The power of marriage is not just legal but social. It seals its promise with the smiles and tears of family, friends and neighbors. It shrewdly exploits ceremony (big, public weddings) and money (expensive gifts, dowries) to deter casual commitment and to make bailing out embarrassing. Stag parties and bridal showers signal that what is beginning is not just a legal arrangement but a whole new stage of life. "Domestic partner" laws do none of these things.

I'll go further: far from being a substitute for the real thing, marriage-lite may undermine it. Marriage is a deal between a couple and society, not just between two people: society recognizes the sanctity and autonomy of the pair-bond, and in exchange each spouse commits to being the other's nurse, social worker and policeman of first resort. Each marriage is its own little society within society. Any step that weakens the deal by granting the legal benefits of marriage without also requiring the public commitment is begging for trouble.

So gay marriage makes sense for several of the same reasons that straight marriage makes sense. That would seem a natural place to stop. But the logic of the argument compels one to go a twist further. If it is good for society to have people attached, then it is not enough just to make marriage available. Marriage should also be *expected*. This, too, is just as true for homosexuals as for heterosexuals. So, if homosexuals are justified in expecting access to marriage, society is equally justified in expecting them to use it. I'm not saying that out-of-wedlock sex should be scandalous or that people should be coerced into marrying. The mechanisms of expectation are more subtle. When grandma cluck-clucks over a still-unmarried young man, or when mom says she wishes her little girl would settle down, she is expressing a strong and well-justified preference: one that is quietly echoed in a thousand ways throughout society and that produces subtle but important pressure to form and sustain unions. This is a good and necessary thing, and it will be as necessary for homosexuals as heterosexuals. If gay marriage is recognized, single gay people over a certain age should not be surprised when they are disapproved of or pitied. That is a vital part of what makes marriage work. It's stigma as social policy.

If marriage is to work it cannot be merely a "lifestyle option." It must be privileged. That is, it must be understood to be better, on average, than other ways of living. Not mandatory, not good where everything else is bad, but better: a general norm, rather than a personal taste. The biggest worry about gay marriage, I think, is that homosexuals might get it but then mostly not use it. Gay neglect of marriage wouldn't greatly erode the bonding power of heterosexual marriage (remember, homosexuals are only a tiny fraction of the population)—but it would certainly not help. And heterosexual society would rightly feel betrayed if, after legalization, homosexuals treated marriage as a minority taste rather than as a core institution of life. It is not enough, I think, for gay people to say we want the right to marry. If we do not use it, shame on us.

QUESTIONS

1. Is withholding the right to marry "inhumane" or unfair to some citizens? Do you agree that it is an "extraordinary deprivation"? What evidence from the text can you offer to support your perspective?
2. Explain Rauch's argument about the pros and cons of marriage. How would you evaluate his proposition that married couples should privately absorb the cost of care for children, the sick, and/or the elderly?
3. Do "domestic partner" laws and benefits undermine marriage as an institution? Why or why not? What evidence can you offer to support your assessment?

Are Women Really Moving Up? (1995)

René A. Redwood

René A. Redwood's query in this brief Washington Post *article elicits a complicated answer—both yes and no. Many women have moved up the corporate ladder, yet the majority are kept from advancing by an array of workplace barriers that remain firmly in place. Redwood describes the factors associated with successful workplace initiatives to break the "glass ceiling."*

Are women moving up the corporate ladder, particularly into senior management and decision making positions? According to the fact-finding report issued in March 1995 by the Federal Glass Ceiling Commission, there are several answers to this question.

The report "Good for Business: Making Full Use of the Nation's Human Capital," found that women are indeed moving into leadership positions in corporate America. Between 1982 and 1992, the proportion of women holding the title of executive vice president rose from four to nine percent; those at the senior vice president level rose from 13 to 23 percent; and almost half of the Fortune 500 companies have at least one woman on the board of directors. Each of the 10 most profitable Fortune 500 companies has at least one female director and five have two.

CEOs now recognize more than ever, that diversity at the top is a bottom line issue essential to business success in today's global marketplace. Thanks in part to the Commission's report, the dialogue on race and gender is moving beyond the ethical and legal arenas to a realization that it is an economic imperative to diversify. The pace of change, however, remains painfully slow.

The positive gains made by women over the years are still hampered by "glass ceiling" barriers that continue to deny them—as well as men of color—the opportunity to compete for and hold senior level positions in the private and public sectors. It's still overwhelmingly a white man's world in the executive suite.

Surveys of the Fortune 1000 industrials and Fortune 500 service companies found that 95 percent of senior level managers are men and of that 95 percent, 97 percent are white. That translates into slightly more than 2100 senior women executives in these companies. And only five percent of these senior women are minorities.

These statistics are hardly representative of the 58.4 million women in the work force—more than 45 percent and growing. Nor are they reflective of their educational attainment—the percentage of women earning college degrees in business and management has increased from 8.1 percent in 1970 to 46.7 percent in 1990. A similar growth has also occurred in graduate degrees. The Commission's report also shows that when women do reach executive levels, they work the same long hours, are more willing to relocate than their male colleagues and rarely take leaves of absence except for maternity and family reasons.

So what are we to conclude from evidence that shows women vastly underrepresented in the executive suite? Clearly, we do not yet live in a gender or color blind society. Discrimination, sexism, racism, and xenophobia live side-by-side with unemployment, underemployment, and poverty; they feed on one another and perpetuate a cycle of unfulfilled aspirations among women and people of color.

But the Commission also reports on signs of change and strategies that help women and minorities achieve their fair share of the American dream, and there are some positive signs to report.

Studies show a positive correlation between workforce diversity and corporate financial performance. High performing organizations are heeding the message of these studies and are using the talents of women and minorities at the highest levels to address changing consumer markets and work force demographics, both here and abroad.

Research indicates that corporate initiatives to break glass ceiling barriers are most likely to succeed where:

- There is visible and continuing commitment from the CEO and the culture of the organization is supportive of work force and management diversity.
- The CEO and senior line managers recognize that it makes good business sense to advance women and minorities and the objective of diversification is incorporated into the strategic business plan.
- Managers are held accountable for the hiring, development, and advancement of all qualified employees. That means tying pay and rewards systems to successful performance in these areas.
- Internal corporate research identifies the specific barriers that impede women and minorities and training for the entire work force addresses stereotypes and misconceptions.
- Personnel systems identify and monitor the progress of high potential women and minorities to ensure that they acquire a broad range of experience in core business areas so that they will be able to compete for leadership positions.

As companies increasingly recognize the "bottom line" benefits of fully utilizing the talents of all their employees, and as women and minorities enter the work force in increasing numbers as the landmark study Workforce 2000 indicates they will, the character of corporate structures in this country will be transformed. The change is as inevitable as it is beneficial.

Some of us may be impatient about the pace at which that change is occurring. But when the glass ceiling in America is forever shattered, we will have succeeded in using our greatest asset—our working people—to their fullest potential. And we will have come a long way to achieving the full promise of our society by making its bounty equally available to all.

QUESTIONS

1. What is the "glass ceiling"? Why is it a difficult phenomenon to battle? What benefits can be gained by workplace diversity?
2. What workplace initiatives have been successful in advancing women and people of color? Why are such initiatives necessary?
3. If businesses have been financially successful with white men at the helm, why would executives want to alter their hiring and promotion practices to bring in more women and people of color?

The Transformation of Silence into Language and Action (1978)

Audre Lorde

An African-American lesbian scholar, Audre Lorde uses provocative language to challenge us to hear the enormous strain of silence on the possibilities for social change. Lorde urges those of us who are silent, and who have been silenced, to find our voices and reclaim the power of language. She reminds us of both the dangers of silence and the empowerment that can result from the expression of one's own voice.

I have come to believe over and over again that what is most important to me must be spoken, made verbal and shared, even at the risk of having it bruised or misunderstood. That the speaking profits me, beyond any other effect. I am standing here as a black lesbian poet, and the meaning of all that waits upon the fact that I am still alive, and might not have been. Less than two months ago, I was told by two doctors, one female and one male, that I would have to have breast surgery, and that there was a 60 to 80 percent

"The Transformation of Silence into Language and Action," by Audre Lorde, reprinted from *Sinister Wisdom 6*, Summer, 1978.

chance that the tumor was malignant. Between that telling and the actual surgery, there was a three week period of the agony of an involuntary reorganization of my entire life. The surgery was completed, and the growth was benign.

But within those three weeks, I was forced to look upon myself and my living with a harsh and urgent clarity that has left me still shaken but much stronger. This is a situation faced by many women, by some of you here today. Some of what I experienced during that time has helped elucidate for me much of what I feel concerning the transformation of silence into language and action.

In becoming forcibly and essentially aware of my mortality, and by what I wished and wanted for my life, however short it might be, priorities and omissions became strongly etched in a merciless light, and what I most regretted were my silences. Of what had I *ever* been afraid? To question or to speak as I believed could have meant pain, or death. But we all hurt in so many different ways, all the time, and pain will either change, or end. Death, on the other hand, is the final silence. And that might be coming quickly, now, without regard for whether I had ever spoken what needed to be said, or had only betrayed myself into small silences, while I planned someday to speak, or waited for someone else's words. And I began to recognize a source of power within myself that comes from the knowledge that while it is most desirable not to be afraid, learning to put fear into a perspective gave me great strength.

I was going to die, if not sooner then later, whether or not I had ever spoken myself. My silences had not protected me. Your silence will not protect you. But for every real word spoken, for every attempt I had ever made to speak those truths for which I am still seeking, I had made contact with other women while we examined the words to fit a world in which we all believed, bridging our differences. And it was the concern and caring of all those women which gave me strength and enabled me to scrutinize the essentials of my living.

The women who sustained me through that period were black and white, old and young, lesbian, bisexual, and heterosexual, and we all shared a war against the tyrannies of silence. They all gave me a strength and concern without which I could not have survived intact. Within those weeks of acute fear came the knowledge—within the war we are all waging with the forces of death, subtle and otherwise, conscious or not, I am not only a casualty, I am also a warrior.

What are the words you do not yet have? What do you need to say? What are the tyrannies you swallow day by day and attempt to make your own, until you will sicken and die of them, still in silence? Perhaps for some of you here today, I am the face of one of your fears. Because I am woman, because I am black, because I am lesbian, because I am myself, a black woman warrior poet doing my work, come to ask you, are you doing yours?

And, of course, I am afraid—you can hear it in my voice—because the transformation of silence into language and action is an act of self-revelation and that always seems fraught with danger. But my daughter, when I told her of our topic and my difficulty with it, said, "Tell them about how you're never really a whole person if you remain silent, because there's always that one little piece inside of you that wants to be spoken out, and if you keep ignoring it, it gets madder and madder and hotter and hotter, and if you don't speak it out one day it will just up and punch you in the mouth."

In the cause of silence, each one of us draws the face of her own fear—fear of contempt, of censure, or some judgment, or recognition, of challenge, of annihilation. But most of all, I think, we fear the very visibility without which we also cannot truly live. Within this country where racial difference creates a constant, if unspoken, distortion of vision, black women have on one hand always been highly visible, and so, on the other hand, have been rendered invisible through the depersonalization of racism. Even within the women's movement, we have had to fight and still do, for that very visibility which also renders us most vulnerable, our blackness. For to survive in the mouth of this dragon we call america, we have had to learn this first and most vital lesson—that we were never meant to survive. Not as human beings. And neither were most of you here today, black or not. And that visibility which makes us most vulnerable is that which also is the source of our greatest strength. Because the machine will try to grind you into dust anyway, whether or not we speak. We can sit in our corners mute forever while our sisters and our selves are wasted, while our children are distorted and destroyed, while our earth is poisoned, we can sit in our safe corners mute as bottles, and we still will be no less afraid.

In my house this year we are celebrating the feast of Kwanza, the African-American festival of harvest which begins the day after Christmas and lasts for seven days. There are seven principles of Kwanza, one for each day. The first principle is Umoja, which means unity, the decision to strive for and maintain unity in self and community. The principle for yesterday, the second day, was Kujichagulia—self-determination—the decision to define ourselves, name ourselves, and speak for ourselves, instead of being defined and spoken for by others. Today is the third day of Kwanza, and the principle for today is Ujima—collective work and responsibility—the decision to build and maintain ourselves and our communities together and to recognize and solve our problems together.

Each one of us is here now because in one way or another we share a commitment to language and to the power of language, and to the reclaiming of that language which has been made to work against us. In the transformation of silence into language and action, it is vitally necessary for each one of us to establish or examine her function in that transformation, and to recognize her role as vital within that transformation.

For those of us who write, to scrutinize not only the truth of what we speak, but the truth of that language by which we speak it. For others, it is to share and spread also those words that are meaningful to us. But primarily for us all, it is necessary to teach by living and speaking those truths which we believe and know beyond understanding. Because in this way alone we can survive, by taking part in a process of life that is creative and continuing, that is growth.

And it is never without fear; of visibility, of the harsh light of scrutiny and perhaps judgment, of pain, of death. But we have lived through all of those already, in silence, except death. And I remind myself all the time now, that if I were to have been born mute, and had maintained an oath of silence my whole life long for safety, I would still have suffered, and I would still die. It is very good for establishing perspective.

And where the words of women are crying to be heard, we must each of us recognize our responsibility to seek those words out, to read them and share them and examine them in their pertinence to our lives. That we not hide behind the mockeries of separations that have been imposed upon us and which so often we accept as our own: for instance, "I can't possibly teach black women's writings—their experience is so different from mine," yet how many years have you spent teaching Plato and Shakespeare and Proust? Or another: "She's a white woman and what could she possibly have to say to me?" Or, "She's a lesbian, what would my husband say, or my chairman?" Or again, "This woman writes of her sons and I have no children." And all the other endless ways in which we rob ourselves of ourselves and each other.

We can learn to work and speak when we are afraid in the same way we have learned to work and speak when we are tired. For we have been socialized to respect fear more than our own needs for language and definition, and while we wait in silence for that final luxury of fearlessness, the weight of that silence will choke us.

The fact that we are here and that I speak now these words is an attempt to break that silence and bridge some of those differences between us, for it is not difference which immobilizes us, but silence. And there are so many silences to be broken.

Questions

1. What does Lorde suggest are the consequences of remaining silent? What is her concept of the tyrannies of silence?
2. How do speech and language function as actions? How does Lorde channel her own voice?
3. In what ways does fear work to silence human speech? How have you encountered fear as a silencer in your own experiences?

IMAGINE MY SURPRISE (1995)

Ellen Neuborne

In this 1995 first person narrative, journalist Ellen Neuborne discusses the potential of third wave feminism as a strategy for counteracting the contemporary subtlety of sexism. Suggesting that the factors influencing the development of first and second wave feminism continue to exist today, Neuborne describes her own experiences in the workplace to illustrate how women can unconsciously internalize the subtle messages of sexism.

When my editor called me into his office and told me to shut the door, I was braced to argue. I made a mental note to stand my ground.

It was behind the closed door of his office that I realized I'd been programmed by the sexists.

We argued about the handling of one of my stories. He told me not to criticize him. I continued to disagree. That's when it happened.

"Imagine My Surprise," by Ellen Neuborne, reprinted from *Listen Up: Voices From the Next Feminist Generation*, edited by Barbara Findlen, 1995, by permission of Seal Press.

He stood up, walked to where I was sitting. He completely filled my field of vision. He said, "Lower your voice when you speak to me."

And I did.

I still can't believe it.

This was not supposed to happen to me. I am the child of professional feminists. My father is a civil rights lawyer. My mother heads the NOW Legal Defense and Education Fund. She sues sexists for a living. I was raised on a pure, unadulterated feminist ethic.

That didn't help.

Looking back on the moment, I should have said, "Step back out of my face and we'll continue this discussion like humans."

I didn't.

I said, "Sorry."

Sorry!

I had no idea twenty-some years of feminist upbringing would fail me at that moment. Understand, it is not his actions I am criticizing; it is mine. He was a bully. But the response was my own. A man confronted me. My sexist programming kicked in. I backed off. I said, "Sorry."

I don't understand where the programming began. I had been taught that girls could do anything boys could do. Equality of the sexes was an unimpeachable truth. Before that day in the editor's office, if you'd asked me how I might handle such a confrontation, I never would have said, "I'd apologize."

I'm a good feminist. I would never apologize for having a different opinion.

But I did.

Programming. It is the subtle work of an unequal world that even the best of feminist parenting couldn't overcome. It is the force that sneaks up on us even as we think that we are getting ahead with the best of the guys. I would never have believed in its existence. But having heard it, amazingly, escape from my own mouth, I am starting to recognize its pattern.

When you are told you are causing trouble, and you regret having raised conflict, that's your programming.

When you keep silent, though you know the answer—programming.

When you do not take credit for your success, or you suggest that your part in it was really minimal—programming.

When a man tells you to lower your voice, and you do, and you apologize—programming.

The message of this programming is unrelentingly clear: Keep quiet.

I am a daughter of the movement. How did I fall for this?

I thought the battle had been won. I thought that sexism was a remote experience, like the Depression. Gloria had taken care of all that in the seventies.

Imagine my surprise.

And while I was blissfully unaware, the perpetrators were getting smarter.

What my mother taught me to look for—pats on the butt, honey, sweetie, cupcake, make me some coffee—are not the methods of choice for today's sexists. Those were just the fringes of what they were really up to. Sadly, enough of them have figured out how to mouth the words of equality while still behaving like pigs. They're harder to spot.

At my first newspaper job in Vermont, I covered my city's effort to collect food and money to help a southern town ravaged by a hurricane. I covered the story from the early fund-raising efforts right up to the day before I was to ride with the aid caravan down South. At that point I was taken off the story and it was reassigned to a male reporter. (It wasn't even his beat; he covered education.) It would be too long a drive for me, I was told. I wouldn't get enough sleep to do the story.

He may as well have said "beauty rest." But I didn't get it. At least not right away. He seemed, in voice and manner, to be concerned about me. It worked. A man got the big story. And I got to stay home. It was a classic example of a woman being kept out of a plum project "for her own good," yet while in the newsroom, hearing this explanation about sleep and long drives, I sat there nodding.

Do you think you would do better? Do you think you would recognize sexism at work immediately?

Are you sure?

Programming is a powerful thing. It makes you lazy. It makes you vulnerable. And until you can recognize that it's there, it works for the opposition. It makes you lower your voice.

It is a dangerous thing to assume that just because we were raised in a feminist era, we are safe. We are not. They are still after us.

And it is equally dangerous for our mothers to assume that because we are children of the movement, we are equipped to stand our ground. In many cases, we are unarmed.

The old battle strategies aren't enough, largely because the opposition is using new weaponry. The man in my office who made a nuisance of himself by asking me out repeatedly did so through the computer messaging system. Discreet. Subtle. No one to see him being a pig. Following me around would have been obvious. This way, he looked perfectly normal, and I constantly had to delete his overtures from my E-mail files. Mom couldn't have warned me about E-mail.

Then there is the danger from other women. Those at the top who don't mentor other women because if they made it on their own, so should subsequent generations. Women who say there is just one "woman's slot" at the top power level, and to get there you must kill off your female competition. Women who maintain a conspiracy of silence, refusing to speak up when they witness or even experience sexism, for fear of reprisals. These are dangers from within our ranks. When I went to work, I assumed other women were my allies.

Again, imagine my surprise.

I once warned a newly hired secretary that her boss had a history of discrimination against young women. She seemed intensely interested in the conversation at the time. Apparently as soon as I walked away, she repeated the entire conversation to her boss. My heart was in the right place. But my brain was not. Because, as I learned that day, sisterhood does not pay the bills. For younger women who think they do not need the feminist movement to get ahead, sisterhood is the first sentiment to fall by the wayside. In a world that looks safe, where men say all the right things and office policies have all the right words, who needs sisterhood?

We do. More than we ever have. Because they are smooth, because they are our bosses and control our careers, because they are noting we will kill each other off so they won't have to bother. Because of all the subtle sexism that you hardly notice until it has already hit you. That is why you need the movement.

On days when you think the battle is over, the cause has been won, look around you to see what women today still face. The examples are out there.

On college campuses, there is a new game called rodeo. A man takes a woman back to his room, initiates sexual intercourse, and then a group of his friends barges in. The object of this game is for the man to keep his date pinned as long as possible.

Men are still afraid of smart women. When Ruth Bader Ginsburg was nominated to the Supreme Court, the *New York Times* described her as "a woman who handled her intelligence gracefully." The message: If you're smarter than the men around you, be sure to keep your voice down. Wouldn't want to be considered ungraceful.

A friend from high school calls to tell me he's getting married. He's found the perfect girl. She's bright, she's funny and she's willing to take his last name. That makes them less likely to get divorced, he maintains. "She's showing me she's not holding out."

In offices, women with babies are easy targets. I've seen the pattern played out over and over. One woman I know put in ten years with the company, but once she returned from maternity leave, she was marked. Every attempt to leave on time to pick up her baby at day care was chalked up as a "productivity problem." Every request to work part-time was deemed troublemaking. I sat just a few desks away. I witnessed her arguments. I heard the editors gossip when she was absent. One Monday we came into work and her desk had been cleaned out.

Another woman closer to my age also wanted to work part-time after the birth of her son. She was told that was unacceptable. She quit. There was no announcement. No good-bye party. No card for everyone in the office to sign. The week she disappeared from the office, we had a party for a man who was leaving to take a new job. We also were asked to contribute to a gift fund for another man who had already quit for a job in the Clinton administration.

But for the women with babies who were disappeared, nothing happened. And when I talked about the fact that women with babies tended to vanish, I was hauled into my boss' office for a re-education session. He spent twenty minutes telling me what a great feminist he was and that if I ever thought differently, I should leave the company. No question about the message there: Shut up.

I used to believe that my feminist politics would make me strong. I thought strong thoughts. I held strong beliefs. I thought that would protect me. But all it did was make me aware of how badly I slipped when I lowered my voice and apologized for having a divergent opinion. For all my right thinking, I did not fight back. But I have learned something. I've learned it takes practice to be a strong feminist. It's not an instinct you can draw on at will—no matter how equality-minded your upbringing. It needs exercise. You have to think to know your own mind. You have to battle to work in today's workplace. It was nice to grow up thinking this was an equal world. But it's not.

I have learned to listen for the sound of my programming. I listen carefully for the *Sorrys*, the *You're rights*. Are they deserved? Or did I offer them up without thinking, as though I had been programmed? Have you? Are you sure?

I have changed my ways. I am louder and quicker to point out sexism when I see it. And it's amazing what you can see when you are not hiding behind the warm, fuzzy glow of past feminist victories. It does not make me popular in the office. It does not even make me popular with women. Plenty of my female colleagues would prefer I quit rocking the boat. One read a draft of this essay and suggested I change the phrase "fight back" to "stand my ground" in order to "send a better message."

But after falling for the smooth talk and after hearing programmed acquiescence spew from my mouth, I know what message I am trying to send: Raise your voice. And I am sending it as much to myself as to anyone else.

I've changed what I want from the women's movement. I used to think it was for political theory, for bigger goals that didn't include my daily life. When I was growing up, the rhetoric we heard involved the theory of equality: Were men and women really equal?

Were there biological differences that made men superior? Could women overcome their stigma as "the weaker sex"? Was a woman's place really in the home?

These were ideas. Important, ground-breaking, mind-changing debates. But the feminism I was raised on was very cerebral. It forced a world full of people to change the way they think about women. I want more than their minds. I want to see them do it.

The theory of equality has been well fought for by our mothers. Now let's talk about how to talk, how to work, how to fight sexism here on the ground, in our lives. All the offices I have worked in have lovely, right-thinking policy statements. But the theory doesn't necessarily translate into action. I'm ready to take up that part of the battle.

I know that sitting on the sidelines will not get me what I want from my movement. And it is mine. Younger feminists have long felt we needed to be invited to our mothers' party. But don't be fooled into thinking that feminism is old-fashioned. The movement is ours and we need it.

I am one of the oldest of my generation, so lovingly dubbed "X" by a disdainful media. To my peers, and to the women who follow after me, I warn you that your programming is intact. Your politics may be staunchly feminist, but they will not protect you if you are passive.

Listen for the attacks. They are quiet. They are subtle.

And listen for the jerk who will tell you to lower your voice. Tell him to get used to the noise. The next generation is coming.

QUESTIONS

1. Why is Neuborne surprised? Explain the significance of the title. What is her goal in this narrative?
2. How does Neuborne experience her own internalized vulnerability to sexism? Why does she decide to write this narrative?
3. What are contemporary challenges for women and third wave feminism in the United States? What is sexist programming? How does sexist programming affect both contemporary challenges and third wave feminism?
4. What is your sense of the differences between third wave feminism and previous feminisms based on the information in this selection?

"Womanist" from *In Search of Our Mothers' Gardens* (1983)

Alice Walker

Alice Walker is an activist, a poet, and a Pulitzer Prize winning novelist. Born in Georgia in 1944, Walker attended Sarah Lawrence College, and began publishing poetry after she became active in both the voter registration movement and the welfare rights movement in the 1960s. She has published numerous novels over the course of her career, including The Third Life of Grange Copeland *(1970),* In Love and Trouble *(1973),* Meridian *(1976),* The Color Purple *(1982),* In the Temple of My Familiar *(1989),* Possessing the Secret of Joy *(1992) and* Warrior Marks *(1995).*

Since Walker's coining of the term "womanist," womanism has evolved into an academic, political and spiritual framework. The following selection presents her definition of "womanist," capturing the unique-

ness and importance of Black feminism in the United States.

Womanist 1. From *womanish.* (Opp. of "girlish," i.e., frivolous, irresponsible, not serious.) A black feminist or feminist of color. From the black folk expression of mothers to female children, "You acting womanish," i.e., like a woman. Usually referring to outrageous, audacious, courageous or *willful* behavior. Wanting to know more and in greater depth than is considered "good" for one. Interested in grown-up doings. Acting grown up. Being grown up. Interchangeable with another black folk expression: "You trying to be grown." Responsible. In charge. *Serious.*

2. *Also*: A woman who loves other women, sexually and/or nonsexually. Appreciates and prefers women's culture, women's emotional flexibility (values tears as natural counterbalance of laughter), and women's strength. Sometimes loves individual men, sexually and/or nonsexually. Committed to survival and wholeness of entire people, male *and* female. Not a separatist, except periodically, for health. Traditionally universalist as in: "Mama, why are we brown, pink, and yellow, and our cousins are white, beige, and black?" Ans.: "Well, you know the colored race is just like a flower garden, with every color flower represented." Traditionally capable, as in: "Mama, I'm walking to Canada and I'm taking you and a bunch of other slaves with me." Reply: "It wouldn't be the first time."

3. Loves music. Loves dance. Loves the moon. *Loves* the Spirit. Loves love and food and roundness. Loves struggle. *Loves* the Folk. Loves herself. *Regardless.*

4. Womanist is to feminist as purple to lavender.

Questions

---

1. What is the significance of the final line of Walker's definition? How does Walker distinguish a womanist and a feminist? What evidence from the definition can you offer to support your interpretation?

2. What is significant about the format Walker has chosen for this presentation of the definition womanist? Why?

Becoming the Third Wave (1992)

Rebecca Walker

Rebecca Walker is the editor of To Be Real *(1995) and co-founder of the Third Wave Direct Action Corporation, a national non-profit organization that promotes young women's leadership and activism in the United States. In this 1992 selection, Walker explores what it means to be part of Third Wave feminism. In her first person narrative, she insists on the need to move beyond political theory and toward "tangible action."*

I am not one of the people who sat transfixed before the television, watching the Senate hearings. I had classes to go to, papers to write, and frankly, the whole thing was too painful. A black man grilled by a panel of white men about his sexual deviance. A black woman claiming harassment and being discredited by other women. . . . I could not bring myself to watch that sensationalized assault [of] the human spirit.

To me, the hearings were not about determining whether or not Clarence Thomas did in fact harass Anita Hill. They were about checking and redefining the extent of women's credibility and power.

"Becoming the Third Wave," by Rebecca Walker, reprinted from *Ms. Magazine*, January/February 1992.

Can a woman's experience undermine a man's career? Can a woman's voice, a woman's sense of self-worth and injustice, challenge a structure predicated upon the subjugation of our gender? Anita Hill's testimony threatened to do that and more. If Thomas had not been confirmed, every man in the United States would be at risk. For how many senators never told a sexist joke? How many men have not used their protected male privilege to thwart in some way the influence or ideas of a woman colleague, friend, or relative?

For those whose sense of power is so obviously connected to the health and vigor of the penis, it would have been a metaphoric castration. Of course, this is too great a threat.

While some may laud the whole spectacle for the consciousness it raised around sexual harassment, its very real outcome is more informative. He was promoted. She was repudiated. Men were assured of the inviolability of their penis/power. Women were admonished to keep their experiences to themselves.

The backlash against U.S. women is real. As the misconception of equality between the sexes becomes more ubiquitous, so does the attempt to restrict the boundaries of women's personal and political power. Thomas's confirmation, the ultimate rally of support for the male paradigm of harassment, sends a clear message to women: "Shut up! Even if you speak, we will not listen."

I will not be silenced.

I acknowledge the fact that we live under siege. I intend to fight back. I have uncovered and unleashed more repressed anger than I thought possible. For the umpteenth time in my 22 years, I have been radicalized, politicized, shaken awake. I have come to voice again, and this time my voice is not conciliatory.

The night after Thomas' confirmation I ask the man I am intimate with what he thinks of the whole mess. His concern is primarily with Thomas' propensity to demolish civil rights and opportunities for people of color. I launch into a tirade. "When will progressive black men prioritize my rights and well-being? When will they stop talking so damn much about 'the race' as if it revolved exclusively around them?" He tells me I wear my emotions on my sleeve. I scream "I need to know, are you with me or are you going to help them try to destroy me?"

A week later I am on a train to New York. A beautiful mother and daughter, both wearing green outfits, sit across the aisle from me. The little girl has tightly plaited braids. Her brown skin is glowing and smooth, her eyes bright as she chatters happily while looking out the window. Two men get on the train and sit directly behind me, shaking my seat as they thud into place. I bury myself in *The Sound and the Fury*. Loudly they begin to talk about women. "Man, I fucked that bitch all night and then I never called her again." "Man, there's lots of girlies over there, you know that ho, live over there by Tyrone? Well, I snatched that shit up."

The mother moves closer to her now quiet daughter. Looking at her small back I can see that she is listening to the men. I am thinking of how I can transform the situation, of all the people in the car whose silence makes us complicit.

Another large man gets on the train. After exchanging loud greetings with the two men, he sits next to me. He tells them he is going to Philadelphia to visit his wife and child. I am suckered into thinking that he is different. Then, "Man, there's a ton of females in Philly, just waitin' for you to give 'em some." I turn my head and allow the fire in my eyes to burn into him. He takes up two seats and has hands with huge swollen knuckles. I imagine the gold rings on his fingers slamming into my face. He senses something, "What's your name, sweetheart?" The other men lean forward over the seat.

A torrent explodes: "I ain't your sweetheart, I ain't your bitch, I ain't your baby. How dare you have the nerve to sit up here and talk about women that way, and then try to speak to me." The woman/mother chimes in to the beat with claps of sisterhood. The men are momentarily stunned. Then the comeback: "Aw, bitch, don't play that woman shit over here 'cause that's bullshit." He slaps the back of one hand against the palm of the other. I refuse to back down. Words fly.

My instinct kicks in, telling me to get out. "Since I see you all are not going to move, I will." I move to the first car. I am so angry that thoughts of murder, of physically retaliating against them, of separatism, engulf me. I am almost out of body, just shy, of being pure force. I am sick of the way women are negated, violated, devalued, ignored. I am livid, unrelenting in my anger at those who invade my space, who wish to take away my rights, who refuse to hear my voice.

As the days pass, I push myself to figure out what it means to be a part of the Third Wave of feminism. I begin to realize that I owe it to myself, to my little sister on the train, to all of the daughters yet to be born, to push beyond my rage and articulate an agenda. After battling with ideas of separatism and militancy, I connect with my own feelings of powerlessness. I realize that I must undergo a transformation if I am truly committed to women's empowerment. My involvement must reach beyond my own voice in discussion, beyond voting, beyond reading feminist theory. My anger and awareness must translate into tangible action.

I am ready to decide, as my mother decided before me, to devote much of my energy to the history, health, and healing of women. Each of my choices will have to hold to my feminist standard of justice.

To be a feminist is to integrate an ideology of equality and female empowerment into the very fiber of my life. It is to search for personal clarity in the midst of systemic destruction, to join in sisterhood with women when often we are divided, to understand power structures with the intention of challenging them.

While this may sound simple, it is exactly the kind of stand that many of my peers are unwilling to take. So I write this as a plea to all women, especially the women of my generation: Let Thomas' confirmation serve to remind you, as it did me, that the fight is far from over. Let this dismissal of a woman's experience move you to anger. Turn that outrage into political power. Do not vote for them unless they work for us. Do not have sex with them, do not break bread with them, do not nurture them if they do not prioritize our freedom to control our bodies and our lives.

I am not a postfeminism feminist. I am the Third Wave.

QUESTIONS

1. What characteristics of third wave feminism are evident in Walker's article? How does Walker see these characteristics as different from previous concerns of the women's movement?

2. Why does Walker begin and end the article with references to the Hill/Thomas decision? What effects of sexism are evident in that decision?

3. How does Walker's story of her train ride through New York support the idea that words are powerful actions? How do the other riders on the train illustrate the effects of sexism?